This strikingly original and impeccably researched account offers an unique insight into the workings of a complex society through the experiences of social, political and economic upheavals brought about by a people's war. Rich in paradoxes, Punam Yadav's powerfully argued thesis is supported by the wealth of idiographic detail, and sureness of touch in assessing micro-level changes, that only an insider can offer. It is, at the same time, firmly situated in a framework of cutting-edge scholarship, to which it makes a significant contribution.

Jake Lynch, *Director, Centre for Peace and Conflict Studies, University of Sydney*

This volume is timely in presenting us with a new and sophisticated analysis of social transformation as we experience ever-changing global relations in conflict and post-conflict settings. In reclaiming our 'humanness' as central to any notion of social transformation: gender emerges as a defining category in our tool kit.

Lynda-ann Blanchard, *Centre for Peace and Conflict Studies, University of Sydney, Australia*

Offering a unique insight into the lives and views of Nepali women post-conflict, Punam Yadav's book is a great read and will be of interest to anyone interested in processes of social change. Her interview material is fascinating and by foregrounding the experiences of women she provides an important and novel contribution to theorizing social transformation from an under-represented perspective.

Kiran Grewal, *Senior Research Fellow, Institute for Social Justice, Australian Catholic University*

A major contribution in the field of social transformation and post-conflict studies which examines in details the insights of women's lived experiences and the first study to provide empirical evidence on the relationship between armed conflict and social transformation through women's perspectives in Nepal.

Erik Paul, *Vice President, Centre for Peace and Conflict Studies, University of Sydney, Australia*

This book gives unique insight into the lives of Nepalese women and women's determination to exploit the changes wrought by war.

Lucy Fiske, *Chancellor's Post Doctoral Research Fellow, University of Technology, Sydney*

Social Transformation in Post-conflict Nepal

The concept of social transformation has been increasingly used in social science to study significant political, socio-economic and cultural changes affected by individuals and groups. This book explores the ways in which social transformation may be understood and its underlying dynamics constructed if women's lived experiences become a basis for theorizing.

Through extensive interviews with women in post-conflict Nepal, this book analyses the intended and unintended impacts of conflict and traces the transformations in women's understandings of themselves and their positions in public life. It raises important questions for the international community about the inevitable victimization of women during mass violence, but it also identifies positive impacts of armed conflict. The book also discusses how the Maoist insurgency had empowering effects on women.

The first study to provide empirical evidence on the relationship between armed conflict and social transformation from gender's perspectives, this book is a major contribution to the field of transitional justice and peacebuilding in post-armed-conflict Nepal. It is of interest to academics researching South Asia, Gender, Peace and Security Studies and Development Studies.

Punam Yadav is a Visiting Scholar at the Centre for Women, Peace and Security at London School of Economics, UK. Prior to starting her academic career, she worked in the Development Sector for over ten years. She is interested in examining women's lived experiences in post-conflict spaces.

Routledge Research on Gender in Asia Series

For a full list of titles in this series, please visit www.routledge.com

Social Transformation in Post-conflict Nepal

A gender perspective

Punam Yadav

Routledge
Taylor & Francis Group

LONDON AND NEW YORK

First published 2016
by Routledge
2 Park Square, Milton Park, Abingdon, Oxon OX14 4RN

and by Routledge
711 Third Avenue, New York, NY 10017

Routledge is an imprint of the Taylor & Francis Group, an informa business

British Library Cataloguing in Publication Data
A catalogue record for this book is available from the British Library

Library of Congress Cataloging-in-Publication Data
Names: Yadav, Punam K. (Punam Kumari), author.
Title: Social transformation in post-conflict Nepal : a gender perspective /
    Punam Yadav.
Description: Abingdon, Oxon ; New York, NY : Routledge, 2015. | Series:
    Routledge research on gender in Asia series ; 11 | Includes bibliographical
    references and index.
Identifiers: LCCN 2015047130 | ISBN 9781138955813 (hardback) |
    ISBN 9781315666037 (ebook)
Subjects: LCSH: Women—Social conditions—21st century. | Feminism—
    Nepal. | Nepal—Social conditions—21st century. | Nepal—History—Civil
    War, 1996-2006—Social aspects.
Classification: LCC HQ1735.9 .Y33 2015 | DDC 305.4095496—dc23
LC record available at http://lccn.loc.gov/2015047130

ISBN: 978-1-138-95581-3 (hbk)
ISBN: 978-1-315-66603-7 (ebk)

Typeset in Times New Roman
by Apex CoVantage, LLC

In memory of my mother, my brother Satish, and my best friend Gyanendra Tripathi, who disappeared during the civil war in Nepal in 2003.

Contents

Figures

Foreword

In her analysis of the lives of women following the 10-year People's War in Nepal, Punam Yadav reveals only a little of herself. Yet this exhaustive and always fascinating account of the transformation in Nepalese women's lives could not have been unearthed without Punam's understanding of her country coupled to her sensitivity regarding the hopes and aspirations of women of different caste and class. Without Punam's understanding and the respondents' trust in her, the research would have barely begun. As it is, we are given a highly encouraging story of empowerment which tells, at least implicitly, of the biography of the author. That merits attention though it can't be the preoccupation of this foreword.

Social transformation sounds at first like an abstract notion. If a researcher focused only on structural changes in a society and heard only from male leaders and other somewhat predictable opinion makers, we might have learned a little about powerful individuals' perceptions of change but not much else. Such accounts can be stereotyped as the top-down manner of conducting social science.

Punam rejected this way of inquiring into the consequences of a civil war on what she calls the lived experiences of women, from Maoist combatants to widows, from members of the Constituent Assembly to drivers of tempos – the distinct Nepalese three-wheeler taxis. By adopting a bottom-up approach to her research, she gave wonderful opportunities for women to speak about their image of themselves before and after the war. As a result, each chapter hurries along with a sense of blood coursing through the quotes and paragraphs. The work also has that mark of authenticity which should enable readers to comprehend how women's lives have changed and how women are changing the culture and the politics of post-conflict Nepal.

Dramatic change is revealed in the case of women who become widows, a predicament massively increased following a war. In pre-war Nepal, widows were ostracized, punished, excluded, labelled and stigmatized by being made to wear a white sari. That exclusion was challenged by war widows. Transformation occurred. No longer obliged to wear the white sari, widows started to be included in social life and felt sufficiently powerful to reject previous cruelties. There is convincing evidence that men's attitudes changed too.

As befits an impressive story derived from research in the best traditions of social and political science, Punam has been influenced by and has contributed to social theory. She acknowledges her debt to the appraisals of social transformation passed on by Michel Foucault, Pierre Bourdieu and Judith Butler. Such significant theorizing is given a separate chapter, but this book is in no way overwhelmed by others' claims and counterclaims about social transformation. Those other social scientists' accounts of the important ways in which power relations are transformed have influenced the revealing insights into the lives of Nepalese women. This book therefore makes an invaluable contribution to a more general understanding of theories about ways women's lives can be transformed even in a male-dominated and conservative society.

In conjuring an idea for the research, in handling the project and in writing this book, Punam shows her own changed understanding of power, though she is characteristically hesitant to admit it. That's a delightful personal touch.

Nepal remains a beautiful country though burdened by poverty and by natural disasters such as the recent devastating earthquakes. That makes transformation seem like one step forward and at least two steps back. Yet this book indicates that previously powerless women have changed in confidence, in views of themselves, in their political understanding and in the increasingly diverse roles they can play in their families and in a wider society. They are making persistent earthquakes of their own, and Punam has eloquently told us how.

Stuart Rees
Professor Emeritus, University of Sydney

Preface

My research journey began in 2009, with an informal discussion at dinner with a group of friends in Nepal. We discussed the consequences of the People's War in Nepal, which started in 1996 and ended with the Comprehensive Peace Agreement (CPA) in 2006. It was an intense conversation where we all agreed that armed conflict, even with political motives, was certainly not the best way to achieve one's goals. However, we also agreed that armed conflicts could have a positive impact on people and society, as it may also provide opportunities for empowerment, especially for marginalized and excluded groups such as women, the poor and people from lower castes. Hence, the initial interest was to explore the positive effects of armed conflict on women. Later, my research interests shifted from the perceived positive impacts of armed conflict to the notion of 'social transformation'. As my research journey progressed, I realized that a 'positive' and 'negative' dichotomy, as applied to impacts of war, does not capture the multiplicity and complex nature of people's lived experiences. People's experiences of armed conflict can be simultaneously positive and negative. For instance, women performing different roles in diverse sociopolitical and geographical locations experienced the People's War differently. The focus of this research project then became to explore these fluid and dynamic social processes and to understand the dynamics of social change – which transformed individual lives as well as social arrangements – taking place with extraordinary speed in post–People's War Nepal.

As a result of the post-war changes and people's expectations about building a new Nepal, the term social transformation has become a buzzword in Nepal, especially after the CPA. It has become one of the main topics in national and local newspapers, and gender equality is prominent in all the discussions. In one instance, a national newspaper wrote, 'women's access to decision making is necessary for social transformation in Nepal' (*Kathmandu Post*, 25 January 2011). At most events, political or organized by development organizations alike, social transformation for a new Nepal has been one of the main topics for discussion.

There are ongoing campaigns for social transformation. Some non-governmental organizations (NGOs) were established after the CPA with the specific aim of 'bringing' about social transformation in Nepal. Meanwhile, other organizations are working to bring social transformation through their specific areas of expertise, for example, social transformation through media, theatre, or community forestry.

The term 'social transformation' in post–People's War Nepal has not only received attention from NGOs, activists and political leaders, but it has also caught the attention of many scholars. The academic studies suggest that positive social change is taking place in Nepal. However, they also suggest that social transformation is yet a long way away.

During the course of this study, I observed changed attitudes among people in two respects: first, an increased recognition of discrimination based on gender, caste, class, religion and region; and second, a desire to 'bring' social transformation by improving the conditions of those discriminated against. Interestingly, those (politicians, civil society leaders, NGOs, media) who were talking about social transformation spoke as if they lived in a different world to the one they were determined to transform, and they strongly believed that something needed to be done 'by them' in order to transform the society. The shifts in people's perceptions about caste and gender were remarkable. However, the way social transformation was understood led me to question how the discourse of social transformation was constructed in Nepal. What were the indicators that determined whether social transformation had occurred, and what was the basis for choosing these indicators? Why were some indicators weighted more heavily than others, and why are indicators so important to study social transformation? My initial research suggested that critical approaches to these questions were absent.

In post–People's War Nepal, social transformation was clearly visible to me on the streets and in the villages. Women were driving tempos – battery-operated three-wheeled vehicles – which was unheard of before the war. Further examples include women being recruited for combat roles in the Nepalese army and widows no longer having to wear a white sari. Social transformation also became increasingly visible in the political sphere, where women and marginalized groups were included in mainstream politics. In 2008, Dr Ram Baran Yadav became the first president of Nepal. These changes represent significant developments in Nepalese history and a radical departure from deeply entrenched sociocultural and political traditions. Yet these radical shifts seemed under-reported and undervalued in much of the popular writing about social transformation in Nepal. These developments and discursive changes are also largely ignored by the organizations working to bring social transformation in Nepal.

The lack of recognition of women's agency in the post–People's War period, particularly in political contexts, appears counter-intuitive, given (1) the widespread currency of social transformation as a desired political goal and (2) the prominence, in discussions at multiple levels, of concepts of gender equality. For some reason, women's agendas appear to lose traction in such discussions, so their achievements – and need for further opportunities – become disconnected somewhere in the transition from theory to practice. This missing gender dynamic is the basis for my investigation. This book explores the ways in which social transformation might be understood and its underlying dynamics differently constructed if women's lived experiences were the foundation for theorizing.

By providing an alternative, bottom-up approach to a study of social transformation there is a focus on individual lived experiences as well as perceived collective social change. I aim to deconstruct the existing understanding of social transformation by placing women's lived experiences of changing social relations at the centre of my analysis, a perspective usually lacking from studies of social transformation in Nepal. Therefore, instead of going to the field with predetermined indicators to measure social transformation, I have listened to many women's stories of how their lived reality has changed.

The writing of this book has been possible because of the support from various institutions and individuals. This book is based on my doctoral thesis. I would like to express my thanks to Australia Awards for recognizing my potential and awarding me with such a prestigious scholarship, enabling me to pursue my PhD. I would like to thank all of my research participants; without their generous participation, this project would not have been possible. My special thanks go to the Centre for Peace and Conflict Studies at the University of Sydney for hosting me and providing me with an opportunity to engage in an excellent academic environment. I would like to express my deep gratitude to Professor Emeritus Stuart Rees for reading my manuscript and giving me insightful feedback. My thanks are due to my PhD supervisors, Associate Professor Jake Lynch, Dr Lynda-ann Blanchard, Dr Kiran Grewal and Dr Lucy Fiske for their continued support and encouragement; without them this book would not have been possible. I am grateful to the Centre for Women, Peace and Security, London School of Economics for hosting me as a Visiting Fellow while I was finishing my book. My thanks also go to Dr. Ken Macnab and all my friends who directly and indirectly helped me to complete this project.

I cannot give enough thanks to my husband and my two lovely children Abinash Yadav and Abisha Yadav, who have been so understanding and supportive throughout this journey. I am grateful to all my family in Nepal and in the UK, especially my father Bhola and my brothers Saroj and Manoj, for their unconditional love and support throughout my life.

Abbreviations

ANWA-R	All Nepal Women's Association – Revolutionary
BBC	British Broadcasting Corporation
BICC	Birendra International Convention Centre
BS	*Bikram Sambat* (Nepali calendar)
CA	Constituent Assembly
CBS	Central Bureau of Statistics
CNAS	Centre for Nepal and Asian Studies
CPA	Comprehensive Peace Agreement
CPN	Communist Party Nepal
CPN-M	Communist Party Nepal – Maoist
CPN-UML	Communist Party Nepal – United Marxist Leninist
CREHPA	Centre for Research on Environment, Health and Population Activities
CRLP	Centre for Reproductive Law and Policy
DFID	Department for International Development
FGD	focus group discussion
FWLD	Forum for Women, Law and Development
IDEA	Institute for Democracy and Electoral Assistance
IDMC	Internal Displacement Monitoring Centre
IDP	internally displaced people
INGO	international non-governmental organization
MJF	Madhesh Janadhikar Forum (Madhesi People's Rights Forum)
MoHP	Ministry of Health and Population
NC	Nepali Congress
NDHS	Nepal Demographic Health Survey
NGO	non-governmental organization
PLA	People's Liberation Army
PW	People's War
RNA	Royal Nepal Army
RPP	Rastrya Prajatantra Party (National Democratic Party)
SLRM	Sanghiya Loktantrik Rastrya Manch (Federal Republic National Front)
UCPN-M	United Communist Party of Nepal – Maoist

UN	United Nations
UNDP	United Nations Development Programme
UNMIN	United Nations Mission in Nepal
WHR	Women for Human Rights
YCL	Young Communist League

1 Locating social transformation in current discourse

The term social transformation carries echoes of the European Enlightenment, or the Age of Reason, a period when notions of a fixed inherited natural, social and political order were increasingly challenged by scientists and philosophers (Senghaas, 1985). Towards the end of the seventeenth century, European intellectuals started challenging traditional ideas, which were based on faith, and began to emphasize reason and individualism and developing scientific methods. The basic philosophy of the Enlightenment was that problems could be understood and solved by reason (rather than through reference to religious dogma), and that a person's character could be transformed by understanding and manipulating the subject's mental and physical environment, which meant that 'man' was perfectible.

In recent years, social transformation as a research paradigm has been increasingly used in social science literature (Castles, 2001). In terms of principles, approaches, assumptions and explanatory logic, there is a significant diversity in attitudes to social transformation across different disciplines (Sanderson, 1999). For example, the approaches to social transformation that are common among peace scholars differ from those of academics working on education. Sociologists, economists and political scientists have their own explanations as to how social transformation should be understood. Despite their varied approaches, most scholars see social transformation as a top-down, intentional process, which often has specific and defined goals. Moreover, the focus of these studies remains mostly on structural developments, and thus economic changes become the basis for measuring the sustainability of social transformation. Above all, the underlying assumptions as to how a transformed society should look still rely on Western models of progress (Castles, 2001).

The Great Transformation by Karl Polanyi, first published in 1944, has been very important for many scholars working on social transformation. Polanyi's theory of 'embeddedness' introduced a new direction to the study of social transformation (Castles, 2015). Polanyi argued that the economy is not independent from society, but is embedded in social order and associated with religious, cultural and political relations (Polanyi, 2001). Polanyi, through his notion of 'double movement' – the two-way relationship between agency and social structure – demonstrated how the economy is embedded in society (Polanyi, 2001). This was a radical shift in the field of economics that opened up a new area of research.

Although Polanyi was an economist, his work has influenced scholars in various other disciplines (see Castles, 2001, 2010, 2015; Pickel, 2002; Sharma & Donini, 2010).[1] Castles, who uses Polanyi's notion of double movement to explore the link between human mobility and social transformation, argues that Polanyi's "idea of the 'double movement' can be seen through the modern lens of the concept of agency" (Castles, 2010, p. 1576). He claims that Polanyi's notion of double movement can be used to examine the two-way relationship between human agency and social structure (Castles, 2010). Despite the emphasis on human agency, the studies that utilize Polanyi's framework to examine social transformation seem to focus primarily on structures rather than agency.

Joseph Stiglitz (1998, p. 5) insists that, "development represents a transformation of society." According to him, social transformation is

> a movement from traditional relations, traditional ways of thinking, traditional ways of dealing with health and education, traditional methods of production, to more 'modern' ways.
>
> (Stiglitz, 1998, p. 5)

According to Stiglitz, a traditional society accepts the world as it is, while a modern society understands and acknowledges its capacity and potential to change that world. He argues that "it recognizes that we, as individuals and societies, can take actions that, for instance, reduce infant mortality, increase lifespan and increase productivity" (Stiglitz, 1998, p. 5). He maintains that this can only be achieved through changing attitudes and ways of thinking, from traditional ways to more scientific ways (Stiglitz, 1998). He claims that development strategies help empower people in traditional societies, so that they can control their own destiny (Stiglitz, 1998).

Stiglitz (1998) offers an updated reading of Polanyi's original concept. His notion of development recognizes the embeddedness of local communities in the development process. However, his notion of social transformation "as a representative of development" is problematic for four overlapping reasons. First, his notion of social transformation rests on a modernizing view of development, in which developing countries should be seen as progressing along a trajectory towards conditions that are already established in the 'developed' world. However, such notions sit uneasy in Nepal, where political change was brought about by popular participation both in the People's War (1996–2006) and in a nonviolent uprising (2006). Second, the 'modernization view' considers social transformation as something performed by experts and/or outsiders to achieve a defined end goal. This theory centres on values that may be alien to the people of the community it purports to support. This may acquire further impetus in a setting, such as post–People's War Nepal, where donor aid is channelled through international financial institutions which impose increasingly stringent conditions (Dreher, 2003), thus controlling the direction of and agendas for reform. Third, it universalizes the process of transformation, situating the social change within a homogeneous model society. Fourth, it reduces the gender needs only to measurable indicators, such as a reduction of maternal mortality and an increase in school enrolments. Maternal mortality is certainly a significant issue, but it is one of many gendered concerns facing women in Nepal.

It is also worth noting that Stephen Castles, a prominent sociologist who has written extensively about social transformation, sees a strong link between globalization and social transformation (Castles, 2001, 2015). According to him, globalization is one of the major contributing factors of social transformation (Castles, 2010). He argues that "studying social transformation means examining the different ways in which globalizing forces affect local communities and national societies with highly diverse historical experiences, economic and social patterns, political institutions, and cultures" (Castles, 2001, pp. 18–19). As an alternative to the developmentalist and modernist views, Castles offers a comprehensive, localized and multidisciplinary approach to social transformation. Social transformation, for him, is "a shift in social relationships so profound that it affects virtually all forms of social interaction, and all individuals and communities simultaneously" (Castles, 2015, p. 4).

For Castles, social transformation is more comprehensive than the normal process of social change, as existing social mechanisms such as political, economic and cultural life are questioned and reconfigured (Castles, 2015). His approach to social transformation recognizes the impact of local historical and cultural contexts on the process of social transformation. Castles (2001) offers an interesting and important perspective on social transformation as he does not take social transformation as a predetermined goal. He sees social transformation as an effect of some kind of intervention, rather than a planned action. This is an important contribution to the study of social transformation, as it refuses the preconceived notion of social transformation as 'intended progress' and allows more space to explore the possible effects. However, his emphasis remains on institutional arrangements, such as transformation in economic, political and strategic relations (Castles, 2010) rather than the lived experience of individuals or the reality of social relations.

Bishnu Upreti, a scholar from Nepal who has written about social transformation in post-conflict Nepal, understands social transformation as a mega-project. According to Upreti, social transformation can only be achieved by replacing the existing socio-economic and political structures with new ones (Upreti, 2008). He argues that a "new [transformed] Nepal is possible only when the existing obstructions (political, economic, social, cultural, and psychological) are dismantled and commitments are made with a new vision" (Upreti, 2008, p. 215). He sees social transformation as a top-down process that focuses on institutional arrangements moving towards a predetermined goal.

In his personal reflections on social transformation in Nepal, Dev Raj Dahal, head of the Nepal Office of the non-governmental organization (NGO) Friedrich-Ebert-Stiftung, focuses primarily on political transformation. He claims that social transformation can only be achieved when there is increased political participation by the public, endorsement of basic human rights, abolition of feudalism and establishment of social democratic forces (Dahal, 2010). Although the indicators he presents are more people-focused, he also seems to understand social transformation as a political project, with goals that can only be achieved through overwhelming structural reforms.

The increase in academic research – including recent work of Jeevan Raj Sharma and Antonio Donini (2010), which explores the nature of social transformation in rural areas of post-conflict Nepal – suggests that there is clear evidence of a qualitative 'step-change' in Nepal which is beyond the continual and 'normal' process of incremental change. They also suggest that "the process of current transition is leading towards major shifts in dominant political, economic, and sociocultural relationships" (Sharma & Donini, 2010, p. 20). Although this study recognizes that the Maoist conflict accelerated the social transformation process and documents some of the evidence of social transformation taking place in Nepal, it does not offer an in-depth analysis of people's lived experiences. No attention is paid to the gains women achieved during the war and, as a consequence, how the intended and unintended transformations are taking place in society, not only in terms of gender relations but also in the effects on the social structure.

Renu Rajbhandari, a prominent women's rights activist in Nepal, presents a different view of social transformation. Rajbhandari (2008, p. 83) argues:

> For the feminists of Nepal, transformation involves not only bringing women into politics, or giving them positions at decision making levels; but it also means ensuring women's rights to means of production, and involvement in education, health, food security and in other areas. It should be made the dominant agenda of all political parties as well as Government. It is not just getting political positions within the same structures which have been dominant for centuries and been responsible for all forms of discrimination to women. Rather, it is a conscious effort to transform them.

Rajbhandari offers a more comprehensive explanation of social transformation. Although she highlights genuine needs and concerns of women in Nepal, she fails to recognize the transformations Nepalese society has already undergone, especially the gains that women have achieved since the beginning of the war. She also fails to recognize the meaning of these social changes. Rajbhandari also sees social transformation as a top-down, intentional process where structural changes are indicators of social transformation.

Although the notion of social transformation has evolved to become more comprehensive since its inception, it still reflects a structuralist position within a modernist paradigm. Current thinking on social transformation is shaped within the tradition of modernity, which provides the foundations in understanding the causes of historical transformations (Portes, 1973). Tradition is considered a default social state, positioned as opposite to the modern (Portes, 1973). Ulrich Beck defines modernity as disembedding the traditional order and re-embedding industrial social forms (Beck, 1994). In other words, modernity is a fundamental shift from a traditional way of life to an industrialized way. However, modernity is not solely about industrialization, capitalization and individualization; it is also about universalization of the notion of equality and freedom that ignores the heterogeneity and diversity among people from different cultures.

The problem with modernity is not only the homogenization or universalization of certain values; it is also the "Western hegemony over other cultures," according to Anthony Giddens (1994, p. 57), who argues that "modern is Western." For Alejandro Portes (1973, p. 252), modernity is "the ideology of successful Westernization." The problem with all modern ideologies is not only assumptions about a Western way of life as the norm; it is also about the affirmation that 'progress' and positive transformation can occur only through adopting Western values (Portes, 1973, p. 252).

The notion of modernity is, therefore, problematic both in conceptualizing social transformation in theory and as a political project. Giddens (1994) identifies two aspects of the social transformation project that can be problematic. First, the extensional spread of modern institutions universalized via globalizing processes. Second, the processes of intentional change that can be associated with radical modernization (Giddens, 1994, p. 57). In other words, the process of social transformation tends only to be measured through universalized indicators, often used to prove progress as achieved through intentional intervention. For instance, development intervention by NGOs, governments, political parties and civil society are considered important steps towards social transformation, while women gathering in a tea stall is not. This approach runs the risk of reproducing the same problems as much of the theoretical work on the subject. First, it endorses the Western global hegemony. Second, it still considers social transformation as a goal-driven project for intentional change, instead of a home-grown process of social interaction. For instance, when the Maoists started the People's War in Nepal, the intentional goal was to eliminate all kinds of discrimination and to create a new structure for an egalitarian society. The fundamental goal – to replace the elite centric political organizations with an egalitarian, equality-based sociopolitical system – has not been realized, and therefore some conclude that the Maoist conflict was a failure (Giri, 2006). However, this does not capture the reality of post-conflict Nepal. There have been significant transformations in Nepal, transformations that were neither expected nor planned.

As discussed earlier, the study of social transformations is heavily influenced by structuralist assumptions, focusing largely on structural transformations. As a result of this focus, there is an increased risk of forgetting or minimizing the subjective experiences or agency of people in the society studied. The indicators that are considered valid to measure social transformation are mostly derived from and measured at a structural level; examples of such indicators include economic and political transformations. In recent studies, although other forms of change, such as increased participation and cultural developments, are taken into consideration, the economic aspects of transformation are still dominant indicators of social transformation (Portes, 1973, p. 255). This narrow definition of social transformation not only emphasizes the importance of economic transformation to ensure the sustainability of these developments; it also reinforces the notion that structural transformation is essential for social transformation. Lidia Puigvert

(2001, p. 37) strongly opposes the structuralist approach and claims that "structuralism paralyzes social transformation" as it dismisses the subject and focuses only on "the structural possibilities of our society." She questions how someone can control their destiny if social life is so deeply influenced by social structures (Puigvert, 2001, p. 37).

The assumption that a social transformation study needs to have predetermined indicators is problematic for two reasons: (1) these indicators are generic, capture only changes at the macro level, and ignore the lived experiences of people; and (2) it assumes social transformation as a predetermined goal, ignoring the fact that social transformation is an effect, not simply an expected outcome of a planned intervention. Judith Butler, in her closing remarks at a conference on women and social transformation, said "I will leave here not the exact same person I was when I came. I think this transformation [in me] will take place in many ways" (Beck-Gernsheim, Butler and Puigvert, 2001, p. 119). She claims that social transformation can be generated through dialogue and believes that "all women have the capacity for dialogue and transformation" (Beck-Gernsheim et al., 2001, p. 117). In short, structural transformation is certainly one possible approach when considering transformations that have taken place in society, but it ignores the subjective aspects – the lived experiences – of social life.

Gendered critiques of social transformation

The oversimplification of social transformation processes leaves the lived experiences of people unexamined. People may, for instance, be assigned membership in a political community, conditioned by a common legal system, but may simultaneously inhabit multiple social and cultural systems, with multiple orientations to different axes of power and dominance, which may defy easy categorization using terms such as progress and modernization. Nowhere is this more evident than in the need to take account of gender dynamics – the interplay of factors bearing upon the lived experiences of women. This perception has given rise to gendered critiques of social transformation, one such important argument being that indicators, often used to determine the extent and direction of social transformation, are not gender-sensitive. Moreover, as Beck (1994, pp. 3–4) points out, change is not always obvious or easily measured:

> More participation by women in work outside the home, for instance, is welcomed and encouraged by all political parties, at least on the level of lip service, but it also leads to an upheaval on the snail's pace of the conventional occupational, political and private order of things . . . it breaks up the old boundary lines drawn between work and non-work. Precisely *because* such small measures with large cumulative effects do not arrive with fanfares, controversial votes in parliament, programmatic political antagonisms or under the flag of revolutionary change, the reflexive modernization of industrial society occurs on cats' paws, as it were, unnoticed by sociologists, who unquestioningly continue gathering data in the old categories. The

insignificance, familiarity and often the desirability of the changes conceal their society-changing scope. More of the same, so people believe, cannot produce anything qualitatively new.

Closer inspection of unnoticed, silent changes may lead to the revision and even the reversal of familiar assumptions. The dominant image of women in war has been as victims. However, this idea has been contested, and while conflict indeed negatively impacts women, it can also provide empowering opportunities (see Aguirre & Pietropaoli, 2008; Bop, 2001; Gardam & Charlesworth, 2000; Manchanda, 2001, 2004; Meintjes, 2001; Pankhurst, 2007; Pettigrew & Shneiderman, 2004; Pillay, 2001; Sideris, 2001). Rita Manchanda (2004, p. 237), referring specifically to the People's War in Nepal, argues that amidst the hardship and pain of the conflict, "intended and unintended spaces for empowering women [became available], effecting structural social transformations and producing new social, economic and political realities that redefine gender and caste hierarchies." Turshen, Meintjes, and Pillay (2001, p. 7) expand on that and argue that it is necessary to acknowledge women's pain and suffering during the war, but that the war also offers opportunities for women to transform their own lives and their self-image, how they think about others and their ability to live independently.

Codou Bop (2001) suggests that war can bring profound changes to the family structure and significantly increases the number of households led by women due to the higher rates of mortality, displacement and migration among men. Due to the absence of men, the responsibilities of managing the household, including financial undertakings, falls on women's shoulders (Turshen, 2001). This certainly increases their burden and is a painful experience, but it also exposes women to the public sphere (Pillay, 2001). Likewise, while "negotiating to survive in the difficult situation, women were empowered through social, economic and political exposure" (Turshen et al., 2001). When a large number of women in Nepal took on jobs that were traditionally performed by men, they became "active outside the home, asserting their rights as citizens. Many women had no choice but to become primary decision makers and heads of household" (Aguirre & Pietropaoli, 2008, p. 361). This was certainly not a planned social transformation, but became a positive development for women (Aguirre & Pietropaoli, 2008). Although women's social gains during war have been well recognized, they are not adequately captured in more structural analysis of social transformation. "The lack of a critical analysis to determine the processes of change wrought in conflict limits the sustainability of these gains after the conflict ends" (Manchanda, 2001, p. 100).

This book emphasizes two perspectives: (1) it utilizes a bottom-up approach to study social transformation; and (2) it uses women's lived experiences to capture the fluidity and multiplicity within the experiences of social transformation. In this book, I examine how conflict produced intended and unintended structural changes, which had considerable impact on the expanding space available for women's agency (Manchanda, 2001), and how this opened up the possibility for widespread social transformation. I also look at the structural causes that have constrained or liberated women's experiences of social transformation.

It should also be remembered that gender is a social construct. Not all women in a war zone are the same. Their experiences of conflict are different just as their connection to conflict may be different. Some women can be directly involved as combatants and soldiers, whereas others may join organizations as mobilizers. As their involvement in the conflict differs, so does their experience in the aftermath; combatants will have different experience than social mobilizers (Turshen et al., 2001). The claim that conflict provides spaces for empowerment is not to homogenize their experiences as women whose experiences are mediated through other factors such as class, caste, ethnicity and religion, which make a significant difference in individuals' experiences. Despite these variations, however, women also share some common experiences. Most women are hardest hit by conflict and they have much to lose, but unexpectedly, women also benefit from war (Turshen et al., 2001).

I am not proposing that there is only one way of looking at social transformation. The purpose of this book is to shed light on the highly personal and localized aspects of social transformation that are often ignored or overlooked. In this book, I will consider social transformation not as an end goal but as a continuous process that requires constant checking (Foucault, 1982).

This book contains nine chapters. Chapter 1, *Locating Social Transformation in Current Discourse*, introduces the book, outlines its scope and identifies the gap in existing literature about social transformation. It also provides a detailed methodological framework and describes the methods used in this study. Chapter 2, *Understanding the Processes of Social Transformation: Thinking Beyond Structures*, presents theoretical frameworks and explains the processes of social transformation from the bottom up, with specific attention to women's lived experiences.

Chapter 3, *Social Structure of Nepal: A Historical Overview*, presents a detailed background of the historical, social, cultural, economic, legal and political context of Nepal, with an emphasis on gender dynamics. Chapter 4, *Women in Politics and the Unintended Consequences*, analyzes various cases of women in post-conflict politics, especially female Constituent Assembly (CA) members. This chapter discusses women who came from various educational, cultural, ethnic, regional and political backgrounds and were working together to ensure a woman-friendly constitution. These women were not only contributing to the constitution making process but were also changing their society.

Chapter 5, *Tea Stall Story: The Power of One*, is a case study of a small community located in the plains of Nepal. I discuss a significant role model who was a housewife prior to becoming a CA member. Her involvement in politics has not only changed her life but has also affected the social fabric of her community.

Chapter 6, *Women Combatants: Challenging Habitus*, analyzes how the lives of female ex-combatants have changed. Despite some challenges, women who were directly involved in the war as combatants have not just experienced a transformation in their own lives; they have also made a great contribution towards the changing discourse on womanhood in Nepal. Prior to the People's War, women were not considered for combat roles as they were seen as weak and emotional beings, but women's involvement in the Maoist movement challenged that notion. As a result, the government of Nepal has recruited thousands of women into the army and thus challenged perceptions of womanhood.

Chapter 7, *White Sari: Transforming Widowhood in Nepal*, analyzes the experiences of war widows and presents a unique perspective on social transformation. It discusses how the performance of widows has changed the discourse around widowhood in Nepal.

Chapter 8, *Women Tempo Drivers: Challenging Doxa*, discusses the case of women at work. In this chapter, I have used the case of women tempo drivers to demonstrate how women's involvement in non-traditional roles has challenged doxa, social norms that are taken for granted. How have these women, who were housewives before the conflict, experienced a radical transformation in their own lives? Only a few years ago, when one woman started driving tempo, it became a national concern. Now, although occasionally sensationalized in newspapers, the discourse has largely shifted from questioning their entry into the profession, to recognition and appreciation of their contribution in changing gender stereotypes.

Chapter 9, *Conclusion: Rethinking Social Transformation*, concludes this book by arguing that if one considers the life experiences most common to women, social transformation appears very different from how it has been described in previous studies. Our understanding of transformations can be enhanced when viewed not only through structural indicators, but also through individuals' lived experiences. In this respect, social transformation is a non-linear process, not always with 'win-win' outcomes.

Research methodology

The findings of any social research are greatly influenced by the research approach utilized, and it is extremely important to acknowledge the relationship between the researcher and the subject matter. As David Marsh and Paul Furlong (2002, p. 17) emphasize:

> Each social scientist's orientation to their subject is shaped by their ontological and epistemological position. Most often those positions are implicit rather than explicit, but, regardless of whether they are acknowledged, they shape the approach to theory and the methods which the social scientist utilizes.

Marsh and Furlong (2002, p. 17) argue that the researcher's ontological and epistemological positions are "like a skin not a sweater: they cannot be put on and taken off whenever the researcher sees fit." Therefore, they argue that identifying or locating the researcher's positionality is important in social scientific studies because the findings are influenced by these positions.

This book has drawn ideas from multiple disciplines and different scholarly works have been used from various fields of study. Within an interpretist framework (Denzin, 1997), feminist standpoint theory (see Brooks, 2007; Collins, 1991, Harding, 1987, 1991, 1992, 2004; Harding & Norberg, 2005; Hekman, 1997;

Smith, 1990, 1999) has been identified as the primary epistemological position of the researcher.

Feminist standpoint epistemology is a theory of knowledge building which emphasizes the need to examine the world from women's perspectives via women's lived experiences. Sandra Harding (1987, p. 3), one of the founders of feminist epistemology, argues:

> Feminists have argued that traditional epistemologies, whether intentionally or unintentionally, systematically exclude the possibility that women could be 'knowers' or *agents of knowledge*; they claim that the voice of science is a masculine one; that history is written from only the point of view of men (of the dominant class and race); that the subject of a traditional sociological sentence is always assumed to be a man.

She further argues that women have been the objects of study in the past, but studying women from their own perspective does not have a long history (Harding, 1987, p. 8); therefore, as discussed earlier, social transformation study also lacks a gender perspective. By putting women at the centre of my research, I aim to examine women's experiences of social change and social transformation in Nepal.

Due to the nature of the study, aiming to examine women's lived experiences of social transformation, there are no claims to objectivity, neutrality or value-free standpoints. On the contrary, given that I am a Nepali woman who has experienced life in post–People's War Nepal, the auto-ethnographic contributions to the project are clearly subjective and arguably provide key insights.

Being an insider

The positioning of the researcher as an insider or outsider is a much debated concern in social research (Chavez, 2008; Geleta, 2014). For the positivists, outsiders are more reliable and accurate than insiders as they do not have biases for people, places and events (Chavez, 2008, p. 474). I have been influenced by the view that researchers are neither outsiders nor insiders, a view that considers researchers as co-participants in the process. The researcher's identity and position influence the research outcomes no matter if one is an insider or an outsider (Chavez, 2008). Denzin (1997) borrows from C. Wright Mills (1963) and Stuart Hall (1985), who argue that we do not have direct access to reality, but reality is mediated through symbolic representation, such as narrative texts and televisual structures. We see our world through these prisms; they are modes of interpretation standing between us and the 'lived' world (Denzin, 1997).

An African development ethnographic researcher, Esayas B. Geleta (2014), argues that her political and cultural identity shaped her research process. She argues that the subjectivity of researchers is influenced by their political affiliation, social status, ethnic background and gender identity.

There are various advantages in being an insider. The researcher's knowledge of a language and culture may contribute to a more in-depth understanding of the subject. For example, female CA members were one of the categories of my research participants. These women were from various parts of the country and all spoke different languages and dialects. There was no common language fluency in Nepal. Therefore, if the interviews needed to be conducted in Nepali, language would have been the barrier. Because I am an 'insider' and can speak many local languages, I was able to conduct these interviews in the language the women felt most comfortable with.

Another distinct advantage of being an insider was my knowledge of the extraordinarily complex cultural, social and geographical differences between regions, ethnicities and castes. Perhaps the most significant advantage to being an insider, in the context of my research, was related to geography. Since I am from the low lands (*Terai*), my interviewees could share experiences that would be 'forbidden' to share with an outsider. Hence, the researcher's identity also influences the outcomes of research, as well as the research design.

A constructivist version of grounded theory has been adopted as a method for data collection and analysis (Charmaz, 2006). Grounded theory is "theory that is grounded in words and actions of those individuals under study" (Goundling, 2005, p. 296). This study aims to capture the fluidity and multiplicity of a social structure in post-conflict Nepal, where actors perform their roles differently at different times and in different contexts. As it provides flexibility to explore the subjective aspects of lived experiences, the constructivist grounded theory fits well with this research framework.

Michel Foucault emphasizes the importance of historical awareness to analyze the current context (Sawicki, 1986, p. 778). Pierre Bourdieu also emphasizes the importance of understanding the historical context, but adds that, as these conditions have been constructed and reconstructed many times over the years, it is necessary to have an end point when studying social transformation. This study focuses on women's status at present, compared to their status prior to the People's War (1996) in Nepal. Fieldwork for this study was carried out between May 2011 and June 2012. However, some of the data was updated in November and December 2014.

Foucault argues that focusing "attention on specific situations may lead to more concrete analysis of particular struggles and thus to a better understanding of social change" (see Sawicki, 1986, p. 31). Therefore, although some men were also interviewed, the main focus of this study is to understand the lived experiences of women in relation to their experience of social transformation.

Kathy Charmaz (2006, p. 15) emphasizes that "*how* you collect data affects which phenomena you will see, *how*, *where*, and *when* you will view them, and *what* sense you will make of them." I was interested in understanding the experiences of women in categories that had newly emerged in Nepal. The categories were identified based on my knowledge as an insider researcher. Using purposive sampling, I identified four categories of women to consider in this study: female CA members, female ex-combatants, war widows and tempo drivers. I consider these to be new categories of women because prior to the People's War either they did not feature at all or they had a minimal presence. The identity of 'woman tempo driver' or 'woman combatant' was not the feature of pre-conflict society. These identities emerged in contrast to traditional gender roles. I was interested in exploring how these shifts in traditional gender roles might have influenced women's lives and whether it had led to any transformation in the social structure more broadly, in terms of gender relations in both public and private spheres.

Moreover, I wanted to understand what other women, who personally did not experience these changed identities, thought about these groups of women and what they thought about the changing nature of gender roles and relations. Furthermore, my research objectives included the larger picture; for instance, how these changes in gender performances were perceived by people knowledgeable on the subject, who are working for these groups or writing about them. I applied four key tools for data collection: individual in-depth interviews, focus group discussions (FGD), key informant interviews and non-participant observation.

A total of 57 in-depth interviews were undertaken with: 31 women CA members, 15 war widows, 6 ex-combatants and 10 tempo drivers. These categories overlap; for instance, there were some widows and ex-combatants among the women CA members. The aim of individual interviews was to examine individual women's experiences of social transformation, both at a personal and a societal level, whereas the information collected through the FGDs and the key informant interviews were used to contextualize patterns of social transformation, as outlined by the participants, within a larger understanding of Nepalese society. The non-participant observation was mainly used to study living conditions, the relationships of my research participants with their families and communities, and their appearance in terms of clothing. Questionnaires and checklists were pretested prior to the field work. The consent of the participants was sought prior to interviews.

More than half of the 57 participants were married (51 per cent), 30 per cent were widows, 11 per cent were unmarried, 4 per cent were separated and 4 per cent had a missing husband. Caste dynamics play an important role in the social organization of Nepal, particularly in terms of gender relations. It is therefore important to look at what castes and ethnic groups were included in this study. The research participants represented the following castes and ethnic groups:[2]

- 17 women were from Janajati, representing both Hill Janajati (10) and Terai Janajati (7);
- 12 were from Terai/Madhesh caste groups;
- 16 were Brahmin/Chhetri, representing both Hill Brahmin/Chhetri (14) and Terai Brahmin/Chhetri (2),
- 9 were Dalits, representing both Hill Dalits (3) and Terai Dalits (6);
- 2 were Newar;
- 1 was Muslim.

The participants represented a good cross section of the caste and ethnic groups in Nepal.

Age was an important consideration because the participants who were in their twenties and thirties had experienced the conflict differently to people who were in their forties. Women who had lost their husbands when they were only in their twenties had a very different experience of widowhood to women who were in their forties and fifties. I used intervals of 5 years because I wanted to examine the experiences of various age groups. Among the 57 research participants, the majority were aged between 21 and 45 years.

Education also plays an important role in women's understanding and experience of the world. I wanted to examine the experiences of women from various educational backgrounds. I looked, for example, at whether the experiences of women who had completed a master's degree were different from the experiences of women who had no educational qualifications. This was particularly interesting among women CA members, as they all acted as political agents at a national level with varied educational backgrounds. I will discuss in detail the demographic background of each category of women later in the chapters. However, it is important to mention that a significant number of research participants (24) had never been to school. They were either illiterate or they had only recently learned to write their names and, in some cases, to read. Only seven women had completed an undergraduate degree or other tertiary qualifications.

Each region in Nepal is culturally distinct. Therefore, it was important to identify where the participants came from. A third were from the Eastern region, 29 per cent from the Mid-western region, 24 per cent from the Central region, 10 per cent from the Western region and only 4 per cent from the Far Western region.

Notes

1 A. Pickel in his article argues that social transformation is a political project, not a scientific theory. Social scientists, as political actors, have played a significant role in the process of social transformation (see Pickel, 2002).
2 The classification of caste/ethnicity in this book is based on Lynn Bennett's classification (see Bennett, Dahal, & Govindasamy, 2008).

References

Aguirre, D., & Pietropaoli, I. (2008). Gender Equality, Development and Transitional Justice: The Case of Nepal. *International Journal of Transitional Justice, 2*(3), 356–377.

Beck, U. (1994). The Reinvention of Politics: Towards a Theory of Reflexive Modernization. In A. Giddens, U. Beck, & S. Lash (Eds.), *Reflexive Modernization: Politics, Tradition and Aesthetics in the Modern Social Order* (pp. 1–55). Cambridge: Polity Press.

Bennett, L., Dahal, D. R., & Govindasamy, P. (2008). *Caste, Ethnic and Regional Identity in Nepal: Further Analysis of the 2006 Nepal Demographic and Health Survey*. Retrieved on 14 December 2014 from http://pdf.usaid.gov/pdf_docs/PNADM638.pdf

Bop, C. (2001). Women in Conflicts, Their Gains and Their Losses. In M. Turshen, S. Meintjes, & A. Pillay (Eds.), *The Aftermath: Women in Post-Conflict Transformation* (pp. 19–34). London: Zed Books.

Brooks, A. (2007). Feminist Standpoint Epistemology. In S. N. Hesse-Biber & P. L. Leavy (Eds.), *Feminist Research Practice: A Primer* (pp. 53–82). Thousand Oaks, CA: Sage.

Beck-Gernsheim, E., Butler, J., & Puigvert, L. (2001). Gender and Social Transformation: A Dialogue (J. Vaida, Trans.). In E. Beck-Gernsheim, J. Butler, & L. Puigvert (Eds.), *Women and Social Transformation* (pp. 116–136). New York: Peter Lang.

Castles, S. (2001). Studying Social Transformation. *International Political Science Review, 22*, 13–32.

Castles, S. (2010). Understanding Global Migration: A Social Transformation Perspective. *Journal of Ethnic and Migration Studies, 36*(10), 1565–1586.

Castles, S. (2015). International Human Mobility: Key Issues and Challenges to Social Theory. In S. Castles, D. Ozkul, & M. Cubas (Eds.), *Social Transformation and Migration: National and Local Experiences in South Korea, Turkey, Mexico and Australia* (pp. 3–14). Basingstoke: Palgrave Macmillan. doi:10.1057/9781137474957.

Charmaz, K. (2006). *Constructing Grounded Theory: A Practical Guide through Qualitative Analysis*. Los Angeles: Sage.

Chavez, C. (2008). Conceptualizing from the Inside: Advantages, Complications and Demands on Insider Positionality. *Qualitative Review, 13*(3), 474–494.

Collins, P. H. (1991). *Black Feminist Thought: Knowledge, Consciousness, and the Politics of Empowerment*. New York: Routledge.

Dahal, D. R. (2010). *Social Transformation in Nepal: A Personal Reflection*. Retrieved 16 October 2014 from http://www.nepaldemocracy.org/civic_education/Discourse%20 on%20Transformation.pdf

Denzin, N. (1997). *Interpretive Ethnography: Ethnographic Practices for the 21st Century*. Thousand Oaks, CA: Sage.

Dreher, A. (2003). A Public Choice Perspective of IMF and World Bank Lending and Conditionality. *Public Choice, 119*, 445–464.

Foucault, M. (1982). The Subject and Power. *Critical Inquiry, 8*(4), 777–795.

Gardam, J., & Charlesworth, H. (2000). Protection of Women in Armed Conflict. *Human Rights Quarterly, 22*(1), 148–166. doi:10.2307/4489270.

Geleta, E. B. (2014). The Politics of Identity and Methodology in African Development Ethnography. *Qualitative Research, 14*(1), 131–146.

Giddens, A. (1994). Living in a Post-traditional Society. In A. Giddens, U. Beck, & S. Lash (Eds.), *Reflexive Modernization: Politics, Tradition and Aesthetics in the Modern Social Order* (pp. 56–109). Cambridge: Polity Press.

Giri, S. (2006). Social Transformation and Political Power: Maoists in Nepal. *Economic and Political Weekly, 41*(21), 2147–2156.

Goundling, C. (2005). Grounded Theory, Ethnography and Phenomenology: A Comparative Analysis of Three Qualitative Strategies for Marketing Research. *European Journal of Marketing, 39*(3/4), 294–308.

Harding, S. (1987). Introduction: Is There a Feminist Method? In S. Harding (Ed.), *Feminism and Methodology: Social Science Issues* (pp. 1–14). Bloomington: Indiana University Press.

Harding, S. (1991). *Whose Science? Whose Knowledge?: Thinking from Women's Lives*. Ithaca, NY: Cornell University Press.

Harding, S. (1992). Subjectivity, Experience and Knowledge – An Epistemology from/for Rainbow Coalition Politics. *Development and Change, 23*(3), 175–193.

Harding, S. (2004). *The Feminist Standpoint Theory Reader: Intellectual and Political Controversies*. New York: Routledge.

Harding, S., & Norberg, K. (2005). New Feminist Approaches to Social Science Methodologies: An Introduction. *Signs: Journal of Women in Culture and Society, 30*(4), 2009–2015.

Hekman, S. (1997). Truth and Method: Feminist Standpoint Theory Revisited. *Signs, 22*(2), 341–365.

Manchanda, R. (2001). Ambivalent Gains in South Asian Conflicts. In M. Turshen, S. Meintjes, & A. Pillay (Eds.), *The Aftermath: Women in Post-conflict Transformation* (pp. 99–121). London: Zed Books.

Manchanda, R. (2004). Maoist Insurgency in Nepal: Radicalizing Gendered Narratives. *Cultural Dynamics, 16*(2–3), 237–258. doi:10.1177/0921374004047750.

Marsh, D., & Furlong, P. (2002). A Skin, Not a Sweater: Ontology and Epistemology in Political Science. In D. Marsh & G. Stoker (Eds.), *Theory and Methods in Political Science* (pp. 17–41). New York: Palgrave Macmillan.

Meintjes, S. (2001). War and Post-war Shifts in Gender Relations. In M. Turshen, S. Meintjes, & A. Pillay (Eds.), *The Aftermath: Women in Post-conflict Transformation* (pp. 63–77). London: Zed Books.

Pankhurst, D. (2007). *Gender Issues in Post-war Contexts: A Review of Analysis and Experience, and Implications for Policies* (Vol. 9). Bradford: Department of Peace Studies, University of Bradford.

Pettigrew, J., & Shneiderman, S. (2004). Ideology and Agency in Nepal's Maoist Movement. *Himal Magazine*. Retrieved 15 October 2015 from http://old.himalmag.com/component/content/article/1700-ideology-and-agency-in-nepals-maoist-movement.html

Pickel, A. (2002). Transformation Theory: Scientific or Political? *Communist and Post-Communist Studies, 35*(1), 105–114. doi:10.1016/S0967-067X(01)00027-7.

Pillay, A. (2001). Violence against Women in the Aftermath. In M. Turshen, S. Meintjes, & A. Pillay (Eds.), *The Aftermath: Women in Post-conflict Transformation* (pp. 35–44). London: Zed Books.

Polanyi, K. (2001). *The Great Transformation: The Political and Economic Origins of Our Time*. Boston, MA: Beacon Press.

Portes, A. (1973). Modernity and Development: A Critique. *Studies in Comparative International Development, 8*(3), 247–279. doi:10.1007/BF02800432.

Puigvert, L. (2001). Dialogic Feminism: "Other Women's" Contributions of the Social Transformation of Gender Relations (J. Vaida, Trans.). In E. Beck-Gernsheim, J. Butler, & L. Puigvert (Eds.), *Women and Social Transformation* (pp. 29–60). New York: Peter Lang.

Rajbhandari, R. (2008). Transformative Politics and Women in Nepal. In K. N. Pyakuryal, B. R. Upreti, & S. R. Sharma (Eds.), *Nepal: Transition to Transformation* (pp. 77–100). Kathmandu: Human and Natural Resources Studies Centre, Kathmandu University and South Asia Regional Coordination Office of NCCR North South.

Sanderson, S. K. (1999). *Social Transformations: A General Theory of Historical Development*. Lanham, MD: Rowman & Littlefield.

Sawicki, J. (1986). Foucault and Feminism: Toward a Politics of Difference. *Hypatia, 1*(2), 23–36.

Senghaas, D. (1985). *The European Experience: A Historical Critique of Development Theory*. Leamington Spa: Berg.Sharma, J. R., & Donini, A. (2010). *Towards a "Great Transformation"? The Maoist Insurgency and Local Perceptions of Social Transformation in Nepal*. Boston, MA: Tufts University.

Sideris, T. (2001). Problems of Identity, Solidarity and Reconciliation. In M. Turshen, S. Meintjes, & A. Pillay (Eds.), *The Aftermath: Women in Post-conflict Transformation* (pp. 46–62). London: Zed Books.

Smith, D. E. (1990). *The Conceptual Practices of Power: A Feminist Sociology of Knowledge*. Boston, MA: Northeastern University Press.

Smith, D. E. (1999). *Writing the Social: Critique, Theory, and Investigations*. Toronto: University of Toronto Press.

Stiglitz, J. (1998). *Towards a New Paradigm for Development: Strategies, Policies and Processes*. Ninth Raul Prebisch Lecture Delivered at the Palais des Nations, Geneva, 19 October 1998. Retrieved 15 September 2015 from http://unctad.org/en/Docs/prebi sch9th.en.pdf

Turshen, M. (2001). Engendering Relations of State to Society in the Aftermath. In M. Turshen, S. Meintjes, & A. Pillay (Eds.), *The Aftermath: Women in Post-conflict Transformation* (pp. 78–96). London: Zed Books.

Turshen, M., Meintjes, S., & Pillay, A. (2001). There Is No Aftermath for Women. In M. Turshen, S. Meintjes, & A. Pillay (Eds.), *The Aftermath: Women in Post-conflict Transformation* (pp. 3–18). London: Zed Books.

Upreti, B. R. (2008). Moving Ahead: From Transition to Transformation. In K. N. Pyakuryal, B. R. Upreti, & S. R. Sharma (Eds.), *Nepal: Transition to Transformation* (pp. 201–222). Kathmandu: Human and Natural Resources Studies Center, Kathmandu, University & South Asia Regional Coordination Office of NCCR North-South.

2 Understanding the processes of social transformation

Thinking beyond structures

> Our vision is not equality with men . . . What we want goes beyond equality to the transformation of social relations . . . Our desire is to describe the conditions that favour social transformation and to outline our vision of a society that respects women's autonomy and bodily integrity.
>
> (Turshen, Meintjes, & Pillay, 2001, p. 16)

In an interview with Gary A. Olson and Lynn Worsham (2004, p. 334), Judith Butler argued that the concept of 'liberation' has the potential to minimize and distort the discourse on social transformation. This misrepresentation of social transformation often occurs when it is understood as identical to liberation. The confusion of these two terms seems to have an impact on studies of social transformation. Since social transformation is understood as identical to liberation, it is often taken as a mega-project where the notions of liberation (e.g. liberation from sociocultural, economic and political repressions), holistic transformation (e.g. radical transformation in all structures: social, cultural, economic and political) and sustainability (e.g. continuity of those changed structures) seem to have more relevance. As a consequence, social transformation often seems unattainable.

Social transformation means different things in different contexts, or there may be different qualifiers for a transformative exercise (Butler, 2001, p. 1). For instance, there may be different qualifiers for social transformation in rural Nepal than in the capital city, Kathmandu. There is no universal theory of social transformation that can be applied to all contexts. Pierre Bourdieu, Michel Foucault and Judith Butler reject the idea of a singular universalized theory of social transformation. For Foucault, "there is no theory of global transformation to formulate, no (singular) revolutionary subject whose interest the intellectual or theoretician can represent" (Sawicki, 1986, p. 31). Likewise, Butler (2001, p. 2) argues that "in the very act of social transformation, we are all lay philosophers, presupposing a vision of the world, of what is right, of what is just, of what is abhorrent, of what human action is and can be, of what constitutes the necessary and sufficient conditions of life."

Butler questions:

> What is the good life? How has the good life been conceived such that wom-
> en's lives have not been included in its conceptualization? . . . Whose preroga-
> tive is it to live? . . . [H]ow do we weigh one life against another?
>
> (Butler, 2001, p. 2)

To understand the dynamics of social transformation, how power relations are
challenged and reconfigured, it is necessary to chart how the actors, individuals
and groups, relate to each other and the larger social order. It is important that the
theoretical framework applied allows for exploration of the dynamic relationship
between social structure and individual agency. Bourdieu's theory of social life is
useful, since it focuses on the potentially asymmetrical and variable relationship
between, as well as within, both social structures and individual agency.

Randal Johnson, in his editor's introduction to Bourdieu's *The Field of Cultural
Production*, summarizes Bourdieu's notion of field. He writes:

> Any social formation is structured by way of a hierarchically organised series
> of fields (the economic field, the educational field, the political field, the cul-
> tural field and so on), each defined as a structured space within its own laws
> of functioning and its own relations of force . . . each field is relatively autono-
> mous but structurally homologous with the others. Its structure, at any given
> moment, is determined by the relations between the positions agents occupy
> in the field.
>
> (Johnson, in Bourdieu, 1993, p. 6)

For example, small, localized improvements to one aspect of women's lives in one
community can be conceptualized as simultaneously contributing to subtle altera-
tions of power relations in many other levels and in other fields, what Foucault
(1978, p. 93) calls "the complex strategic situation in a particular society." Each
field, Bourdieu (1998, p. 39) argues, is "a microcosm with its own laws, defined
both by its position in the world at large and by the attractions and repulsions
to which it is subject from other such microcosms." Social transformation does
not therefore depend on detecting, or even positing, a clearly delimited source of
political agency following a predetermined agenda. However, groups with clear
agendas working towards a set of goals can and do affect society. For example,
the polity of Nepal in the period under consideration was greatly influenced by the
Unified Communist Party Nepal, the Maoists. But while "there is no form of power
that is exercised without a set of aims and objectives," Foucault (1978, p. 95) notes
that it would be futile to look for "the headquarters that presides over its rational-
ity." Likewise, Steven Lukes's (1974/2005, p. 25) third dimension of power allows
that "the bias of the system can be mobilized, recreated and reinforced in ways that
are neither consciously chosen nor the intended result of particular individuals'
choices." Social transformation is not the unfolding of a plan written in advance,
but a development suddenly noticed after a multitude of small changes, as agents

adjust to the subtly altered balance of attraction and repulsion within fields and between them.

The processes of social transformation have been explained differently by different scholars. For example, Pierre Bourdieu's theory of social life emphasizes processes of change and continuity through the concepts of *field, habitus* and *practice*. Michel Foucault explains how social relations are constructed within a set of power relations through particular discourses. His theory of subject positions complements Bourdieu's notion of reflexivity, that is when there is a misfit between field and habitus. Similarly, Judith Butler's notion of gender as performative identifies how the changing portrayals of masculinity and femininity make critical reflexivity possible and shows how such changes affect both individual and collective habitus.

Foucault, Bourdieu and Butler provide the language to articulate the interaction between social structures and the people who are involved in the construction, reconstruction and application of those structures. For that reason, it is important to further explore and elaborate on their views.

Bourdieu's theory of social life

Bourdieu outlines the relationships and interactions between social structures within an overarching framework, the symbolic order that is masculine domination. According to him, "the social order functions as an immense symbolic machine tending to ratify the masculine domination on which it is founded" (Bourdieu & Nice, 2001, p. 9). A woman feeling guilty for not fulfilling her duty as a 'good wife' is an example of how masculine domination constructs a particular discourse. Although it may vary between different times and contexts in terms of "their relative weights and their functions" (Bourdieu & Nice, 2001, pp. 82–83), the practice of the dominant social order in everyday life ensures its permanence – at least until it is challenged (Bourdieu & Nice, 2001). Male domination is maintained and affirmed through the practice of social roles and through institutions such as family. Bourdieu argues that due to the historical nature of masculine domination, it is not possible to be entirely liberated from such constructions (Bourdieu & Nice, 2001) because our actions and practices are neither fully conscious nor fully unconscious.[1] These are ongoing processes of a lifestyle which have been learned since birth (Jenkins, 1992).

Moreover, Bourdieu (1989, p. 20) argues that our perception of "the social world is the product of a double structuring" as it is shaped by both a subjective view and an objective understanding of the world around us. Subjective structures are, for Bourdieu, mental constructs, the embodiments of sociocultural rules (Jenkins, 1992). He perceives the subjective structure as an established system that helps make sense of the distribution of resources or the organization of the objective structure (Dick, 2008). It is an internalization of the objective structures of the world (Bourdieu, 1989). Examples of these external structures manifested in the body include how gender is performed, but also other, more specific roles, such as widowhood. Bourdieu (1989, p. 18) explains that it is interesting to see how "even the most disadvantaged ones, tend to perceive the world as natural and to accept it much more readily than one might imagine." This sentiment is echoed in the following statement by a widow from Nepal, whose husband was killed during the People's War:

> I was only 22 when my husband died. I had to wear a white sari. I was not allowed to eat (meat, spicy food) like other married women. I was not supposed wear any make up. It was a painful experience but I thought this is what a widow is supposed to do.
>
> (Sumedha)

As the restriction on widows' lives has a long history and this behaviour became the norm, widows themselves thought it was normal. Sumedha only realized that this practice amounted to discrimination against widows when she joined a single women's group where she attended several training sessions and heard similar stories from others.

Another example of how the dominated themselves participate in discriminatory acts, considering them to be normal, is a festival called *Teej*. It is a festival for women celebrated throughout Nepal. The day is a public holiday 'only for women'. Hindu women, especially from Brahmin/Chhetri castes, fast for 24 hours, going without food and water, and worship lord Shiva to lengthen the lives of their husbands. The belief is so strong that even when women fall sick, they do not drink water because it is believed that to drink water on this day is analogous to consuming their husband's blood. Women follow these practices strictly, without any direct external social pressures. In 2011, a national newspaper reported that 15 women fainted at Pashupatinath temple, a famous temple of lord Shiva in Kathmandu (*Kathmandu Post*, 2011).

There are many discussions and debates, especially among feminists and women's rights activists of Nepal, around the relevance and importance of Teej in the twenty-first century. There have also been some awareness-raising programs, but Teej celebrations have become larger and more women participate now than in the past. Initially it was a 3-day event. The first day, *dar khane din*, is the day when families and relatives sit and eat food together. The second day is *Teej*, when women fast, worship lord Shiva and dance. On *Rishipanchami*, the third or the fourth day (depending on the Hindu calendar), women wake up before the sunrise, go to the river or pond, wash their body with holy soil, and clean their teeth with *datiwan* (stem of a medicinal plant). This ritual cleansing is performed 108 times, for instance, a woman will clean her teeth with 108 *datiwan*. After washing, the women return home and gather in a place where a worshiping ceremony, led by a male Brahmin *Purohit* (Priest/Pandit), takes place. It is believed that by performing these rituals they will be forgiven any sin (knowingly or unknowingly) committed by a women during menstruation (see Bennett, 2004).[2]

Recently some interesting patterns have emerged in the festival practices. It is no longer exclusively a festival for the Brahmin/Chhetri castes; women from various castes and ethnic groups, who follow the Hindu religion, celebrate this festival. For example, women from the Plains of Nepal (*Terai*) have historically never participated; now, however, they frequently take part in this festival. Despite having a long history, the *Teej* festival has become modernized and commercialized. Depending on their wealth, women buy new red saris and gold jewellery in conjunction with the event. The festival is now celebrated for a full month, mostly through eating in the company of family, friends and relatives.

By objective structure, Bourdieu means material conditions, such as money, property, rules and institutions, within which agents organize their life (Dick, 2008; Jenkins, 1992). According to Bourdieu (1985, p. 727), the objective structure is also "socially structured because the properties attached to agents or institutions do not offer themselves independently to perception, but in combinations that are very unequally probable." Bourdieu further argues that perception of objective structure also vary unpredictably over time (Bourdieu, 1985, pp. 727–728).

In his book *Development as Freedom*, Amartya Sen (1999) compares the notion of wealth and poverty in two different countries, India and the United States. Sen shows that class structure is a relative term and cannot be measured through capital or wealth alone. If one solely uses a person's income and assets to measure their social status, a person who is considered rich in India may not even be considered middle class in the United States (Sen, 1999). Similarly, a landlord from a rural village of Nepal would have a different status if s/he migrated to Kathmandu.

Although subjective and objective structures appear different, they are inseparable because each contributes to the production and reproduction of the other (Jenkins, 1992). They are "in a close dialectic" (Dick, 2008, p. 329). For instance, material conditions influence people's position and people can influence material conditions. Both structures have their own limitations. A subjective approach to social theory focuses on individuals as agents, assuming that people are free to make their own choices based on their own interests and desires (Calhoun, LiPuma, & Postone, 1993, p. 3). Meanwhile, an objectivist approach to social theory focuses on the influence of social structures – economic, cultural and material relations – on people's lives (Calhoun et al., 1993, p. 3). A subjective method can place too much emphasis on individuals as agents of change without considering how the social order may constrain or limit their ability to act. Conversely, focusing on objective structures emphasizes material conditions, which risks overlooking the capacity of people to create social change.

Bourdieu's theory on the phenomenology of social space provides an inclusive framework bridging the gap between these two approaches (Calhoun et al., 1993). He opposes the two extremes and demonstrates the importance of both the subjective and the objective structures in the construction of our lives and analyzes how the two are interlinked. He argues:

> Microsociological vision leaves out a good number of other things: as often happens when you look too closely, you cannot see the wood for the tree; and above all, failing to construct the space of positions leaves you no chance of seeing the point from which you see what you see.
>
> (Bourdieu, 1989, p. 19)

In short, the same person can have different positions in different contexts and a different set of habitus (Bourdieu, 1989). He argues that the "social reality" that an objectivist believes is also a perception (Bourdieu, 1989, p. 18).

Bourdieu claims that although the objective structures (cultural, social, political, economic and material) have an impact on individuals' lives, a person's life is not fully shaped by the structure of the society (Calhoun et al., 1993, p. 3). While we often perform actions without knowing why, we may nevertheless reflect on them and modify our behaviour if given the opportunity (Jenkins, 1992). Individuals as agents have the capacity to reflect on their own actions. Since humans are reflexive, they arrange their actions and behaviours around their own interests and desires (Calhoun et al., 1993). In other words, individuals have agency, making them not only the constructors of society but also agents of change.

Bourdieu's theory of social life can be compared to a game. As in all games, there are rules for the players. Society, he contends, operates in a similar way where there are certain rules that agents acting within society must follow. These rules are taught since childhood, as well as instilled through practice in everyday life (Jenkins, 1992). People's social competencies are defined by their knowledge of and adherence to these rules (Jenkins, 1992). Although certain knowledge is important for the production and reproduction of social order (Jenkins, 1992), the system is not fixed and does not depend upon the intention of individuals, but rather on individuals obeying the rules at particular times and within specific contexts (Bourdieu, 1977, p. 2). For instance, female tempo drivers in Nepal might have to adhere to strict social rules when visiting their family in a village; they may, for example, have to wear a sari, but they may not necessarily follow the same strict rules when they are in the city. However, while they do not have to wear a sari, they still do not wear shorts or the type of clothing worn by male drivers. There is a significant departure from the previous habitus, but not a full departure from gender roles, although this may change over time.

For Bourdieu, social structure has three tiers: field, habitus and practice. Field has its "own history, logic and agents" (LiPuma, 1993, p. 15). Habitus is another relation of embodied social rules and norms, which shape how individuals see the world and operate in it. Practice is embodied social knowledge. These tiers are interconnected and one can influence the other. Thus, practice can influence the habitus, field can feed into habitus, and habitus can affect field and guide practice.

Bourdieu's notion of field as objective structure

Field, for Bourdieu, is a "network, or a configuration, of objective relations between positions" (Bourdieu & Wacquant, 1992, p. 97). It is a "separate social universe having its own laws of functioning independent of those of politics and the economy" (Bourdieu & Johnson, 1993, p. 89). Jenkins simplifies Bourdieu's notion of field as "a structured system of social positions – occupied either by individuals or institutions – the nature of which defines the situation for their occupants" (Jenkins, 1992). These are not limited to economic, social, cultural or religious fields. Field can be any structured social space with its own rules and stakeholders (Jenkins, 1992, p. 84). One such example is a university. The university has its own logic and well-defined structure, where academics, students and staff have to obey certain rules. Although these rules determine identities and competencies (e.g. 'good academic' or 'poor student'), they are nevertheless often taken for as norms by the agents who operate within the field. There can be many fields within the same university, divided by faculties, schools and departments. These various fields may have some shared rules and some that are specific to that field. Depending on the context and scope, there may be fields operating together despite having different rules. Although each field has its own boundaries, they are not very restrictive and always shifting (Jenkins, 1992).

Fields are autonomous and have their own rules and logic (Dick, 2008; Jenkins, 1992); they are like a "prism which refracts every external determination: demographic, economic or political events are always retranslated according to the specific logic of the field" (Bourdieu, 1993, pp. 89–90). In other words, although these fields are autonomous, the logic of a field is constructed within a broader discourse, reflecting larger social structures. For instance, the logic of a political institution is constructed within a broader discourse but is adjusted and practiced according to a local context. For example, the Women's Caucus in Nepal is a political body; while it can be a politically autonomous field it can never be entirely separate from Nepali politics. The Women's Caucus is a reflection of various political parties and of varied sociocultural fields within Nepalese society.

The concept of the field in Bourdieu's theory on social life provides a framework for "relational analysis" of "the multidimensional space of positions and the position taking of agents" (Calhoun et al., 1993, p. 5). Although each field has its own agents, logic, history and a form of capital, the fields are interrelated (Calhoun et al., 1993, p. 5) and influence each other. Changes in the economic field, for example, will have an impact on social and cultural fields, and changes within the political field may have an effect on various national and international institutions.

Penny Dick (2008) argues that Bourdieu's notion of field is an analytical category which provides space for the systematic investigation of complex and dynamic social orders. The notion of field contributes to an understanding of social order and avoids homogenizing the processes of social transformation. If there is a transformation in one field, it may not necessarily have an impact on all other fields. A concrete example of the complex interrelation between fields can be found when considering widowhood in Nepal, where widows no longer have to wear a white sari. While this is certainly a significant transformation in the cultural field, it does not necessarily mean the social structure has been completely transformed. Widows may still face various forms of discrimination. Moreover, these social transformations are also dependent on geographical context, as the discourse of widowhood remains more restrictive in the western regions of Nepal than in the eastern regions.

The independent logic of these varied fields and their interconnected nature illustrates two key points: (1) the assumption that social transformation is a megaproject, where all fields will transform at the same time, is incorrect; and (2) the understanding of social transformation as an intentional process, where external intervention (with predetermined goals) is necessary, is erroneous. When the Maoist movement began in Nepal, there was no intended goal to transform discourses surrounding widowhood.

Bourdieu's notion of habitus as subjective structure

Bourdieu's notion of habitus is an important concept, which is key when examining of the process of social transformation. Habitus, for Bourdieu, is the way people "carry themselves" (Jenkins, 1992, p. 75). It is an embodiment of social rules that exists 'inside the head' and is made visible through practice and behaviours (Jenkins, 1992, pp. 74–75). "Habitus is both a system of schemes of production of practices and a system of perception and appreciation of practices" (Bourdieu, 1989, p. 19). In other words, we act according to our habitus, and people who view/ perceive our acts as 'normal' or 'natural' are also a product of habitus, as their own habitus shapes how they view the world.

Bourdieu (1989, p. 19) argues that habitus provides a sense of belonging, the 'sense of one's place' and the 'sense of the place of others'. First, it presupposes and classifies what 'family' should be like and then provides it with meaning (Bourdieu, 1989, p. 19), which we understand through our practice in everyday life. Habitus also guides appropriate actions and behaviours, which are not necessarily conscious decisions. Habitus directs practice "in a subconscious, unreflective manner" (Brubaker, 1993, p. 225). We act without being conscious of it and we believe that the actions are normal and therefore acceptable. As previously discussed, social actions are neither wholly determined nor completely arbitrary; instead, habitus generates and shapes social actions according to the rules and internal logic of the field (Adkins, 2003, p. 23).

The habitus is the integration of past experiences into the present as perceptions and natural actions. Bourdieu claims that everyone is a "producer and reproducer of objective meaning," which indicates that our actions are "the product of a modus operandi of which we are not the producer and of which we do not possess conscious mastery, they contain an 'objective intention' which is beyond their consciousness" (Bourdieu, 1973, p. 70). Habitus is social competence that is characterized as durable and transposable (Adkins, 2003, p. 23). McNay (1999, p. 102) argues:

> Habitus suggests a layer of embodied experience that is not immediately amenable to self-fashioning. On a pre-reflexive level, the actor is predisposed or oriented to behave in a certain way because of the 'active presence' of the whole past embedded in the durable structures of the habitus.

Bourdieu's notion of habitus is important in the study of social transformation because it provides a language to articulate the non-linear nature of social transformation.

Bourdieu's notion of practice as place for reflexivity

Another of Bourdieu's key ideas about social life is his theory of practice (LiPuma, 1993). According to Bourdieu, people act according to their feel (habitus) for the game (field), meaning that their actions are not just a reflection of the field but also of their habitus (Jenkins, 1992). Practice of social rules cannot be expected to be the same at different times and in different contexts. Each practice has its own context and operates within a temporal framework (Jenkins, 1992, p. 69).

Jenkins argues that nothing is random and no response is out of context. One action leads to another and they are not always performed in full consciousness (Jenkins, 1992, p. 70). Individuals do not always think before they act and their thoughts may not be rational. An individual's actions can be automatic responses to a particular situation, which can be understood in relation to a practical logic or common sense appropriate in a particular context. Bourdieu (1977, p. 22) contends:

> The agent who 'regularizes' his situation or puts himself in the right is simply beating the group at its own game; in abiding by the rules, falling into line with good form, he wins the group over to his side by ostentatiously honouring the values the group honours . . . It is therefore not sufficient to say that the rule determines the practice when there is more to be gained by obeying it than by disobeying it.

There are three points to note here. First, human being do not always act consciously. Even when rationales are given, they are constructed within a particular field and subject to the field's internal logic. Second, 'doxic practices', the social constructions that we take for granted, make our lives easy and enable us to feel that we are part of society. Third, we think these doxic acts are natural because we have learned them since birth; for instance, the understanding that a girl is supposed to walk in a particular way, dress and speak in certain ways and so on (Bourdieu & Eagleton, 1992, p. 115). Following the rules assigned by the society means "conforming to the social order, and . . . not falling out of line" (Bourdieu, 1977, p. 161).

We often perform gendered norms without question because they are considered normal and innate. Bourdieu calls these accepted situations, which are perceived as natural, 'doxa', or practical knowledge (Bourdieu, 1989; Bourdieu & Eagleton, 1992). These doxic attitudes reproduce a given understanding of the world where, for example, rules for each gender are considered essential and universal (Calhoun, 2006, p. 1405). Although doxic practices occur in every society, traditional societies have many more of such practices where the world is considered as natural and "self-evident" (Bourdieu, 1977, p. 164). In rural areas of Nepal, traditional social beliefs are considered more natural and normal than in cities. However, doxa is not the same as 'orthodoxy' (Moi, 1991, p. 1026). Doxa is something that is understood as natural without question; one such example is the practice of the wife moving to her husband's home after marriage in Nepal. This routine is usually never questioned unless or until there are some special circumstances. These doxic practices may put people into a subordinated position, which they accept as normal without question. Since actors operate within a constructed discourse, they tend to accept their situation as reality as they do not have the capacity to imagine alternatives or options (Bourdieu & Eagleton, 1992, p. 118).

While describing his notion of habitus as a generative structure, Bourdieu argues that crisis leads to questioning of doxic practices (Bourdieu, 1977, p. 168), which then contributes to change. One example can be found in Nepal: when men died in the war, there was a sudden increase in the number of young widows. These widows started working outside the home in order to survive. It was initially difficult for them, but through this process they gained access to public life. They not only learned new things; they were also able to reflect and examine their own lives. However, it is important to note that not every crisis is "a sufficient condition for the production of a critical discourse" (Bourdieu, 1977, p. 168). Bourdieu's theory of *practice* explains how traditional norms, even though they are discriminatory, are produced and reproduced. This theory is particularly important for the study of social transformation, as it helps us understand how social transformation takes place, why some norms are continued, some are reproduced in a new form and some are abandoned.

Although Bourdieu's theory of social life is a comprehensive theory with which to capture the multiplicity and fluidity of social relations, he faces criticism from feminist scholars. The main criticism is that he underrepresents gender in his work. He only started considering gender in his article "La Domination Masculine" (Moi, 1991; Thorpe, 2010). He has also been criticized for not responding appropriately to existing feminist theory. Since his scholarship is mostly limited to analyzing the structural constraints of masculine domination, his views on gender are considered as ahistorical and androcentric (Fowler, 2003; Thorpe, 2010).

Bourdieu also faces the charge of determinism. In response, he argues that habitus is not a principle of determination but a generative structure. Despite the criticism, there is an increasing number of feminist scholars who are using Bourdieu (Adkins, 2003; Adkins & Skeggs, 2004; Krais, 1993; McLeod, 2005; McNay, 1999; Moi, 1991). Toril Moi (1991, p. 1019) argues that he provides a "microtheory of social life" that enables us "to incorporate the most mundane details of everyday life in our analyses." Although only a few scholars have used his theory to examine social transformation (see Adkins, 2003; Calhoun, 2006; Fowler, 2012; McNay, 1999), it is nevertheless an emerging area for exploration. Julie McLeod argues that the unevenness of the relationship between field and habitus offers scope to study social change and continuity within feminist analysis (McLeod, 2005, p. 12). Although Bourdieu's model of masculine domination was formulated with reference to advanced capitalist countries (Fowler, 2003, p. 469) in the 1960s, it not only "exemplifies the ways in which gender hierarchies are maintained in modern industrial society" (Thorpe, 2010, p. 291), but it can also be applied to the gender structures of present-day Nepal.

Foucault's power and subject

While Bourdieu's theory of social life is useful to explore the interconnected-ness of subjective and objective structures, Foucault's theory of power provides a language to articulate how different subjects and structures are constructed and how they are reproduced. According to Foucault (1982), subjects are constituted through power. It is a system of power that establishes someone as a subject, such as a minister, prime minister or head of the department. Foucault further clarifies his notion of 'subject' by separating it into two forms. He writes:

> There are two meanings of the word 'subject': subject to someone else by control and dependence; and tied to his own identity by a conscience or self-knowledge. Both meanings suggest a form of power which subjugates and makes subject to.
>
> (Foucault, 1982, p. 781)

Subjectivity, for Foucault, is constructed by a discourse within the location of the subject (Minson, 1995, p. 84). Different discourses construct different subject-positions (Heller, 1996, p. 93). According to Foucault,

> although all subject-positions are 'subjected' to discourses that temporally and ontologically precede them, the inevitable multiplicity of those discourses ensures that subjectification invariably produces structurally incompatible (i.e., hegemonic and counter-hegemonic) subject-positions.
>
> (Heller, 1996, p. 94)

Within each field, there are actors with their own subject positions determined both by the distribution of resources within a given field and by the structural rela-tions between that field and others. Foucault's notion of subject position is signifi-cant as it allows examination of how society can undergo social change originating within the lower social echelons, as well as the multiplicity of the social positions of each individual. For example, a female CA member, who used to be a housewife with one set of powers, becomes a politician working in national government; thus the power associated with her position has changed, as has her status in society.

The social field is "a multi-dimensional space of positions" where each position "can be defined in terms of a multi-dimensional system of co-ordinates whose val-ues correspond to the values of the different pertinent variables" (Bourdieu, 1985, p. 724). There are two aspects to this theory. First, each individual has their posi-tion according to their overall social capital. The second dimension is the relative merit or importance of that capital (Bourdieu, 1985, p. 724). For instance, a person from a remote village of Nepal can be classified as a powerful person in her/his village, but when s/he is displaced to a new city where no one knows her/him, their power and status will not remain the same. Bourdieu further clarifies this theory regarding the position of an actor: "the position of a given agent within the social space can thus be defined by the positions he occupies in the different fields, that is, in the distribution of the powers that are active within each of them" (Bourdieu, 1985, p. 724). These powers are the product of both embodied and materialized capital which defines "the state of the power relations" which are "institutional-ized," "socially recognized" and "legally guaranteed." "It determines the actual or potential powers within the different fields and the chances of access to the specific profits that they offer" (Bourdieu, 1985, p. 724). Bourdieu's notion of subject posi-tion explains how power relations are institutionalized and recognized.

Foucault's notion of subject position explains how power is experienced, chal-lenged and changed. Power does not always determine the subject's position in the field; the subject's place is relational and can be experienced through the exer-cise of power. Foucault's notion of subject position enables the understanding of transformation in Nepal; it helps locate the multi-dimensional power relations that a single person can experience in a multi-dimensional society. Foucault's notion of subject position is also helpful in exploring how changes in subject positions contribute to social change.

Discourse

Changing discourse is another key aspect to consider in the process of transfor-mation. Discourse can be understood as a group of statements and practices that define how people engage with everyday life (Pringle & Markula, 2006, p. 52). According to Foucault, everything is constructed through discourse (Mills, 2003, p. 55), even the understanding of our bodies. It is not something that is imposed on an individual level, but a system through which we perceive our reality that may enable or constrain our actions (Mills, 2003, p. 55). Discourse can be both a tool and an effect of power (Mills, 2003, p. 54). Foucault argues that knowledge and power are interlinked through discourse (Heller, 1996; Pringle & Markula, 2006). "Knowledge is defined by the possibilities of use and appropriation offered by discourse . . . there is no knowledge without discursive practice; and any discursive practice may be defined by the knowledge that it forms" (Foucault, 1972, as cited in Pringle & Markula, 2006, pp. 53–54).

While Bourdieu discusses the embodiment of social norms, Butler focuses on the performative aspect of these norms. This framework enables scholars to articulate how changes in gender performance (practice, in Bourdieu's terminol-ogy) can lead to social transformation. Butler's notion of gender is also useful in understanding gender construction in Nepalese society.

Exploring the performative nature of gender: Butler

A central question in this book is how social transformation is understood when women's lived experiences are at the centre of the analysis. This is explored by considering the changing performances of women in post-conflict Nepal. Butler's notion of gender as performative is useful, as it provides an insight into how the social norms and rules that constrain our actions and govern our reality are main-tained, produced and reproduced (Butler, 2001, p. 15).

Butler shows that while performance is a crucial part of gender performativity, 'performance' and 'performativity' are two different but related concepts. Gender performance is performing gender roles within cultural situations or as a response to a set of norms. It is the performance of identity and the actions of individuals that are governed by cultural norms. According to Butler, agency is constrained by culture and "what I can do is, to a certain extent, conditioned by what is available for me to do within the culture and by what other practices are and by what practices are legitimizing" (Olson & Worsham, 2004, p. 345). Gender performativity is "not just drawing on the norms that constitute, limit, and condition [the individual]; it's also delivering a performance within a context of reception, and [the individual] cannot fully anticipate what will happen" (Olson & Worsham, 2004, p. 345).

Butler also draws attention to the fact that context or the audience has an impact on gender performativity, which is similar to Bourdieu's theory of practice. One performs their gender and modifies their gender performance depending on *where* they are – socially, politically and geographically. Thus, "gender performativity . . . produces hermeneutic rifts, questions of whether a common understanding (of gender) is even possible" (Olson & Worsham, 2004, p. 345). What is performed is determined not just by the agent's actions, but also by the context and the recipient's responses. "What are being performed are the cultural norms that condition and limit the actor in the situation" (Olson & Worsham, 2004, p. 345).

Butler's notion of agency is particularly relevant for this study. For instance, as I discuss in Chapters 4–8, no matter how profound the social transformation Nepalese widows, ex-combatants, and female tempo drivers have experienced, the context in which they act still limits their performance. The women who left their homes to fight against discrimination in the war have all the knowledge and capacity to exercise their agency – in theory. This is not the case in practice, however. They are still daughters and/or wives, and while they live in a society that has been transformed to some extent, it has not changed as radically or as quickly as these individuals have. However, this does not mean they cannot do anything to change their position; it means that what they can and what they cannot do is limited. These limitations are not only imposed on them, explicitly or implicitly, by society, but are often endorsed by the women themselves, as they are attached to their discourses, habitus or fields – their normal way of being.

Conclusion: Foucault, Bourdieu and Butler combined

Society is a relational space regulated by certain discourses and social relations made visible through the performative acts of individuals. Each of these relational spaces, or fields in Bourdieu's terms, have their own rules and logics followed by stakeholders and agents. These rules are constructed by individuals or subjects within the society or objective structure. According to Bourdieu, social realities are not constructed in a vacuum but within the structural constraints of a particular social order. Likewise, cognitive structures are socially mandated, and this social reality is not an individual perception but a collective belief (Bourdieu, 1989). Once these structures and beliefs are created, they are then taken as 'essential' or 'normal' aspects of social life, and they often remain unquestioned (Mills, 2003, p. 56); this is similar to what Bourdieu calls doxa. The social universe is often implicitly assumed and not questioned until this becomes unavoidable (Bourdieu & Eagleton, 1992, p. 118).

Doxa, for Bourdieu, is a practical experience (Bourdieu & Eagleton, 1992, p. 118). People assume their history to be an objective reality which, in turn, is the foundation of habitus. Thus, our actions and practices are the products of that habitus (Jenkins, 1992). Habitus also affects history. According to Bourdieu's theory, agents are not just those who maintain the rules; habitus also leads practice (Adkins, 2003, p. 24). It is possible to observe different practices performed by different actors in each field, and the action of the agents thus shapes the habitus (Adkins, 2003, p. 24).

Social realities and beliefs are constructed within an overarching framework. Bourdieu explains, for example, how masculine domination influences both subjective and objective structures. He argues:

> The social world functions (to a greater or lesser extent, depending on the field) as a market in symbolic goods, dominated by the masculine vision: for women, as has been noted, to be is to be perceived, and perceived by the male eye or by an eye informed by masculine categories.
>
> (Bourdieu & Nice, 2001, p. 99)

Bourdieu shows that knowledge about the social world is constructed within a masculine discourse (Bourdieu & Nice, 2001). Although in Nepal these constructions are experienced differently by people from different castes, ethnic background or geographical regions, the masculine order influences all the other social variables. There are a number of factors, such as family structures or public institutions, which ensures continuity and durability of such practices.

Foucault argues that everything is constructed through discourse, including our understanding of our own body (Mills, 2003, p. 55). Therefore, knowledge is discursive, and discourse both influences and forms knowledge (Markula & Pringle, 2006). Drawing on all three theorists, I argue that structures are the 'discursive construction of collective beliefs'. In other words, social structure is a discursive habitus. It is discursive because each social structure is constructed through a particular discourse. Not just subjective but also objective structures such as social rules, laws, and rituals are constructed through a particular discourse. Due to the repeated practice of these discursively constructed rules, they become the habitus of individuals and society. Although habitus is generative, it is durable and lasts for a long time. Habitus thus resemble doxa, self-evident knowledge. People follow the rules and logics of a particular field, as these are considered normal and natural. Thus, a social structure is neither fixed nor material or virtual. It is a discursive habitus located within its material and embodied conditions, which become visible through the performance or acts of individuals.

So when does the possibility of social transformation arise? The notion of social reproduction seems to be key to understanding social transformation. According to Bourdieu, social transformation is possible when there is an "objective crisis, which, in breaking the immediate fit between the subjective structures and the objective structures, destroys self-evidence practically" (Bourdieu, 1977, pp. 168–169). In other words, social transformation is possible when there is "a critical reflexive stance towards formerly normalized – or at least taken-for-granted – social conditions" (Adkins, 2003, p. 21). For Bourdieu, reflexivity arises when there is a misfit between field and habitus, "when synchronicity between subjective and objective structures is broken" (Adkins, 2003, p. 21). Adkins argues that "in late modernity there is a lack of fit between habitus and field in certain public spheres of action via an increasing transposition or movement of the feminine habitus from private to public spheres" (Adkins, 2003, p. 21). Likewise, when women in Nepal joined the Maoist movement, their roles suddenly changed and they were no longer confined to the household. They lived and performed within an entirely new sociopolitical and military field. When people were displaced from their villages to the cities, women's exposure to the public sphere increased. Their habitus no longer matched the field, and possibilities for reflectivity about their own practices were created.

Bourdieu further argues that "crisis is a necessary condition for a questioning of doxa but is not in itself a sufficient condition for the production of a critical discourse" (Bourdieu, 1977, p. 169). The reason a crisis alone is not sufficient to trigger critical discourse is that dominant groups, and society at large, will resist the alteration of doxic practices from which they benefit (Bourdieu, 1977, p. 169). For instance, when women started driving tempos in Nepal they were criticized strongly, not because they were unable to do the job but because female tempo drivers would alter the established social structure. It was not the normal social behaviour of women. Therefore, there was a misfit between social field and social habitus regarding women's roles. Moreover, when women joined the tempo driving profession, it clearly created a disarticulation between their previous lives and their current roles at an individual level, which led to the possibility for reflexive experiences. With an increasing number of women joining the profession, the social boundaries for women were also pushed.

Bourdieu's social theory of practice leads to the situated reflexivity which is linked with our everyday activities as unconscious categories of habit which shape our action (Adkins, 2003, p. 25). Reflexivity is not a generalized capacity of subjects, but something that emerges from "distanciation" triggered by conflict or tension within or across the fields and which "arises unevenly from their embeddedness within differing sets of power relations" (McNay, 1999, p. 110). Bourdieu does not deny the normal process of reflexivity that arises from practice in everyday life through self-awareness as well as from outsider intervention (McNay, 1999, p. 106). The possibility of reflexivity emerges where there is a distanciation between the field and the habitus. Butler adds to that by arguing that only those who have internalized the norms can reflect on them (Olson & Worsham, 2004). In other words, only those who have a good understanding of the norms can subvert them.

For Butler (1997), reflexivity is conscience, by which she means that a person's ability to be self-reflexive is closely tied to conscience (Butler, 1997, p. 22). She further elaborates her notion of reflexivity:

> In order to curb desire, one makes of oneself an object for reflection; in the course of producing one's own alterity, one becomes established as a reflexive being, one who can take oneself as an object. Reflexivity becomes the means by which desire is regularly transmitted into the circuit of self-reflection.
>
> (Butler, 1997, p. 22)

Reflexivity appears to be central to social transformation, which arises when there is a misfit between field and habitus. The misfit or the distanciation of the field and the habitus is possible through conflict, external interventions or increased self-awareness. Foucault argues that individuals are the *subject* of transformation, not its passive *objects* (Heller, 1996, p. 83). The notion of critical reflexivity reconciles the gap between the two approaches, between subjective and objective structures, and provides findings that are interactive and more comprehensive. This approach is particularly useful when considering social change from a gender perspective, as it assists in an examination of women's lived experiences of social transformation.

As argued earlier, social structure is a discursive habitus, and thus social transformation occurs when there is a shift in the discursive habitus that goes beyond the normal process of change. The armed conflict in Nepal created a crisis and challenged both subjective and objective structures. For example, when a policeman died, his wife was appointed to take that position. It was something which could never have been imagined in peacetime, as the social expectations placed on widows were different before the war. During a decade of war, many social norms and social institutions were challenged, and new social groups emerged which were not a feature of traditional Nepali society. I will shed light on some of the newly emerged categories of women in Chapters 4–8 and examine the misfit between the field and the habitus which led to social transformation.

Notes

1 Bourdieu understands masculine domination as an overarching structure that influences both 'subjective structures' and 'objective structures'. He does not talk about the varied experiences of masculine domination by the people from different class/caste/ethnic groups. However, his notion of habitus does explain these differences very well.

2 See Lyn Bennett for more details about the practice of Teej and Panchami, available at http://himalaya.socanth.cam.ac.uk/collections/journals/kailash/pdf/kailash_04_02_04. pdf. Also see http://blog.nepaladvisor.com/rishi-panchami/.

References

Adkins, L. (2003). Reflexivity: Freedom or Habit of Gender? *Theory, Culture & Society*, *20*(6), 21–42. doi:10.1177/0263276403206002.

Adkins, L., & Skeggs, B. (2004). *Feminism after Bourdieu*. Malden, MA: Blackwell.

Bennett, L. (2004). The Wives of the Rishis: An Analysis of the Tij-Rishi Panchami Women's Festival. Retrieved 30 October 2015 from http://himalaya.socanth.cam.ac.uk/collections/journals/kailash/pdf/kailash_04_02_04.pdf

Bourdieu, P. (1973). The Three Forms of Theoretical Knowledge. *Social Science Information, 12*(1), 53–80. doi:10.1177/053901847301200103.

Bourdieu, P. (1977). *Outline of a Theory of Practice* (Vol. 16). Cambridge: Cambridge University Press.

Bourdieu, P. (1985). The Social Space and the Genesis of Groups. *Social Science Information, 24*(2), 195–220. doi:10.1177/053901885024002001.

Bourdieu, P. (1989). Social Space and Symbolic Power. *Sociological Theory, 7*(1), 14–25.

Bourdieu, P. (1993). *The Field of Cultural Production: Essays on Art and Literature* (R. Johnson, Ed.). Cambridge: Polity Press.

Bourdieu, P. (1998). *On Television* (P. P. Ferguson, Trans.). New York: New Press.

Bourdieu, P., & Eagleton, T. (1992). Doxa and Common Life. *New Left Review, 191*, 111–121.

Bourdieu, P., & Nice, R. (2001). *Masculine Domination*. Cambridge: Polity Press.

Bourdieu, P., Sapiro, G., & McHale, B. (1991). First Lecture. Social Space and Symbolic Space: Introduction to a Japanese Reading of Distinction. *Poetics Today, 12*(4), 627–638.

Bourdieu, P., & Wacquant, L.J.D. (1992). *An Invitation to Reflexive Sociology*. Chicago: University of Chicago Press.

Brubaker, R. (1993). Social Theory as Habitus. In C. Calhoun, E. LiPuma, & M. Postone (Eds.), *Bourdieu: Critical Perspectives* (pp. 212–134). Chicago: University of Chicago Press.

Butler, J. (1997). *The Psychic Life of Power: Theories in Subjection*. Stanford, CA: Stanford University Press.

Butler, J. (2001). The Question of Social Transformation (J. Vaida, Trans.). In J. Butler, E. Beck-Gernsheim, & L. Puigvert (Eds.), *Women and Social Transformation* (pp. 1–28). New York: Peter Lang.

Calhoun, C. (2006). Pierre Bourdieu and Social Transformation: Lessons from Algeria. *Development and Change, 37*(6), 1403–1415. doi:10.1111/j.1467-7660.2006.00535.x.

Calhoun, C.J., LiPuma, E., & Postone, M. (1993). *Bourdieu: Critical Perspectives*. Cambridge: Polity Press.

Dick, P. (2008). Resistance, Gender, and Bourdieu's Notion of Field. *Management Communication Quarterly, 21*(3), 327–343. doi:10.1177/0893318907309930.

Foucault, M. (1972). *The Archaeology of Knowledge and Discourse on Language*. New York: Pantheon Books.

Foucault, M. (1978). *The History of Sexuality, Vol. 1: An Introduction*. London: Penguin Books.

Foucault, M. (1982). The Subject and Power. *Critical Inquiry, 8*(4), 777–795.

Fowler, B. (2003). Reading Pierre Bourdieu's Masculine Domination: Notes towards an Intersectional Analysis of Gender, Culture and Class. *Cultural Studies, 17*(3–4), 468–494. doi:10.1080/0950238032000083908.

Fowler, B. (2012). Pierre Bourdieu, Social Transformation and 1960s British Drama. *Theory, Culture & Society, 29*(3), 3–24. doi:10.1177/0263276412441034.

Heller, K.J. (1996). Power, Subjectification and Resistance in Foucault. *SubStance, 25*(1), 78–110.

Jenkins, R. (1992). *Pierre Bourdieu*. New York: Routledge.

Kathmandu Post. (2011, 31 September). Hindus, Muslims Celebrate Teej, Eid. Retrieved 12 June 2014 from http://www.ekantipur.com/the-kathmandu-post/2011/08/31/metro/hindus-muslims-celebrate-teej-eid/225765.html

Kathmandu Post. (2015, 17 September). Women Throng Temples for Teej. Retrieved 25 October 2015 from http://kathmandupost.ekantipur.com/printedition/news/2015-09-17/women-throng-temples-for-teej.html

Krais, B. (1993). Gender and Symbolic Violence: Female Oppression in the Light of Pierre Bourdieu's Theory of Social Practice. In C. Calhoun, E. LiPuma, & M. Postone (Eds.), *Bourdieu: Critical Perspectives* (pp. 156–177). Chicago: University of Chicago Press.

LiPuma, E. (1993). Culture and the Concept of Culture in a Theory of Practice. In C. J. Calhoun, E. LiPuma, & M. Postone (Eds.), *Bourdieu: Critical Perspectives* (pp. 14–34). Chicago: University of Chicago.

Lukes, S. (1974/2005). *Power: A Radical View* (2nd ed.). Basingstoke: Palgrave Macmillan.

Markula, P., & Pringle, R. (2006). *Foucault, Sport and Exercise: Power, Knowledge and Transforming the Self*. New York: Routledge.

McLeod, J. (2005). Feminists Re-reading Bourdieu: Old Debates and New Questions about Gender Habitus and Gender Change. *Theory and Research in Education, 3*(1), 11–30. doi:10.1177/1477878505049832.

McNay, L. (1999). Gender, Habitus and the Field: Pierre Bourdieu and the Limits of Reflexivity. *Theory, Culture & Society, 16*(1), 95–117. doi:10.1177/026327699016001007.

Mills, S. (2003). *Michel Foucault*. New York: Routledge.

Minson, J. (1995). Strategies for Sociologists? Foucault's Conception of Power. In B. Smart (Ed.), *Michel Foucault: Critical Assessments* (Vol. 5, pp. 79–114). New York: Routledge.

Moi, T. (1991). Appropriating Bourdieu: Feminist Theory and Pierre Bourdieu's Sociology of Culture. *New Literary History, 22*(4), 1017–1049.

Olson, G.A., & Worsham, L. (2004). Changing the Subject: Judith Butler's Politics of Radical Resignification, an Interview with Gary A. Olson and Lynn Worsham. In J. Butler & S. Salih (Eds.), *The Judith Butler Reader* (pp. 325–356). Malden, MA: Blackwell.

Sawicki, J. (1986). Foucault and Feminism: Toward a Politics of Difference. *Hypatia, 1*(2), 23–36.

Sen, A. (1999). *Development as Freedom*. Oxford: Oxford University Press.

Thorpe, H. (2010). Bourdieu, Gender Reflexivity, and Physical Culture: A Case of Masculinities in the Snowboarding Field. *Journal of Sport & Social Issues, 34*(2), 176–214. doi:10.1177/0193723510367770.

Turshen, M., Meintjes, S., & Pillay, A. (2001). There Is No Aftermath for Women. In M. Turshen, S. Meintjes, & A. Pillay (Eds.), *The Aftermath: Women in Post-conflict Transformation* (pp. 3–18). London: Zed Books.

3 Social structure of Nepal

A historical overview

Geography and demography of Nepal

Ethnically and culturally diverse, Nepal is geographically divided into three regions: *Terai* (the Plains, which are also called *Madhesh*), the Hills and the Mountains. Out of 26.6 million people, more than half (50.27 per cent) live in *Terai*, 43 per cent in the Hills and 6.73 per cent in the Mountains. Nepal endorsed its new constitution in September 2015 (*Constitution of Nepal 2072*, 2015) through the Constituent Assembly, which divided the country into seven federal states.[1] These states are further divided into Districts, Municipalities and Village Development Committees.

The majority of the people live in rural areas (83 per cent) with less than one-fifth (17 per cent) in urban areas. However, there has been a significant increase in the urban population (14.99 per cent) in the last 10 years, with the highest population growth in Kathmandu district (61.23 per cent). This leaves 27 districts of Nepal with negative population growth, including extreme population decline in Manang district (a loss of 31.80 per cent). Population density, the average number of people per square kilometer, at the national level was recorded as 180 in 2011. The Kathmandu district has the highest population density, with 4,416 people per square kilometer. The lowest is 3 people per square kilometer in Manang district (CBS, 2011). There are two reasons for the extreme population growth in Kathmandu: (1) people left their villages during the war to look for a safer place, and Kathmandu was perceived as a safe place to live; and (2) resources and opportunities are centralized in the capital city. Therefore, many people want to settle in Kathmandu. Although life is a struggle for many, Kathmandu has become an ultimate destination for the people who want to progress in their lives.

The female population is slightly higher (51.44 per cent) than the male population (48.56 per cent) in Nepal (CBS, 2011). It is important to note that the gender ratio has decreased in the last 10 years. It was 99.8 (males per 100 females) in 2001, which decreased to 94.2 (males per 100 females) in 2011. Likewise, the absentee population has doubled in the last 10 years (1.92 million in 2011 versus 0.762 million in 2001), of which 86.7 per cent are men.[2] There is a correlation between the absentee population and the reduced gender ratio. The 2011 census also confirms that one in every four households (25.42 per cent) has at least one absent member. The average household size has decreased to 4.88 from 5.44 (CBS, 2011).

Nepal is a diverse country also in terms of language. People from different ethnic backgrounds speak different languages. Besides Nepali, there are 123 languages spoken as mother tongues. Some 44.6 per cent of the total population speaks Nepali as their mother tongue, followed by Maithili (11.7 per cent), Bhojpuri (6 per cent), Tharu (5.8 per cent), Tamang (5.1 per cent), Newar (3.2 per cent), Bajjika (3 per cent), Magar (3 per cent), Doteli (3 per cent) and Urdu (2.6 per cent); the remainder speak other languages (CBS, 2011). Although there is recognition of other languages, Nepali is an official language of Nepal.

The literacy rate among the population aged 5 and above has increased in the last 10 years from 54.1 per cent (in 2001) to 65.9 per cent (in 2011). However, there is still a big gap between the literacy rate among men (75.1 per cent) and women (57.4 per cent). The gap between men and women is even wider at higher levels of education. Out of 158,432 people doing postgraduate studies, only one-quarter (39,603) are women (CBS, 2011). The urban population is more literate than the rural population. The highest literacy is in the Kathmandu district (86.3 per cent) and the lowest literacy rate is in Rautahat district, which is in *Terai*, where only 41.7 per cent of the local population can read and write.

Caste and ethnicity are contested issues in Nepal, especially after the establishment of democracy in 1990. There is no clear distinction between caste and ethnicity in colloquial Nepali, as *Jat* (best translated as 'descent group') is used for both (Whelpton, 2005, p. 8). However, it is important to understand this concept, as Nepal's social structure operates according to *Jat*. Everyone in Nepal knows what their caste/ethnicity is. David Gellner (2007, p. 1823) argues that it is "unimaginable" to identify anyone in Nepal without their caste or ethnicity. It is maintained throughout one's life in all the cultural and religious practices from birth to death. Even laws and politics are highly influenced by the interests of different castes and ethnic groups. Though the extent of rigidity or flexibility within and between different castes and ethnicity may vary, castes/ethnicity specific cultures are being practiced in every section of Nepali society.

Although it is not very difficult to identify who is who, meaning who belongs to which caste or ethnic group as their surname indicates their caste or ethnicity, there is no common agreement on the definition of ethnic group or ethnicity. Kailash Nath Pyakuryal (2008), an eminent Nepali sociologist, argues that people are considered members of the same ethnic group if they have some common features, such as common ancestral history, the same culture, religion, race and language. He elaborates:

> An ethnic group can have one or more things in common whereas ethnicity is a 'we feeling' with varying degree of reciprocal, common identification such as symbols of shared heritage, including language, religion, and customs, awareness of similar historical experience, and a sense of in group loyalty or associated with a shared social position, similar values and interests, and often, but inevitably, identification with a specific national origin.
>
> (Pyakuryal, 2008, p. 191)

The population census started in 1911 in Nepal, was just a head counting process. Scientific data collection started in 1952–1954. However, data on caste and ethnicity was first collected in 1991 when 60 castes and ethnic groups were identified. Those groups whose population was more than 1 per cent of the total population were considered as 'major castes/ethnicity' and those who had less than 1 per cent were called 'minor groups' (Niroula, 1998, p. 15). The 2001 census listed 103 caste/ethnic groups. According to this census, 57.5 per cent of the population were caste groups, 37.2 per cent were *Janajati* (indigenous) and the religious minority were 4.3 per cent. Despite the census data, many agencies provided their own estimates about ethnic/caste groups and thus the information about the number of ethnic/caste groups and their population size differ. For example, Dr Dilli Ram Dahal notes that 59 distinct cultural groups within *Janajati* were identified by the National Committee of Nationalities in 2002; and 28 cultural groups were recorded within *Dalits* by the Dalit Commission (Dhahal, n.d., p. 89). Dahal's research demonstrates the complexities and variations within each caste/ethnic group. Each caste group or ethnicity has its own subcategories and these categories change if a high caste male gets married with a woman from a low caste – which makes it complicated, especially for an outsider, to understand the social organization of Nepal (Thapa & Sharma, 2009).

Lyn Bennett's work on caste and ethnicity in Nepal examines the highly complex nature of the caste/ethnic composition of Nepalese society. Her research substantiates a comprehensive list of the different castes and ethnicities used as a benchmark by international non-governmental organizations (I/NGOs) and UN agencies and for government purposes (Bennett, Dahal, & Govindasamy, 2008). The 2011 census recorded 125 caste/ethnic groups, with Chhetri having the largest population (16.6 per cent), followed by Brahmin (12.2 per cent), Magar (7.1 per cent), Tharu (6.6 per cent), Tamang (5.8 per cent), Newar (5 per cent), Kami (4.8 per cent), Musalman (4.4 per cent), Yadav (4 per cent) and Rai (2.3 per cent) (CBS, 2011).[3] It is interesting to note the increase in the number of castes/ethnic groups since 1991, from 60 to 125. This does not mean that new castes and ethnic groups have emerged. Rather, it means that castes which were ignored in the past are now being officially recognized.

Religion has played a key role in social organization in Nepal. Until 2006, Hinduism was the dominant religious ideology. Although some recognition was given to other major religions, such as Islam and Christianity, Hinduism had traditionally been identified as the dominant religion. Until recently, nearly all public holidays were for Hindu festivals. On January 15, 2007, Nepal was officially declared a secular state, and this led to public holidays that recognize festivals of other religions, such as public holidays for Christmas and *Losar*. Religious categories identified in the census 2011 include Buddhism (9.9 per cent), Islam (4.4 per cent), Kirat (3.1 per cent), Christianity (1.4 per cent) and Prakriti (0.5 per cent); bon, Jainism, Bahai and Sikhism make up less than 0.5 per cent (CBS, 2011). Hinduism is still an important aspect of social life in Nepalese society, as the majority of the population (81.3 per cent) identify as practitioners, but there seems to be a growing tolerance and acceptance of other religions (Sharma & Donini, 2010).

Nepal has its own calendar, which is called *Bikram Sambat* (BS), which is about 56.7 years ahead of the Georgian calendar. The new year starts in *Baisakh* (around mid-April). April 14, 2015, was the start of the Nepalese calendar year 2072.

Historical overview

Historical political shifts in Nepal, most recently the People's War, have significantly impacted the social structure of Nepal (Sharma & Donini, 2010). Historical developments here will help to understand the changing attitude towards caste and ethnicity in post–People's War Nepal, which have also influenced women's lived experiences. This section sheds light on five main historical phases: pre-unification; after unification (1768) until 1990; the first people's movement and the establishment of democracy in 1990; the People's War (between 1996–2006); and the post–People's War (2006 onwards).

The first significant historical political period is pre-unification, when Nepal was divided into several small independent kingdoms and principalities or states. Ahirs and Kirant kings were early dynasties, and then Lichchhavi and Thakuri kings took over and ruled until the twelfth century (NDHS, 2011, p. 1). Kathmandu valley, which has now become the capital of Nepal, was also divided into three small kingdoms – Kathmandu, Lalitpur and Bhaktpur – which were ruled by the Malla dynasty (Einsiedel, Malone, & Pradhan, 2012, p. 4). The Malla era began in the twelfth century, which was called 'the golden age', as kings of that era were well known for their contribution to the arts and culture (NDHS, 2011, p. 1). Similarly, there were many small states in the west called *Baise* (22) and *Chaubise* (24), Rajya (states) ruled by various clans. The Eastern Hills were dominated by the Kirant rulers and the Southern Plains were divided into several kingdoms.[4]

It is difficult to trace the history of Nepal prior to unification, especially in terms of caste and ethnic composition. Dr Dilli Ram Dahal, a Professor of Anthropology at the Centre for Nepal and Asian Studies (CNAS) in Tribhuvan University, offers two main reasons why there is little reliable information about the caste/ethnic structure in Nepal: "(i) History of unified Nepal begins only after 1768, (ii) No anthropological/linguistic survey has been carried out in Nepal to date to note the various ethnic/caste groups and their mother tongues" (Dhahal, n.d., p. 88). However, evidence suggests that the caste system existed long before unification (Aziz, 2001, p. xix). The first record of the caste system was found in the Kathmandu Valley, where the King Jaisthiti Malla (1382–1395) allocated different tasks and ranks to 64 different castes (Dhahal, n.d., p. 89). These small states were ruled by indigenous people and had their own languages and cultures. For instance, Kirats were very different from Mallas. Likewise, the *Baisi* and *Chaubisi* states were Hindu states, whereas in the Western Hills the Khas Empire followed Buddhism (Whelpton, 2005, p. 30). It is noted in the literature that these states were significantly different from each other religiously, ethnically and culturally (Thapa & Sharma, 2009, p. 206).

The second historical political period starts from unification until the end of monarchy. The history of unified Nepal starts from 1768. Prithvi Narayan Shah, who was a king of Gorkha, started the unification campaign in 1765. Although the campaign was led by a Chhetri of the Hindu warrior caste, the King had support from Gurungs and Magars.[5] The campaign was successful and he won several states, including three states in Kathmandu Valley (Kathmandu, Bhaktpur and Lalitpur) and expanded the Eastern region up to Sikkim, which is now part of India (Whelpton, 2005, p. 35). Prithvi Narayan Shah became the first king of Nepal in 1768 (Bennett et al., 2008, p. 2). After he died in 1775, his brother, Bahadur Shah, continued the unification movement and expanded the Western region up to Kumaon and Garhwal, which is now part of the Indian state of Uttaranchal (Whelpton, 2005, p. 39). Within a few years, the small Gorkha state became almost double the size of present Nepal (Thapa, 2012, p. 38). However, war broke out with the British East India Company in 1814, and Nepal in defeat had to sign the treaty called *Sagauli Sandhi* on 2 December 1815, forfeiting many states and reducing Nepal to the present size (Whelpton, 2005, p. 56).

The history of unification is important, not only because it united small states into one, but also because it reshaped the entire social structure of Nepal. After unification, the political system depended on one strong individual – a king (Whelpton, 2005, p. 50) – and it was strictly hierarchical (Frieden, 2012, p. 114). All power and authority were assumed by the king and his family. Shah rulers used the concept of caste hierarchy as an organizing principle to consolidate the diverse peoples inhabiting Nepal into a nation state under their authority (Bennett et al., 2008, p. 2). Power was centralized and only those who were nearest and dearest to the king had power, such as *Bhardars* – the ministers, aides, and officials (Einsiedel et al., 2012, p. 5). These people belonged to higher castes, spoke Nepali, and wore a particular style of dress which were emblems of the rulers and gradually became the norm for the people of Nepal (Einsiedel et al., 2012, p. 5). Despite the fact that the unified Nepal was a combination of different states, where people had different cultures, languages, costume and religious backgrounds, the Shah dynasty was successful in institutionalizing a sense of nationalism, embodied by a single religion (Hinduism), a single language (Nepali), and a single costume (*Daura Suruwal* for men and *Gunyo Cholo* for women) (Einsiedel et al., 2012, p. 5).

In 1846, when Jung Bahadur Rana, who was a military official, took over executive power through a bloody coup, the Shah dynasty came to a temporary halt. The Ranas ruled the country for 104 years as prime ministers through a hereditary system and kept the monarchy in place without giving it any power (Einsiedel et al., 2012; Frieden, 2012).

Discrimination against castes other than Brahmins and Chhetris had already started under the Shah dynasty, which was further institutionalized by the Ranas. The first prime minister of the Rana regime, Jung Bahadur Rana, formalized the caste system by providing a legal framework (Hachhethu, 2003, p. 223). The first civil code, *the Muluki Ain*, adopted in 1854 by Jung Bahadur Rana, was based on the classical Hindu laws of Manu (Aziz, 2001, p. xix) which codified Hindu caste structure and institutionalized the hierarchy, justifying official discrimination against some castes. As a result, a large portion of the population was marginalized (Einsiedel et al., 2012, p. 5). The *Muluki Ain* 1854 classified the people in three categories: (1) at the top, *Tagadhari* ('twice born', the sacred thread-wearing castes); (2) in the middle, *Maatwali* (liquor-drinking castes and ethnic groups); and (3) in the lowest position *Sudra* (impure but touchable castes) and *Acchhut* (impure and untouchable castes) (Hachhethu, 2003).

People were not just allocated different tasks according to their caste. The *Muluki Ain* 1854 discriminated against people from different castes in the judicial system as well as in the distribution of state resources, which translated 'diversity into inequality' (Hachhethu, 2003, p. 223). The *Muluki Ain* 1854 benefitted high caste Brahmins and Chhetris who were close to the ruling elites and marginalized others (Pradhan, 1991, as cited in Thapa, 2012, p. 39).

Ranas played an important role in institutionalizing Hinduism as a national religion and Nepali as an official language. As a result the languages, religions, and cultures of non-privileged groups were gradually silenced (Hoefer, 2004, as cited in Thapa, 2012, p. 40). The Rana dynasty came to an end when King Tribhuvan Bir Bikram Shah, with the support from some political parties, assumed power in 1951. Although the first democracy was established in 1951 under the leadership of the king (Einsiedel et al., 2012, p. 6), King Tribhuvan Bir Bikram Shah did not fulfil his commitment to hold a democratic Constituent Assembly election. Instead he assumed all the power, changed the government several times and appointed handpicked prime ministers. After his death, his son, Mahendra Shah, became the king of Nepal in 1955 (Thapa & Sharma, 2009, p. 207).

Responding to significant political unrest, King Mahendra called a first general election in 1959. Bisheshwor Prashad Koirala from the Nepali Congress (NC) became the prime minister of democratic Nepal. However, his leadership did not last long. King Mahendra overthrew the subsequent government with the support of the Royal Army in December 1960, banned all political parties and instituted the party-less *Panchayat*[6] (traditional village councils) system. He justified these actions by arguing that parliamentary democracy was not suitable for the country (Einsiedel et al., 2012; Thapa & Sharma, 2009). Instead he claimed that *Panchayats* were more democratic. From then on, for the next 30 years, Nepal lived through an authoritarian regime that banned all political activity outside the *Panchayat* system.

The *Panchayat* system further institutionalized the privileges of the Kathmandu-based elites, following the policies which favoured the social and economic values of the ruling upper castes. This led to the systematic marginalization of *Dalits* (untouchables of the Hindu caste system), *Janajati* (the group who lived in the Mountains and mainly spoke Tibeto-Burman language), *Madhesis* (whose origin is traced to the *Terai*, the plains of southern Nepal), and religious minorities and their world view (Thapa, 2012, p. 40). Hence, the *Panchayat* system crafted a sense of Nepali nationhood based on a set of features with which more than two-thirds of the population could not identity (Thapa, 2012, p. 40). However, the rapid change in Nepalese society, including Rana's own investment in expanding education, coupled with a failure to increase opportunities in line with expectations, produced growing opposition to the *Panchayat* system (Whelpton, 2005, p. 86). People started organizing and raised their voices, especially marginalized people like the *Madhesi, Janajati* and *Dalits* (see Thapa, 2012, pp. 40–44).

The third historical/political period of interest here is the first nationwide People's Movement, which began in April 1990 and which successfully established a multiparty democracy within the framework of a constitutional monarchy by overthrowing the *Panchayat* system (NDHS, 2011, p. 1). With the promulgation of the Constitution, 30 years of the *Panchayat* system came to an end in 1990. Thapa and Sharma (2009, p. 208) argue that this political shift was significant in three ways: "it transferred sovereignty from the king to the people; it instituted a parliamentary form of government; and it constitutionally guaranteed the democracy and human rights of the people."

The first election, after establishment of democratic, took place in 1991. This saw the Nepali Congress (NC) win the majority of seats and lead the country. Although the government was elected for 5 years, due to the disagreement between parties, a second election was held within 3 years, in 1994. The Communist Party Nepal – United Marxist Leninist (CPN-UML) defeated the NC in the second election. The CPN-UML was also not able to retain power and dissolved in mid-1994. In the third election in November 1994, none of the parties won a majority. As a result, several coalition governments were formed, which created political uncertainty (Thapa, 2012, p. 48). The instability of government created chaos in the country. The four major political parties were also undergoing internal splits.

Moreover, with the success of the first democratic movement, political awareness among people had increased and their expectations of the new government were at a peak. However, the new government failed to fulfil its commitments (Upreti, 2008, p. 37), such as bridging the gap between rich and poor and removing inequality based on caste, ethnicity, gender, religion and region. The radical social transformation that was promised by democracy was left unfulfilled (Thapa, 2012, p. 48). Likewise, after the re-establishment of democracy in 1990, Nepal was open to all kinds of development, such as infrastructure and skills development. A number of I/NGOs started programs to empower people and raise awareness. People had freedom of speech, and the media began to play an important role in spreading awareness about human rights (Thapa & Sharma, 2009).

The fourth historical period is the People's War of 1996. Although after the establishment of democracy in 1990 ethnic diversity was recognized, power remained in the hands of a few elite groups, mainly from Brahmins and Chhetris (Thapa & Sharma, 2009, p. 208). Discrimination based on gender, class, caste/ethnicity, religion and region continued (Thapa & Sharma, 2009, p. 208). The failure by the democratic government to protect human rights led to the Maoist insurgency in Nepal (Aguirre & Pietropaoli, 2008, p. 359). The Communist Party Nepal – Maoist (CPN-M) launched its People's War in 1996 (Thapa, 2012, p. 42) with the aim of abolishing the monarchy and establishing a discrimination-free People's Republic.[7] They believed that "war is essential to liberate the people from all kinds of exclusions, deprivations, marginalizations, injustices and inequalities" (Pathak, 2005, p. 22).

The history of the Communist Party Nepal (CPN) goes back to its founding in 1949. As a result of the *Panchayat* system, which banned all political activities, followers of communism were brutally suppressed. The CPN itself went through several splits. The CPN (United Centre) was formed in 1991 and won some seats in the first parliamentary election in 1991. In 1994, a more radical faction of CPN (United Centre) emerged which was called CPN-M. The CPN-M submitted a 40-point list of demands to the government, calling for the elimination of all kinds of discrimination such as discrimination based on gender, caste, ethnicity, region and religion.[8] The 40 demands were submitted to the prime minister on 4 February 1996; a week the Maoists announced their *Janayudha* (People's War) on 13 February 1996 (Thapa & Sharma, 2009, p. 209).

The People's War initially started from a few districts of Nepal, such as Rukum and Rolpa in the Mid-western region (Thapa & Sharma, 2009, p. 209), Gorkha in the Central region and Sindhuli in the Eastern region (Pathak, 2005, p. 98). The initial targets of the insurgents were political representatives, police, land-lords, teachers and local government officials because they were perceived to be exploiters and oppressors (IDMC, 2006). Although they started from the Western Mid-hills (Thapa, 2012, p. 37), within a short time the movement grew and spread throughout the country. Because of their agenda and advocacy opposing all kinds of social discriminations, the Maoists received massive support from marginal-ized groups such as *Dalits* and *Janajati* and from women. Indeed sources have documented that over 30 per cent of the Maoist militia were women (Aguirre & Pietropaoli, 2008, p. 359).

A number of factors contributed to the sudden growth and success of the Maoist movement: relative deprivation, exclusion and marginalization of women; dis-crimination against lower castes; disparities among regions, different localities, ethnic groups and inhabitants of certain regions; and continuation of an outdated sociopolitical system. All these factors led to frustration among the people (see Frieden, 2012; Panday, 2012; Thapa, 2012). Nepal went through a dark day of vio-lence when the royal family – the king, his wife and children and other relatives – were assassinated on 1 June 2001.[9] After the murder of the family, King Birendra's brother, Gyanendra Bir Bikram Shah, became king of Nepal on 4 June 2001 (Upreti, 2008, p. 37). People were frustrated with such a political situation, and the royal massacre had saddened the entire country. On the one hand, the Mao-ist insurgency was growing; on the other hand, people's frustration was mount-ing due to the political instability. The security situation gradually worsened for both Maoists and non-Maoists after the imposition of a state of emergency in November 2001 severely curtailed people's freedoms. No more than 5 people were allowed to gather in one place. Likewise, people travelling within the country had to go through several check posts; at every one they had to get off the vehicle, go through the checks and walk 600–1,000 meters. On average, people had to go through at least 8–10 check posts in a 200-km journey. People were unnecessarily questioned and harassed by the army. The whole idea of having these checks was to identify Maoists, but in practice it gave a lot of power to security personnel. People were often victims of verbal and sometime physical abuse even though they had nothing to do with Maoists and had not committed any crime. This created a lot of frustrations among people. Normal life was disturbed and slowed down.

The government labelled the Maoists terrorists and began to refer to them under the provisions of the Terrorist and Disruptive Activities Control and Punishment Ordinance (Shakya, Gyawali, & Pokhrel, 2005). Fear generated insecurity in the general population. On the one hand, government forces identified people who were Maoists supporters; on the other hand, Maoists began to accuse people of being informants for the security forces.

Although the government tried to control the Maoist movement through the use of force, this worked against them (Shakya et al., 2005). The People's War escalated and became more organized. Civil society was engaged to the extent that one person per family was asked to support the Maoist struggle of the people against the monarchy. People found themselves trapped in the climate of fear-mongering and began leaving their homes. For example, people from rural areas moved to perceived safer places like district headquarters, cities nearby and to the capital city (IDMC, 2006; Yadav, 2007). The security situation further deteriorated when King Gyanendra assumed executive power on 4 October 2002. Atrocities were committed by both sides. A large number of people were injured, imprisoned or killed; schools and health centres were closed down; people lost their jobs; government officials and local elites were forced to give donations to the Maoists; the livelihoods of villagers deteriorated; and insecurity influenced all aspects of social life.

Government attempts to hold peace talks with Maoist leaders failed. When the first ceasefire was announced in January 2003, the Maoist leaders agreed to sit at the negotiating table. However, government leaders refused to agree to the Maoist demand for a parliamentary election to decide the fate of the monarchy (Thapa & Sharma, 2009, p. 210). As a result, the talks ended inconclusively and a further state of emergency was declared. A second attempt at a general election announcement was presented by Prime Minister Sher Bahadur Deuba in 2005. However, several talks and negotiations with political parties could not reach consensus under the prime minister's leadership, and the monarchy again assumed all executive power (Upreti, 2008, p. 37). In February 2005 parliament was dismissed, which led Nepal into another phase of direct monarchical rule (Frieden, 2012, p. 115).

Although King Gyanendra Bir Bikram Shah tried to win the people's trust and promised to restore peace and improve security, he was not successful. People were unhappy with the dismissal of the parliament and abandonment of the promise of democracy. Political parties – including the Maoists – united and launched a second People's Movement[10] (*Janaandolan*) in April 2006. King Gyanendra was forced to hand power back to the people, to the parliamentary system, after 19 days of continuous nationwide protests (*BBC News*, 2006). After the success of the second People's Movement, a Comprehensive Peace Agreement (CPA) was signed between the Maoists and the Seven Party Alliance in November 2006, which formally ended the 10-year People's War.[11] The Constitution of 1990 was abrogated (Pandey, 2010, p. 1), and the Interim Constitution was promulgated in January 2007 which declared Nepal a secular state (Thapa & Sharma, 2009).

This was a major shift in Nepali politics, from the monarchical democracy to a democratic republic.

The People's War impacted the entire country. During 10 years of war more than 13,000 people were killed, 1,300 disappeared (UNOHCHR, 2012, p. 3) and hundreds of thousands were displaced (IDMC, 2006). However, there is no exact estimation about the number of internally displaced people (IDP) in Nepal. There has not been any extensive survey on the displacement of people, nor have there been camps set up for IDP. Nepal did not have an IDP policy until 2007. When people started moving, they went to various cities and lived like other migrants because there was stigma attached to IDPs. People who were displaced by the Maoists were seen as corrupt or supporters of the government, and they also feared the Maoists even after displacement. Therefore they did not want to disclose their identity as IDPs. The people who were displaced by the security forces were attacked for being Maoists and supporters of Maoists, and were therefore equally scared of disclosing their identity as IDPs.

Only 2,500 people out of thousands displaced registered as IDPs, and there was only one camp in the western district headquarters for IDPs. Initially, only people who were displaced by the Maoists were recognized as IDPs; there was no recognition for those who were displaced by the threat from the security forces (see Yadav, 2007). The stigmatization and confusion behind IDPs and the hidden nature of internal displacement in Nepal made it difficult to estimate the total number of IDPs. There have been several estimates by various organizations, but the most commonly used number is between 150,000 and 200,000, and 80 per cent of those IDPs are women and children (Caritas Nepal, 2005).

The fifth and final period is from the CPA onwards. The first-ever Constituent Assembly (CA) election took place in April 2008, when 601 members were elected from across the country. The problem with the CA was that no one had a clear majority. There was therefore no option other than to form a coalition government. This meant the focus was on forming the government rather than working on the constitution. Several coalition governments were formed after the CA election in 2008. However, none of them was stable, as consensus could not be reached on major political agenda items such as the structure of federalism. On the one hand, as people in Nepal observed, it was difficult for the major political parties to accept Maoists as leaders. On the other hand, the People's War was a testament to Maoist leadership. Democracy was new to Nepal, yet there was increased awareness across Nepali society – due to the People's War – of the political change brought to the society and people from the mobilization of different ethnic groups.

Nepal saw several ensuing ethnic conflicts including the *Madhesh* movement in January and February 2007, led by the Madhesh Janadhikar Forum (MJF);[12] during which people from the Maoist movement and *Madhesi* protesters were killed (see Hachhethu, 2007). The major ethnic conflicts were over after the first Constituent Assembly (CA) election took place (Thapa & Sharma, 2009). However, political parties could not reach consensus about the federal structure for Nepal. Initially CA tenure was for 2 years, but even after several extensions, the CA could not establish a constitution for Nepal. The first CA was dissolved on 27 May 2012 after completion of its fourth year. The challenges at that moment for the country became 'the federal structure'. Each party had different recommendations for the structure of federal states. Subsequently, from 27 May 2012 until March 2013, there was no active government in Nepal. Baburam Bhattarai remained in charge of the caretaker government. In March 2013, Chief Justice Khil Raj Regmi was appointed as head of an interim government with a mandate to hold the second CA election.

The second CA election took place on 19 November 2013. Women's representation in the second CA was reduced to 30 per cent. Like in the previous CA election, none of the political parties was able to win a majority, as a result coalition government. After 2 years of constant disagreement over federal structures, Nepal finally promulgated its new constitution on 20 September 2015. The new 2015 constitution is highly controversial as it was endorsed without a proper consultation. The new constitution has several discriminatory provisions, especially in regards to citizenship rights and boundaries of federal states.

The first CA was not just a historic political moment. The sociocultural ramifications were arguably more monumental. For instance, Dr Ram Baran Yadav was elected as the first president of Nepal on 21 July 2008; this in itself was significant because *Yadav* was not one of the privileged castes. Likewise, people from discriminated and marginalized communities, including Dalits and lesbian, gay, bisexual and transgender individuals, were included in the CA. However, a most significant development was the inclusion, for the first time in Nepalese history, of mandated representation of women in politics. One third (33 per cent) of CA places were allocated for women, who were legislated to represent national level of political positions.

In spite of the political instability following the People's War, there have been some remarkable social changes in Nepal. The institution of the monarchy was discarded and the Maoists – once termed terrorists – became one of the major political parties, winning popular support (220 out of 601 seats) in the first CA election (Pandey, 2010, p. 1). Moreover, social and political spaces have opened up in both the public and private spheres to accommodate voices from diverse locations within the society. People from various castes/ethnic groups are recognized, women's representation in public spheres has increased and there have been several legal reforms, which will be discussed later in this chapter.

Women in Nepal

Nepal is a patriarchal society. Hinduism has played an important role in the social organization (Whelpton, 2005, p. 29). The relationship between men and women is shaped by religious ideologies (WHR, 2010, p. 7). Hinduism is not just a religion but a way of life constructed by a number of beliefs and practices (Organ, 1974, p. 1). Hindu religion and Hindu culture are so connected that it is hard to differentiate which practice is religious and which is cultural (Organ, 1974, p. 10). That is, "even when a person says he is not a Hindu, his acts can be associated with Hinduism" (Organ, 1974, p. 2). The root of Hindu tradition comes from the Vedic period, which is believed to be between 1500 B.C. and 600 B.C. (Embree, 1966, p. 3). The *Manusmriti* (*The Laws of Manu*) was written around the same time. The *Manusmriti* includes laws for every aspect of life and people's behaviour (Doniger & Smith, 1991, p. xvii) and it is considered to be a code of conduct for Hindus. Although the script was written thousands of years ago, it is still being practiced in today's Nepal.

According to the *Manusmriti*, women should not have independent status. The following verses from the *Manusmriti* are revealing in terms of women's status:

> A girl, a young woman, or even an old woman should not do anything independently, even in (her own) house. In childhood a woman should be under her father's control, in youth under her husband's and when her husband is dead, under her son's. She should not have independence.
>
> (*Manusmriti*, Chapter 4, trans.
> Doniger & Smith, 1991, p. 115)

> The wife brings forth a son who is just like the man she makes love with; that is why he should guard his wife zealously, in order to keep his progeny clean. . . . He should keep her busy amassing and spending money, engaging in purification, attending to her duty, cooking food, and looking after the furniture.
>
> (*Manusmriti*, Chapter 9, trans.
> Doniger & Smith, 1991, p. 198)

Uma Maheswari (1995, p. 1) claims:

> The sages of the period imagined the past, surveyed the present and browsed over the future (and derived the code of conduct for the society such as *Manusmriti*). The Vedic literature is nothing but musings of the seers, of what they saw, of what they enjoyed, in the spiritual minds, leaving the mundane to the ordinary.

What she means is that the discrimination against women existed even before the *Manusmriti* was written, and was adopted and manipulated by the sages of that time to fulfil their own needs.

The first national civil code (the *Muluki Ain* 1854) of Nepal was based on the classical Hindu laws of Manu, which define rules for different castes and genders (Aziz, 2001, p. xix). However, Nepal has undergone significant sociocultural and political transformation since then. The question is, social transformation for whom? It appears that Nepal (from above) is no longer bound by the sexist, racist, 'ancient' laws of Manu because recent laws and social changes have promoted women's human rights to gender equality. What it feels like for women in Nepal (from below) is that some of the rules stipulated in the *Manusmriti* are still practiced under the guise of cultural norms.

For various cultural and religious reasons, marriage is extremely important for a Nepalese Hindu family. Indeed, marriage is considered a necessary event in everyone's life (Allendorf & Ghimire, 2012; Bajracharya & Amin, 2010; Thapa, 1996). As is written in the *Manusmriti*, "the wife is traditionally said to be what the husband is" (*Manusmriti*, Chapter 9, trans. Doniger & Smith, 1991, p. 44), and this is a common understanding even in present-day Nepal. The wife is considered as *ardhangini* (half body) of her husband. As described by Sarah Lamb in her research on women in Hindu families in India, women change their last name to their husband's last name and move to their husband's residence after their marriage (Lamb, 2000, p. 231). Her husband's family becomes her own family, and she is expected to accept her husband's world as her own (Lamb, 2000, p. 221). This is true for a majority of families in Nepal, with few exceptions.

In Nepal, child marriage was banned in 1963, but the practice is still common among orthodox Hindu families (Aziz, 2001, p. xxi). In folklore, it is believed if you marry off your daughter before she begins menstruation, you will go to heaven. However, there are many other push factors that encourage child marriage in Nepal. In the *Terai*, although the practice of child marriage is seen less and less, it is still being practiced. Different reasons are suggested for the practice. The honour of the family is attached to their daughter, and only an arranged marriage is culturally recognized as legal. There is a fear that girls will elope with somebody they love or they might be manipulated by someone. Therefore, parents arrange marriages for their girls at an early age.

Another reason for child marriage in the *Terai* is the increasing demand for dowry. If parents wait for their daughters to grow up and become educated before marriage, the family may face greater costs. This is because first, there is a risk that the daughter might elope and the family's honour will be at risk; and second, finding a right match for an educated girl will cost a lot of money because educated men make higher dowry demands. Moreover, due to the low literacy rate in the *Terai*, it is difficult for parents to find a right match (an educated groom) for their daughter.

The practice of considering a daughter as another's property has an enormous impact on social structure – beginning with the general acceptance that parents prefer sons to daughters. There is a saying in Nepal regarding childbirth: "Never mind the delay as long as it is a son." However, when daughters are born, parents start worrying about dowry (see Panday, Mishra, Chemjong, Pokhrel, & Rawal, 2006). If a girl is fair and beautiful, parents (especially in the *Terai/Madhesh*) think that she is not going to cost too much. Even in the Hills, girls have to be pretty. There is a saying in the eastern *Terai/Madhesh*: "*Beta kehno hai ta bela hai*" ("No matter what a son looks like, he is a son"). This view is widespread not only in the eastern *Terai*, but throughout the country. The extent of discrimination and the preference for a son may differ in different ethnic groups, such as in Hill Janajati. However, a son has priority over daughters in most Nepalese communities.

There is a symbolic assumption that women and girls carry the culture of the community and marriage is associated with the prestige of the family. Having unmarried girls at home after they are grown up is considered humiliating. That is why marriage becomes a main event in a woman's life. There is a colloquial saying that a woman's life starts after marriage, which is clearly seen in the day-to-day life of Nepalese people. These practices are changing, but the recent Nepal Demographic Health Survey (NDHS, 2011) suggests that although the age at first marriage is rising, people in Nepal still get married at an early age. More than half (55 per cent) of women are married by age 18; 74 per cent are married by the time they are 20; and 95 per cent of women are married by the time they reach 25 (NDSH, 2011, p. 68). Although the practice of early marriage among men is lower than for women, 70–80 per cent of men are married by the time they reach 25 years of age. Due to the institutionalization of marriage which is structured by patriarchal norms (as examined in relation to widowhood in Chapter 7), women face various consequences.

There are various notable consequences of patriarchal structure which are experienced by women in Nepal in their everyday lives. One of the consequences is the disparity in literacy rates between men (75.1 per cent) and women (57.4 per cent) (CBS, 2011). Even at present, a significant number of women still do not know how to read and write (NDHS, 2011, p. 47). Another consequence is that women still do not own property. The number of women heads of household has increased by 11 per cent since 2001 (CBS, 2011). The 2011 Nepalese National Census records 82 per cent of people in Nepal residing in their own households. However, only 20 per cent of them are owned by women. Even though 25.73 per cent of households are headed by females, this does not mean that all female heads of households own their properties. Although the law prohibits polygamy, it is still practiced; about 4 per cent of women are in polygamous unions. Polygyny is practiced in the hill districts, especially in the Eastern Hills, but not in the Mountains and the *Terai/Madhesh* (NDHS, 2011, p. 66).

Women's lack of rights to their reproductive health is another consequence of patriarchy. Knowledge about contraception is universal in Nepal; almost everyone is aware of at least one contraceptive method (NDHS, 2011). However, only 43 per cent of women are using modern contraception: 7 per cent are using traditional methods; 27 per cent have an unmet need for family planning (NDHS, 2011, p. 93); 12 per cent of pregnancies are mistimed; and 13 per cent of pregnancies are unwanted (NDHS, 2011, p. 90).[13] Half of these unwanted pregnancies are terminated under unsafe conditions, resulting in a high maternal mortality ratio (Tuladhar & Risal, 2010). The maternal mortality rate in Nepal is 380 deaths per 100,000 live births, and half of that rate is associated with unsafe abortion (CREHPA, 1999). Although abortion was legalized in Nepal in September 2002, there are still many challenges to safe abortion services, such as lack of access, high fees and lack of knowledge about new legal provisions.

Only 38 per cent of women aged 15–49 believe that abortion is legal in Nepal (NDHS, 2011, p. 137). Another study conducted in the Nepal Medical College Teaching Hospital, Kathmandu in 2010 suggests that out of 200 comprehensive abortion care clients, only 66.5 per cent were aware of the legal provisions (Tuladhar & Risal, 2010). The majority of people rely on public health services in Nepal. However, until April 2006, there were only 122 approved facilities (76 governments and 46 NGOs) located across 66 districts (CREHPA & MoHP, 2006), which means the rest of the districts have no comprehensive abortion care services. Only 59 per cent of women know where a safe abortion service is available (NDHS, 2011, p. 138). Despite the legal restrictions, sex-selective abortion is still being practiced, if the foetus is female (see Lamichhane et al., 2011).

Women face violence at home and also in the workplace. One-third of married women aged 15–49 experience emotional, physical and/or sexual violence from their spouse. However, it is not common practice in Nepal to report such violence or to seek any kind of assistance. Nearly two in three women have never told anyone about the violence they have experienced (NDHS, 2011, p. 233). Moreover, women face extreme forms of discrimination because of religious based notions of 'purity' and 'pollution'. Women are still considered impure while they are menstruating. In the practice called *Chhaupadi Pratha*,[14] women are separated from their house during menstruation and live mostly in the cowshed; this carries serious health consequences and other dangers, such as "deaths, attacks by wild animals, snakebites, diseases, rapes, poor mental health, and infants dying of pneumonia" (Das, 2014). As Das (2014) calls it, a 'monthly exile' for women. Despite major efforts by NGOs and other state actors, this practice is still observed, mostly in the Far Western region (see UNRHCO, 2011). Likewise, widows face layers of discrimination, which will be discussed in Chapter 7. Women who do not get married in time (the perception about the right time to get married varies across cultures) have to suffer various kinds of discriminations.

Women have always played a key role in all the democratic movements in Nepal, including significant participation in the Maoist movement, but their representation in politics was limited to 3–5 per cent until April 2008. For the first time in Nepalese history, under the constitution women were able to secure 33 per cent of the seats in the Constituent Assembly (CA).

People in Nepal are discriminated against because of their caste, ethnicity, religion, region, class and social status. In addition to this, women also have to face gender-based discrimination. The situation is graphic when a poor woman from a lower caste and from the Western region is compared with a man from the Central region who is well off and belongs to a Brahmin or Chhetri family. Women face multiple layers of discrimination, and their experience becomes even worse when it intersects with other discriminated categories. However, to try to counter this, many sociocultural and legal reforms have been introduced since the establishment of democracy, especially after the People's War.

Promoting women's rights: key legal reforms

There have been many legal reforms in Nepal since 2000. The *Muluki Ain 2020* (the Civil Code of Nepal 1963) had never been amended to address gender discriminatory provisions until September 2002. The *Muluki Ain 2020*, based on the tenets of the Hindu religion, contains numerous gender discriminatory provisions, such as denying women the right to inheritance and negative provisions regarding marriage, divorce and citizenship. Gender-specific caveats were also included, such as abortion being highly restricted. Women were not permitted to terminate their pregnancies, even in cases of rape or incest. A woman could only terminate a pregnancy if her life was at risk. Although the law clearly stated that any person who was involved in an abortion would be jailed, a study carried out by CREHPA (2000) in 1996 showed that 80 per cent of those imprisoned because of abortion were women and only 20 per cent were men. Another study conducted by CRLP and FWLP in January 2001 revealed that 57 women were prosecuted for abortion and infanticide offences, and they were housed in 26 prisons across the country, indicating that abortion was clearly policed and prosecuted.

Human rights organization and women's rights NGOs started to raise their concerns about gender discriminatory laws and policies after the promulgation of the constitution in 1990 (Subedi, 2009, p 37). However, these voices were pushed to the background for several years, even by the democratic government, as transforming politics and 'security' of the nation state took priority over the human security of women in village communities. After several submissions, the 11th Amendment Bill was passed in September 2002 (Subedi, 2009, p. 37). This bill included four main amendments: women's right to inheritance, abortion rights, stricter punishment for child marriage and changes in the provisions for punishment for rape. According to the bill, both son and daughter had equal rights to inherit property for the first time in Nepal.

In the past, only unmarried daughters who were over the age of 35 had rights to claim their ancestral property, which they had to return to their family if they decided to get married. This law was not about protecting a daughter's rights to her parental property. Instead it provided security for their survival if they did not get married. This new bill also provides full rights for widows to claim a share from their husband's property. Before the amendment, a widow had to wait until the age of 30 to be able to claim property, even if she was widowed at the age of 16; and like all women, she had to return the property if she got married again. Widows did not have rights to any property, without certain caveats. They were given a share just for their survival if they remained widows for the rest of their lives.

A study conducted by Women's Human Rights (WHR, 2010, p. 30) reveals that 52 per cent of widows were aged under 40 in the Far Western region, 47.7 per cent in the Mid-western region, 44 per cent in the Western region, 39.7 per cent in the Eastern region and 9.5 per cent in the Central region of Nepal. However, there was no provision for an allowance for widows until they reached 60 years. Widows now do not need to wait until they are 60 to receive the widow allowance; furthermore, those whose husbands were killed during the conflict receive a monthly allowance. Similarly, single women and widows previously needed consent from their sons after they were 16 or older to sell or hand over property to others. If a son was just 6 years old when his mother became a widow, she would have to wait until he turned 16 years to give his permission.

The bill also removed the condition that a woman must reach the age of 35 and complete 15 years of marriage before she can live separately and take her share from her husband. In pre–People's War Nepal, women were denied any right to property from both parents and in-laws in the event of divorce. Only a man had the right to divorce, if he found his wife having sexual relations with another man. Women did not have the right to divorce their husbands on the same basis, meaning even if they found their husband with another woman, they did not have rights to divorce. However, the new bill gives rights to both husband and wife to appeal for divorce in such cases. The bill also guarantees equal rights to education, food, health and clothing for daughters which had not previously been legally mandated. Parents were not allowed to give an only son to anyone for adoption, but they could give an only daughter – there were no restrictions on daughters. The bill now prevents parents from giving their only girl child up for adoption.

The 11th Amendment Bill also legalizes abortion, thus securing women's rights to their reproductive health. The new law allows termination of an unwanted pregnancy up to 12 weeks without requiring anyone's permission if the woman is 16 or older. In the case of girls under 16 years of age, a parent or any family member or friend aged 16 or older could provide consent if she is willing to abort the pregnancy. This was a significant progressive step towards securing women's rights, and Nepal became an example for several developing nations in this regard. Abortion law is more flexible in cases of rape and incest (up to 18 weeks), and women can undertake abortion at any time if their life is at risk or if the baby is not physically or mentally healthy. For this, a doctor's recommendation is needed. Furthermore, the new law provides legal sanction if abortion is performed by force or based on sex selection of the foetus.

The bill amends the legal provisions for rape cases. It requires the victim's statements to be taken by only female police officers. Similarly, during the hearing, only certain people are allowed to appear before the court. The bill provides for an additional punishment of 5 years' imprisonment for the crime of gang rape and also for the rape of a pregnant or disabled woman. The bill also addresses the practice of child marriage. The legal sanction for child marriage has been increased to 3 years in jail and a fine of up to 10,000 Nepali rupees (approximately US$114) to discourage child marriage. The legal age for marriage is 20 years without parental consent and 18 years with consent. Under the previous law, the legal marriage age was 16 for girls and 18 for boys.

Although the bill was progressive in terms of gender equality, there are still discriminatory provisions. For example, only men are entitled to divorce when there are no children, even after 10 years of marriage. Women are not entitled to divorce on the same grounds. Similarly, a married woman is not entitled to adopt a child except in limited situations. A husband has the first right to decide about the adoption of a child. Except in limited situations, a woman whose husband is still living or who has a living son of her own or of co-wives is precluded from adopting a child.

A woman's rights NGO called the Forum for Women, Law and Development (FWLD) had identified 173 clauses/sections/rules, and 102 schedules/annexes/ forms in 83 different laws including the constitution which had gender discrimi-natory provisions. Responding to these, FWLD prepared an amendment proposal for ministers of parliament, the speaker and the Women's Ministry, pressurizing them to amend the particular existing discriminatory laws. The Gender Equality Bill was approved by the House of Representatives on 28 September 2006, and the certification of the bill took place on 3 November 2006. The bill has been heralded as an important step towards eliminating discrimination against women. The bill has repealed and amended 56 discriminatory provisions in various acts and has incorporated some new provisions to ensure women's rights, including punishment of marital rape by 3–6 months' imprisonment.[15]

In 2007, the Supreme Court of Nepal decided that the government should scrap all laws that discriminate against individuals based on sexual orientation or gender. This was a historic step. Now third-gender individuals can obtain citizenship with-out having to identify as male or female. The first passport was issued recently for third-gender individuals, where gender is identified as 'other' (see Pandey, 2015).

Women can now pass their citizenship onto their children, whereas prior to the People's War only men had this right. There is a discriminatory caveat to this pro-vision, however: if a woman marries a foreigner, then her husband is not entitled to apply for citizenship. Furthermore, a child of a foreign man married to a Nepali woman is only eligible for Nepali citizenship if s/he is residing in Nepal since her/his birth and hasn't acquired citizenship in any other country. However, a man married to a foreigner can apply for citizenship immediately after their wedding. Likewise, the children of a foreign woman married to a Nepalese man have the right to Nepalese citizenship without any condition. This reveals the persistence of the patriarchal mindset and long-term impact of habitus. A woman is still con-sidered as someone's property and it is assumed she will go to her husband's place after marriage.

The new Constitution 2015 also clearly states that women shall not be dis-criminated against in any way on the basis of their gender. In the new constitution, women have the right to reproductive health, to protections from gender-based violence and also to equal rights over inheritance.

Besides these improved legal provisions, social and political spaces are open-ing up in both the public and private spheres to accommodate voices from diverse locations within the society. The agenda of inclusion of women is on the rise. Women are being included in all governmental, non-governmental and civil soci-ety organizations, including mandatory provision for inclusion of women in the Nepal army. Ms Bidhya Bhandari was elected as the first female president of Nepal on 28 October 2015 (see *BBC News*, 2015). Likewise, Ms Onsari Gharti Magar has been appointed as the speaker of the parliament (see *Kathmandu Post*, 2015b); she is the first female speaker of the parliament. Ms Bhushan Shrestha has been appointed as the first female vice chancellor of Far-western University of Nepal (*Kathmandu Post*, 2015a). These kinds of appointments and progressive steps, in terms of promoting women in every sector, have been taking place in every section of society at various levels. However, it is not simply the presence of new social spaces that constitutes transformative capacity; rather it is the actual and somatic realization of individual agency to engage the space. In this respect, as this research project uncovers, the agency of women may be a hitherto unacknowledged significant indicator of social transformation.

Conclusion

Nepal does not have a colonial history, but it does have a profound political and social history. Nepal was under an autocratic government for 240 years after the country was unified in 1768, a development which reshaped both political and social structures. The country has also been through several internal conflicts at different times (Thapa & Sharma, 2009). Despite several successful democratic movements in earlier times, power always returned to the autocrats. The People's War was a catalyst for breaking this historical trend and reclaiming Nepali politics from monarchy for a republic. It is incorrect to suggest that this shift in historical precedent was only possible due to the Maoist conflict, as there were various other contributing factors that led to this radical political transformation. However, the decade-long Maoist armed conflict expedited the process of political change (Aasland & Haug, 2011; Pettigrew & Shneiderman, 2004; Sharma & Donini, 2010). That long and fraught struggle not only disrupted the political landscape, but it also created new threads to the social fabric, as others frayed and fell away.

For example, liberating social relations from regional discrimination was an unintended consequence of political change. Traditionally, people living in the *Terai* are discriminated against by people from the Hills and the Mountains; similarly, people living in the Mountains are discriminated against by people living in the Hills. History narrates that the country was united by a king from the Hills and therefore, though Nepal had become a multicultural or multi-ethnic society after unification, the language of the rulers became the national language, their costumes became the national costumes and their culture was recognized as the Nepali culture. The *Parbatiyas* ('people of the Hills and the Mountains') were the original speakers of what is now known as Nepali (Whelpton, 2005, p. 8). However, post–People's War Nepal recognizes Nepali as the official language and also recognizes a plurality of languages; thus the discrimination is *felt* less by people who speak minority languages and are from less privileged districts of Nepal. There is an increasing acceptance of people from different castes and ethnic groups in post–People's War Nepal, where political participation of people from various castes indicates significant social change. The census data also suggests the recognition of various minority groups. Census 2011 recognizes 125 caste/ethnic groups as compared to 60 caste/ethnic groups in 1991. The Central Bureau of Statistics introduced a gender-sensitive policy in 2001 and started collecting gender-disaggregated data since 2001.

Yet, in post–People's War Nepal women's position is still subordinate to that of men. Despite significant policy reforms in legal provisions – under the amendment bills, for example, legalizing all manner of gender equality provisions – cultural persistence of classic patriarchy did not permit women to *feel* the benefits of what on the surface *looked* like social transformation. This observation encourages a more cautious approach to the use of the term transformation that begins with a critical reading of theoretical locations of this concept, before a more nuanced exploratory analysis. In Europe, despite major efforts to reduce the gender gap at work, it still exists because of the long history of women and men in certain professions. Similarly in Nepal, despite many efforts, due to the long history of patriarchy and male domination, women's status remains below that of men. However, there has been significant progress in terms of achieving gender equality in Nepal within a short period of time. The People's War has provided space for several gender reforms.

Notes

1 The new Constitution of Nepal 2072/2015, which is highly controversial, was promulgated on 20 September 2015 without a proper public consultation. Although some people welcomed the new constitution, as it took 8 years to come to this stage, most people were unhappy about it, especially the Madhesi, the Janajati and women. The Madhesi people started protesting since the day the new constitution was promulgated. At least 50 people were killed during the strike. The main problems seem to be the division and boundaries of the Federal states. Other major demands of the Madhesi groups are electoral constituencies based on population, proportional representation of Madhesis in government bodies and Madhesh autonomous province. Women's main concern about the new constitution is with the citizenship rights which is discriminatory to women. The provisions for Madhesis and Janajati were more progressive in the Interim Constitution 2007 of Nepal. The new constitution curtailed some of the rights of the marginalized groups which were already granted by the Interim Constitution (see report by Charles Haviland on BBC, 19 September 2015, available at http://www.bbc.co.uk/news/world-asia-34280015, and also see Sanjay Majumdhar report on BBC, 22 September 2015, available at http://www.bbc.co.uk/news/world-asia-india-34313280).
2 People who were not in the country during the census are called absentees. Nearly half (44.81 per cent) of the absent population is from the age group 15–24 years (CBS, 2011).
3 See CBS (2011) for the list of castes and ethnic groups.
4 See Einsiedel et al. (2012) and Whelpton (2005) for the detailed history of Nepal.
5 Gorkha is one of the districts in the Western Hills of present Nepal.
6 The government formed under the king was known as the *Panchayat* government. It was dissolved after the establishment of democracy in 1990.
7 The People's War in Nepal has been widely studied. Since the beginning of the war in 1996 to date, there have been numerous studies looking at various aspects of the People's War, such as understanding the catalysts for the conflict, strategies applied, people's motivation for joining the armed conflict and its impacts on different categories of people (see Cottle & Keys, 2007; Devkota & Teijlingen, 2010, 2012; Gobyn, 2009; Hall, 2011; Hatlebakk, 2010; Kerttunen, 2011; Nayak, 2007; Nepal, Bohara, & Gawande, 2011; Riaz & Basu, 2007).
8 For the full list of the 40-point demands of the Maoists, see http://www.satp.org/satporgtp/countries/nepal/document/papers/40points.htm.

9 On June 1, 2001, the Royal Massacre occurred in Nepal, where the king and all his family members were killed, including Queen Aswarya, Prince Dipendra, Prince Nirajan and Princess Shruti. Although the report prepared regarding the Royal Massacre suggests that Prince Dipendra killed all his family members and later he killed himself (see http://nepalitimes.com/news.php?id=18246). However, the reliability of this report is highly questioned by the Nepalese people. King Gyanendra, the brother of the late King Birendra, who became the king after the Royal Massacre, is one of the suspects in this killing (see https://americanepali.wordpress.com/2012/06/01/royal-massacre-11-years-later/). There is still no clear answer as to how the massacre happened and who was involved.

10 There is a difference between the People's War and the People's Movement. The People's Movement was a movement led by mainstream political parties with support from the public. So far there have been two such movements. The first People's Movement took place in 1990 and the second in 2006. The second People's Movement was led by the Seven Party Alliance and supported by the Maoists based on their 12-point understanding, which was signed in New Delhi in November 2005. The People's War was a civil war started by the CPN-M in 1996, which ended with a CPA in 2006.

11 The Seven Party Alliance was an alliance of seven political parties in Nepal, which was formed to end the autocratic monarchy. They launched a nationwide peaceful protest known as the second People's Movement. See http://www.politicalaffairs.net/nepal-seven-party-alliance-announces-demands/.

12 Madhesh Janadhikar Forum (MJF; Madhesi People's Rights Forum) was formed in 2007. It was not a political party when it started. It was a political advocacy movement for the right to self-determination and for Madhesh to become an autonomous region. Leaders from various political parties, who were in favour of Madhesi people's rights, joined this movement. Since the aim was to demand rights for the Madhesi people, the MJF got support from everyone in Madhesh. Dozens of people were killed during this movement. The MJF was registered as a political party on 25 April 2007 and took part in the CA election in May 2008. See http://www.mprfn.org/.

13 Mistimed pregnancy means the pregnancy was wanted but not at that time.

14 During the first four days of menstruation, women and girls are not allowed to touch men or participate in any family activities because they are considered impure. This tradition is practiced all over the country, especially among high castes such as hill Brahmin and Chhetri. However, this practice is very restrictive and rigid in the Western region of Nepal, especially among Hill Brahmin and Chhetri. The practice is called *Chhaupadi*. See Rustad (2013) for more details about *Chhaupadi* system. For more details about the prevalence and impacts of *Chhaupadi* system in Nepal, see Chapagain (n.d.), George (2014) and Uprety & Bhandari (2010).

15 See FWLD website at http://www.fwld.org. For the details of the amendments, also see http://www.lawcommission.gov.np.

References

Aasland, A., & Haug, M. (2011). Perceptions of Social Change in Nepal: Are Caste, Ethnicity, and Region of Relevance? *Journal of Asian and African Studies, 46*(2), 184–201.

Aguirre, D., & Pietropaoli, I. (2008). Gender Equality, Development and Transitional Justice: The Case of Nepal. *International Journal of Transitional Justice, 2*(3), 356–377.

Allendorf, K., & Ghimire, D. (2012). *Determinants of Marital Quality in an Arranged Marriage Society*. Population Studies Centre Research Report 12-758, University of Michigan.

Aziz, B. N. (2001). *Heir to a Silent Song: Two Rebel Women of Nepal*. Kritipur, Kathmandu: Centre for Nepal and Asian Studies.

Bajracharya, A., & Amin, S. (2010). *Poverty, Marriage Timing, and Transitions to Adult-hood in Nepal: A Longitudinal Analysis Using the Nepal Living Standards Survey*. Working Paper No. 19. Retrieved from http://www.popcouncil.org/pdfs/wp/pgy/019.pdf

BBC News. (2000, 3 December). Nepal's Women Breaking Barriers. Retrieved 15 May 2014 from http://news.bbc.co.uk/2/hi/south_asia/1052910.stm

BBC News. (2006, 2 June). People's Movement Defines Nepal. Retrieved 20 July 2014 from http://news.bbc.co.uk/2/hi/south_asia/5033512.stm

BBC News. (2015, 29 October). Bidhya Devi Bhandari Elected Nepal's First Female President. Retrieved 30 October 2015 from http://www.bbc.co.uk/news/world-asia-34664430

Bennett, L. (1983). *Dangerous Wives and Sacred Sisters*. New York: Columbia University Press.

Bennett, L., Dahal, D. R., & Govindasamy, P. (2008). *Caste, Ethnic and Regional Identity in Nepal: Further Analysis of the 2006 Nepal Demographic and Health Survey*. Calverton, MD: Macro International. Retrieved from http://pdf.usaid.gov/pdf_docs/PNADM638.pdf

Caritas Nepal. (2005). *Caravan of Conflict: A Study of Dynamics of Conflict-Induced Displacement in Nepal*. Kathmandu: Caritas Nepal.

CBS. (2011). *Population Census 2011*. Kathmandu: Government of Nepal.

Chapagain, B. (n.d.). Shackles of the Chhaupadi System. *Astitwa*. Retrieved 20 October 2015 from http://www.astitwa.com/index.php/shackles-of-the-chhaupadi-system

Constitution of Nepal 2072. (2015). Retrieved on 18 November 2015 from https://drive.google.com/file/d/0B1EyNP0s1r6JUGhoMHBtYmtvdDA/view

Cottle, D., & Keys, A. (2007). The Maoist Conflict in Nepal: A Himalayan Perdition? *Australian Journal of International Affairs, 61*(2), 168–174.

CREHPA. (1999). *Management of Abortion Related Complications in Hospitals of Nepal – A Situational Analysis*. Kathmandu: CREHPA.

CREHPA. (2000). *Women in Prison in Nepal for Abortion. A Study on Implications of Restrictive Abortion Law on Women's Social Status and Health*. Kathmandu: CREHPA.

CREHPA & MoHP. (2006). *Nepal Comprehensive Abortion Care (CAC): National Facility-Based Abortion Study Kathmandu*. Kathmandu: CREHPA.

CRLP & FWLD. (2001). *Abortion in Nepal: Women Imprisoned, Kathmandu*: CRLP and FWLD.

Das, B. (2014, 10 February). Nepal's Menstrual Exiles. *Al Jazeera*. Retrieved 25 September 2015 from http://www.aljazeera.com/indepth/features/2014/02/nepal-menstrual-exiles-201423131149488509.html

Devkota, B., & Teijlingen, E. v. (2010). Demystifying the Maoist Barefoot Doctor of Nepal. *Medicine, Conflict and Survival, 26*(2), 108–123.

Devkota, B., & Teijlingen, E. v. (2012). Why Did They Join? Exploring the Motivations of Rebel Health Workers in Nepal. *Journal of Conflictology, 3*(1), 18–29.

Dhahal, D. R. (n.d.). *Social Composition of the Population: Caste/Ethnicity and Region in Nepal*. Chapter 3, pp. 87–135. Available at http://web.iaincirebon.ac.id/ebook/moon/Geography%26Demography/Chapter%2003%20%20Social%20Composition%20of%20the%20Population.pdf.

Doniger, W., & Smith, B. K. (1991). *The Laws of Manu*. London: Penguin Books.

Einsiedel, S. v., Malone, D. M., & Pradhan, S. (2012). Introduction. In S. v. Einsiedel, D. M. Malone, & S. Pradhan (Eds.), *Nepal in Transition: From People's War to Fragile Peace* (pp. 1–33). New York: Cambridge University Press.

Embree, A. T. (Ed.). (1966). *The Hindu Tradition*. New York: Random House.

Frieden, J. (2012). A Donor's Perspective on Aid and Conflict. In S. v. Einsiedel, D. M. Malone, & S. Pradhan (Eds.), *Nepal in Transition: From People's War to Fragile Peace* (pp. 100–113). New York: Cambridge University Press.

Gellner, D. N. (2007). *Nepal: Towards a Democratic Republic, Caste, Ethnicity and Inequality in Nepal*. Retrieved from http://www.uni-bielefeld.de/midea/pdf/darticle2.pdf

George, R. (2014, 11 March). Blood Speaks. *Jezebel*. Retrieved from http://mosaicscience.com/story/blood-speaks

Gobyn, W. (2009). From War to Peace: The Nepalese Maoist's Strategic and Ideological Thinking. *Studies in Conflict and Terrorism, 32*(5), 420–438.

Hachhethu, K. (2003). Democracy and Nationalism: Interface between State and Ethnicity in Nepal. *CNAS, 30*(2), 217–252.

Hachhethu, K. (2007). Madheshi Nationalism and Restructuring the Nepali State. Paper Presented at an International Seminar on "Constitutionalism and Diversity in Nepal", Centre for Nepal and Asian Studies, Tribhuvan University, Kirtipur, 22–24 August 2007, Kathmandu, Nepal. Retrieved on 8 February 2016 from http://www.uni-bielefeld.de/midea/pdf/Hachhethu.pdf

Hall, A. (2011). Nepal: An Incomplete Peace. *Asian Affairs, 42*(3), 403–418.

Hatlebakk, M. (2010). Maoist Control and Level of Civil Conflict in Nepal. *South Asian Economic Journal, 11*(1), 99–110.

Hoefer, A. 2004 (1979). *The Caste Hierarchy and the State in Nepal: A Study of the Muluki Ain of 1854*. Kathmandu: Himal Books.

IDMC. (2006). *Nepal: IDP Return Still a Trickle Despite Ceasefire*. Geneva: Norwegian Refugee Council.

Kathmandu Post. (2015a, 25 August). PM Koirala Appoints VCs in Five Universities. Retrieved 28 October 2015 from http://kathmandupost.ekantipur.com/news/2015-08-25/pm-koirala-appoints-vcs-in-five-universities.html

Kathmandu Post. (2015b, 16 October). Onsari Gharti Magar Elected First Woman Speaker. Retrieved 17 October 2015 from http://kathmandupost.ekantipur.com/news/2015-10-16/onsari-elected-first-woman-speaker.html

Kerttunen, M. (2011). A Transformed Insurgency: The Strategy of the Communist Party of Nepal (Maoist) in the Light of Communist Insurgency Theories and a Modified Beaufrean Exterior/Interior Framework. *Small War & Insurgencies, 22*(1), 78–118.

Lamb, S. (2000). *White Saris and Sweet Mangoes: Aging, Gender, and Body in North India* Berkeley: University of California Press.

Lamichhane, P., Harken, T., Puri, M., Darney, P. D., Blum, M., Harper, C. C., & Henderson, J. T. (2011). Sex-Selective Abortion in Nepal: A Qualitative Study of Health Workers' Perspectives. *Women's Health Issues, 21*(3), S37–S41.

Maheswari, U. (1995). *Dress and Jewellery of Women: Satavahana to Kakatiya*. Madras, India: New Era.

Nayak, N. (2007). The Maoist Movement in Nepal and Its Tactical Digressions: A Study of Strategic Revolutionary Phases, and Future Implications. *Strategic Analysis, 31*(6), 915–942.

Nepal, M., Bohara, A. K., & Gawande, K. (2011). More Inequality, More Killings: The Maoist Insurgency in Nepal. *American Journal of Political Science, 55*(4), 885–905.

Nepal Demographic and Health Survey (NDHS). (2011). Kathmandu: Ministry of Health and Population, New ERA, ICF International, Calverton, MD. Retrieved from http://dhsprogram.com/pubs/pdf/FR257/FR257%5B13April2012%5D.pdf

Niroula, B. P. (1998). Caste/Ethnicity Composition of Population of Nepal. *CNAS, 25*, 15–56.

Organ, T. W. (1974). *Hinduism: Its Historical Development*. New York: Barron's Educational Series.

Panday, D. R. (2012). The Legacy of Nepal's Failed Development. In S. v. Einsiedel, D. M. Malone, & S. Pradhan (Eds.), *Nepal in Transition: From People's War to Fragile Peace* (pp. 81–99). New York: Cambridge University Press.

Panday, T. R., Mishra, S., Chemjong, D., Pokhrel, S., & Rawal, N. (2006). *Form and Patterns of Social Discrimination in Nepal: A Report*. Kathmandu: UNESCO.

Pandey, L. (2015, 7 August). Passports for Third Gender. *Himalayan Times*. Retrieved 25 September 2015 from http://thehimalayantimes.com/kathmandu/passports-for-third-gender/

Pandey, N. N. (2010). *New Nepal: The Fault Lines*. New Delhi: Sage.

Pathak, B. (2005). *Politics of People's War and Human Rights in Nepal*. Kathmandu: BIMIPA.

Pettigrew, J., & Shneiderman, S. (2004). Ideology and Agency in Nepal's Maoist Movement. *Himal Magazine*. Retrieved 15 October 2015 from http://www.himalmag.com/component/content/article/4272-women-in-the-maobaadi-ideology-and-agency-in-nepals-maoist-movement.html

Pyakuryal, K. N. (2008). Pluralism, Diversity and National Integration. In K. N. Pyakuryal, B. R. Upreti, & S. R. Sharma (Eds.), *Nepal: Transition to Transformation* (pp. 185–199). Kathmandu: Human and Natural Resources Studies Centre, Kathmandu University and South Asia Regional Coordination Office of NCCR North South.

Riaz, A., & Basu, S. (2007). The State-Society Relationship and Political Conflict in Nepal (1768–2005). *Journal of Asian and African Studies, 42*(2), 123–142.

Rustad, H. (2013, 30 April). Nepalese Menstruation Tradition Dies Hard. *Globe and Mail*. Retrieved on 8 February 2016 from http://www.theglobeandmail.com/news/world/nepalese-menstruation-tradition-dies-hard/article11644844/

Shakya, A., Gyawali, V., & Pokhrel, S. (Eds.). (2005). *IDPs Dynamics in the Kathmandu Valley. Auditing of Conflict Induced Internal Displacement*. Kathmandu: HimRights, Popwatch & Plan Nepal.

Sharma, J. R., & Donini, A. (2010). *Towards a "Great Transformation"? The Maoist Insurgency and Local Perceptions of Social Transformation in Nepal*. Boston, MA: Tufts University.

Subedi, N. C. (2009). Elimination of Gender Discriminatory Legal Provisions by the Supreme Court of Nepal with Reference to Women's Rights to Property. *Tribhuvan University Journal, 24*(1), 37–54.

Thapa, D. (2012). The Making of the Maoist Insurgency. In S. v. Einsiedel, D. M. Malone, & S. Pradhan (Eds.), *Nepal in Transition: From People's War to Fragile Peace* (pp. 37–57). New York: Cambridge University Press.

Thapa, G. B., & Sharma, J. (2009). From Insurgency to Democracy: The Challenges of Peace and Democracy-Building in Nepal. *International Political Science Review, 30*(2), 205–219. doi:10.2307/25652899.

Thapa, S. (1996). Girl Child Marriage in Nepal: Its Prevalence and Correlates. *CNAS Journal, 23*(2), 361–375.

Tuladhar, H., & Risal, A. (2010). Level of Awareness about Legalization of Abortion in Nepal: A Study at Nepal Medical College Teaching Hospital. *Nepal Medical College Journal, 12*(2), 76–80. Retrieved from http://www.ncbi.nlm.nih.gov/pubmed/21222401

UNOHCHR. (2012). *Nepal Conflict Report: An Analysis of Conflict-Related Violations of International Human Rights Law and International Humanitarian Law between February 1996 and 21 November 2006*. Kathmandu: UN Human Rights Office of High Commissioner.

UNRHCO. (2011). *Chaupadi in the Far-West*. Kathmandu: UN Resident and Humanitarian Coordinator's Office.

Upreti, B. R. (2008). Resistance Movements in Conflict Transformation and Social Change. In K. N. Pyakuryal, B. R. Upreti, & S. R. Sharma (Eds.), *Nepal: Transition to Transformation* (pp. 15–48). Kathmandu: Human and Natural Resources Studies Centre, Kathmandu University and South Asia Regional Coordination Office of NCCR North South.

Uprety, A., & Bhandari, R. R. (2010). *Midterm Review of Chhaupadi Elimination Project in Accham*. Kathmandu: Save the Children Country Office Nepal.

Whelpton, J. (2005). *A History of Nepal*. Cambridge: Cambridge University Press.

WHR. (2010). *A Journal Towards Empowerment and the Status of Single Women in Nepal*. Baluwatar, Kathmandu: WHR.

Yadav, P. (2007). *Gender Dimension of Conflict-Induced Internal Displacement in Nepal* (Masters), Asian Institute of Technology Thailand.

4 Women in politics and the unintended consequences

Conflict produces both intended and unintended consequences which lead to structural changes by creating an enabling environment for women to exercise their agency (see El Bushra & Piza-Lopez, 1993; Gardam & Charlesworth, 2000; Manchanda, 2001a; Pankhurst, 2007; Turshen, Meintjes, & Pillay, 2001). Turshen (2001, p. 80) argues that "under the hard conditions of civil conflict, women do demonstrate an ability to transform their lives. In changing women's gender roles, war provides opportunities for some women to emerge as leaders." The People's War in Nepal has created an enabling environment for women to participate in politics; as a result even illiterate women who were previously housewives have emerged as leaders. Their participation in politics has not only transformed their own lives but also indicates some broader transformative patterns in post-conflict Nepali society. Case studies of women Constituent Assembly (CA) members from diverse political, economic and cultural backgrounds will be presented in this chapter to discuss and analyze the transformation that is taking place in Nepal.

The experience of conflict is mediated through various factors, such as caste, ethnicity, class, education, religion, region and other contexts. Women's experience of conflict in Nepal is therefore not homogeneous (Manchanda, 2001b). However, one thing is common among all women in Nepal, that despite their diverse experiences of conflict, "they suffer gender discrimination in addition to class, caste, community and regional oppression" (Manchanda, 2001a, p. 117). This chapter acknowledges the heterogeneous experiences among women during the transformative process and focuses on identifying the gains that women have achieved in post-conflict Nepal due to their increased participation in politics.

Women in politics in Nepal

Nepali women have had the right to vote since 1951. However, women's representation in politics remained minimal until 2007 (Falch, 2010; IDEA, 2008). Before the establishment of democracy, when the last *panchayat* cabinet was dissolved (after 240 years of monarchical rule) on 8 April 1990, out of the 25 members there was only one female minister (Kabir, 2003, p. 11). The situation of women's lack of representation in politics did not decrease even after the establishment of democracy in 1990. When the first democratic election took place in 1991, only 7 women out of 205 members were elected (Kabir, 2003, p. 11). Since the 1990 constitution required at least 5 per cent women's representation in the upper house, another three women were nominated to fill the quota (Kabir, 2003, p. 11). Despite women's representation in parliament (although minimal), they did not get a chance to be involved in the formulation of the first democratic constitution in 1990 (Nepali & Shrestha, 2007, p. 70). The second election took place in 1994. However, despite the mandatory provision to have at least 5 per cent women's representation, less than 5 per cent of women were given the chance to stand in the 1994 election. The third election took place in 1999, and although women's candidacy increased to 6.3 per cent, only 5.85 per cent won places in the election (Nepali & Shrestha, 2007, p. 71).

Even though there were some efforts to ensure women's representation in politics, women's participation in politics never exceeded 6 per cent until 2008 before the first CA (Kabir, 2003; Nepali & Shrestha, 2007). And, most of the women who were elected or given the opportunity to run in the election were either high caste women or the close relatives of male politicians such as wives, widows or daughters (IDEA, 2008; UNDP, 2009). The competition was among political elites, people with a long political background (IDEA, 2008; UNDP, 2009). Politics was out of reach for the overwhelming majority of Nepali women. Moreover, even women who were in politics did not have much say in the decision-making process (IDEA, 2008). Only men held leadership roles and made all the decisions for the country.

This trend of not including women in decision-making processes was observed even after the peace agreement. Despite women's active representation in both the People's War (1999–2006) and the second People's Movement (2006), women were not included in the peace negotiations. The Comprehensive Peace Agreement (CPA) was signed in 2006, and not a single woman was included. A committee was set up to develop an Interim Constitution in 2006, after the CPA. No women, from the Maoist or the government side, were included in the initial six-member committee. However, after constant pressure from outside, especially from women politicians and women's rights activists, the committee was expanded to included four women. These four women represented four key political parties of Nepal.

The pressure from outside continued, while the Interim Constitution was being drafted, to have guaranteed women's representation in the new political institutions. As a result a mandated minimum of one-third of women's representation in the Constituent Assembly was secured (Falch, 2010; UNDP, 2008). The achievement of a mandatory increase in political representation from 5 to 33 per cent was an undoubted significant victory.

Nepal was going through a profound political transformation after the CPA (UNDP, 2009). On the one hand, the CPN Maoists joined mainstream politics and became part of the Legislature Parliament (IDEA, 2008). On the other hand, the emergence of ethnic and regional politics had become stronger compared to national politics (UNDP, 2009). Now the success of any party depended on support from regional and ethnic groups. As a result, propositional representation became the bargaining point for all those protesting groups (UNDP, 2009). Although, the

Interim Constitution was more inclusive and advanced compared to the 1990 Constitution, it still did not address the demands of various ethnic and regional groups and as a result various ethnic conflicts broke out throughout the country in 2007. These conflicts were both armed insurgency and non-armed movements.[1] In the Eastern Terai, the Madhesh movement was on the rise; in the Eastern Hills an indigenous movement arose; and in Western Terai the Tharu movement was strong. Similarly, there were several declared and undeclared movements through-out the country in the name of castes/ethnicity and regions. Although there is no formal documentation of the number of conflicting groups, international non-governmental organizations (I/NGOs) working in Nepal had collected the name of 127 ethnic groups.[2] The underlying aim of these ethnic conflicts was to secure a fair share in the Constituent Assembly.

Due to these movements and the fragile political situation, it appeared that everything could be negotiated, including the structure of the state, the symbols of nationhood and the rights of citizens (UNDP, 2009). The government held peace talks and made some agreements with at least 18 groups (see Bogati, Cara-pic, & Muggah, 2003). Finally, with an agreement between the major regional and national competing groups and parties, a long-awaited first CA election took place on 28 May 2008. In this election 601 CA members were elected and nominated from various parts of the country. Out of these, 197 (33 per cent) were women.

Historic representation of women in the first Constituent Assembly

The first CA was historic in many ways. For the first time, the constitution was going to be written by the people's representatives with a significant representation from women, which included women from Dalit, indigenous, *Madhesi*, Muslim and other marginalized communities (IDEA, 2011). To ensure representation from all genders, religions, castes and ethnic groups, the government of Nepal adopted a 'mixed system'[3] which involved both direct elections and nominations. As a result, women won 30 seats in the direct election and 161 women were nominated through the proportional representation system. In addition, six women were nomi-nated by the three major political parties to comply with the quota, which meant that women held one-third of the total seats in the Constituent Assembly (*Constitu-tion of Nepal*, 2015; Falch, 2010; IDEA, 2008). A point to note here is that despite having a clear provision for proportional representation in the CA, women's repre-sentation only reached 33 per cent, due to the mandatory provision in the Interim Constitution, even though they were 51 per cent of Nepal's population.

Despite this achievement and a historic win for women in the CA, when the first cabinet was formed, only four women (16.67 per cent) were appointed out of 24 ministerial positions (Falch, 2010, p. 23). This mixture of acceptance and denial of women in politics by male leaders, acceptance in politics but denial in leadership roles, and using them for their own benefit, reveals the existence of patriarchy in Nepal. However, being able to secure 33 per cent in the CA itself was an important victory for Nepali women. With this, Nepal ranked seventeenth highest worldwide in terms of the percentage of women in parliament (IDEA, 2011, p. 73).

While I was in Nepal to interview women CA members in 2011, the International Institute for Democracy and Electoral Assistance (IDEA) was preparing a report on women CA members. They published a 905-page report on the 197 women CA members, which included a brief biography of each woman CA member. I extracted some data from this report on the background of women CA members. According to the International IDEA, out of 196 (one woman CA member died in an accident), only 26 women CA members were previously members of parliament and 170 were completely new to politics (IDEA, 2011, p. 61). These women were from different castes and ethnic groups, while more than a third were *Janajatis* (indigenous; 35.7 per cent), followed by *Brahmins* (22.4 per cent), *Madhesis* (15.8 per cent), *Dalits* (10.7 per cent), *Chhetris* (10.7 per cent), Muslims (2.6 per cent) and others including *Kirat* (2 per cent) (IDEA, 2011, p. 63). Although most of them were followers of the Hindu religion (57.7 per cent), interestingly more than a quarter (26.5 per cent) categorized themselves as secular and 9 per cent said they were Buddhist (IDEA, 2011, p. 64).

Age and marital status varied among these women CA members. They were between 28 and 78 years old. Most were aged between 30 and 35 and the average age was 43 years (IDEA, 2011, p. 65). The majority of the women CA members (73.5 per cent) were married. It was interesting to note that most of these CA members came from non-political families. About 60 per cent were married to farmers, businessmen, development workers, social activists, consultants, health workers, journalists, legal practitioners, tailors and taxi drivers; only 40 per cent were married to politicians (IDEA, 2011, p. 66). This was not the case in pre-conflict Nepal. Moreover, 7.7 per cent were unmarried and 15.3 per cent were single/widowed, the majority of whom lost their husbands during the decades-long armed struggle (IDEA, 2011, p. 66). Despite their marital status or the association of their husbands with politics, most of the women said they joined politics because they wanted to bring about social change and wanted to fight against injustice, especially gender-based, class-based and caste-based discrimination which they had witnessed while growing up (IDEA, 2011, p. 70).

There were also significant variations in educational level among these women CA members. Although the majority of them had some level of education, 17.9 per cent had never been to school or had no formal education. They could barely read and write. This is something that could never have happened in pre-conflict Nepal. Only educated women from political families got the opportunity to be in politics in the past. While 14.8 per cent had completed postgraduate studies, one quarter had only finished their School Leaving Certificate which is equivalent to grade 10 (see IDEA, 2011, p. 65).

Despite such variations in education levels, all women CA members played a significant role in the constitution drafting process, particularly pushing for women's issues such as increased women's representation in all state organs, women's right to citizenship and law of domestic violence (IDEA, 2011). A Women's Caucus was formed on 2 January 2009 (IDEA, 2011, p. 74); the vice chairperson of the CA was a woman; there were four women chairing different committees in the first CA; and others were leading several subcommittees (IDEA, 2011). Between May 2008 and May 2011, 39 bills were approved by parliament. They included a long-awaited and much-debated bill on domestic violence criminalizing all types of violence, including physical, mental, sexual and financial violence. In addition to this, women CA members participated in the decision making on various bills including the Financial Bill, the Reconciliation Bill and the Caste Discrimination and Untouchability (Crime and Punishment) Bills (IDEA, 2011). Women CA members were also actively involved in other projects such as infrastructure development including drinking water, electricity, education, health, and women's empowerment projects, among other things (IDEA, 2011).

Women CA members of the first CA, collectively (through caucus) or individually, advocated for various issues. One of my research participants, who is highly educated and is one of the top leaders of the Nepali Congress (NC), said:

> All women CA members have one aim, that is, to increase women's representation in every sector. Once women are included in all sectors, they themselves will bring their agendas . . . it is not just participation, but we are demanding a meaningful representation . . . not only members, but at the decision making level . . . if there are two positions such as chair and vice chair then one has to go to a woman . . . We are now 33 per cent women here in the CA, that's why our demand have more weight . . . the more the better . . . once the rights are guaranteed in the constitution there won't be problem to make a law.
>
> (Puspa Bhusal)[4]

Among many other gender initiatives, women were trying to secure 50 per cent representation in all state organs. The gains women have achieved were possible only because of the critical mass of women in the CA. The first CA was dissolved on 28 May 2012 without promulgating the constitution.

The second Constituent Assembly and the continuity of women's historic representation in politics

The second CA election took place on 19 November 2013. Despite having the provision in the Interim Constitution for at least 33 per cent representation, only 30 per cent secured their seats in the second CA. There have been lots of ups and downs in terms of in women's representation since 2008. For instance, despite having one-third of women in the CA, very few women got the chance to be in the cabinet. But on a positive note, although there was a decrease from 33 to 30 per cent, the representation of women was still remarkable; most importantly, these women were not sitting quietly but were demanding their rights to have more women in the CA. The most interesting thing in this whole process was that women who could barely read and write were creating the future of the country. Illiterate women with no political background were sitting with highly educated women and contributing towards making a new constitution. This was undoubtedly a historic event and indicative of revolutionary transformation in Nepal (IDEA, 2011).

Diversity among research participants

I interviewed 31 women CA members from the first CA election. They represented several political parties with various economic, caste/ethnicity, religious and cultural backgrounds. Out of the 31, 10 were *Janajati*, 10 were *Madhesi*, 6 *Dalits*, 3 *Brahmin/Chhetri*, 1 Muslim and 1 *Newar*. The sample includes *Brahmin/Chhetri*, *Janajati* and *Dalits* from both *Terai* and *Pahad*. The women CA members were between 30 and 55 years old. Most were married (18), 7 were widows, 2 were unmarried, 2 were separated and 2 had a missing husband. Thirteen women could read and write but did not have any formal educational background; the remainder (18) had completed grade 10 or above. Among these 18, 7 women were graduates (with bachelor's and master's degree in various subjects).

Among my respondents, 5 were elected in the direct election and 26 were nominated through the PR system. These groups of women represented both big and small parties. Nearly half of them (15) were from the UCPN-M, followed by the MJF (6), the CPN-UML (4), the RPP (2), the NC (1) and three were from other small parties such as the SLRM, Sadbhabhana, and the Terai Madhesh Loktantrik Party.

Opening up space for women to join politics

The People's War in Nepal and other regional and ethnic conflicts that emerged after the CPA created an enabling environment for women to join politics. It has been estimated that at least one-third of Nepali women participated in the People's War (1996–2006); thousands of women participated in the second People's Movement in 2006; and women were in the front line for all the other movements in the country, such as Madhesh movement, Tharu movement and so on. As a result hundreds of women had an opportunity to become involved in politics at the national level, including the highest-ever number (197) of women in the first CA. I asked the 31 women CA members I interviewed why they joined politics, since it was not something most of these women would have thought about prior to the People's War. Although they had very distinct stories to tell, four broad reasons were identified. These women: (1) were already in politics or were family members of politicians; (2) wanted to bring change; (3) were widows whose husbands were killed during the war or were wives of disappeared people; and (4) were social workers who were leaders in their field.

Out of the 31 women, only four had chosen politics as a career and had been in politics for a long time. Puspa Bhusal (Nepali Congress), who has completed her master's degree in political science, became a politician because she wanted to follow in her father's footsteps, Usha Kala Rai (CPN-UML), who was involved in student politics, continued her political journey after she graduated. Pampha Bhusal and Jaypuri Gharti Magar are top leaders of UCPN-M, who started their political career prior to the People's War. However, the majority of women I interviewed started their political careers either after they joined the Maoist movement or after they participated in other ethnic and regional movements. Durgi Devi Paswan, a housewife from a lower caste family, joined the Maoist movement because she was convinced that the UCPN-M was the only party that could bring change in the country and for people like her. Later, in recognition of her contribution, the UCPN-M nominated her to be a CA member. She says:

> Maoists started coming to my house. They said that we all are living for ourselves. There is a lot of injustice and discrimination in the country. We need to fight against injustice. We need to do something. We need to bring change. I also felt like doing something for the country . . . if not me, my children will live in a better world.

Pramila Devi Yadav (UCPN-M) was forced to go underground in 2005 after all the male members of her family (father, two brothers and husband) were killed by the army. Recognizing her contribution and that of her family to the Maoist movement, she was nominated to be a CA member.

A significant number of women joined politics during various ethnic movements after the CPA. The Madhesh movement, which took place in 2007, also provided opportunities for women who otherwise would never have thought about joining politics or becoming politicians. Some women got the opportunity to become CA members because of their own contribution in the movement, while others were given the opportunity because of family contributions in various movements. Durga Devi Mahato and Devi from MJF-Democratic became CA members because of their active involvement in the Madhesh movement in 2007, whereas Sumitra Devi Yadav (MJF-Democratic) won the direct election after her husband was killed during the ethnic movement.

It is evident that the conflicts played the role of a catalyst in increasing women's political participation in Nepal. One thing to note here is that whatever the circumstances were for each woman to join politics, the provision in the Interim Constitution to have at least 33 per cent female representation in the CA and an extremely influential discourse about the inclusion of women in post-conflict Nepal played an important role in securing women's historic representation in Nepali politics. Not only educated women who had adopted politics as a career became CA members; women from diverse educational, regional, political, caste and ethnic backgrounds also joined the CA. For the first time in Nepal's history, diverse groups of women came together to write the constitution. Despite the diversity among the women they all experienced some level of transformation in their lives after they became CA members.

Patriarchy as a challenge

The political transformation in Nepal is remarkable, especially in terms of opening up political space for women. This is clearly a positive step towards gender equality. However, women still face various challenges. Usha Kala Rai

(CPN-UML), who is a former president of the Women's Caucus, said "gender based discrimination and patriarchal thoughts have affected even the CA." She added, "despite having capable women in the CA, men still occupy almost all the decision making positions, which is an indication of strong existence of patriarchy in Nepal." I have identified three key sub-themes which arose repeatedly during my interviews with women CA members: (1) hesitancy on the part of male politicians to entrust decision-making roles to women; (2) difficulties in promoting a distinctive women's agenda in the CA; and (3) discrimination based on gender and social status.

Hesitancy of male politicians to entrust decision-making roles to women

One of the main challenges that almost all the women CA members mentioned during the interviews was the hesitancy of male politicians to entrust women with decision-making roles. Puspa Bhusal, a CA member from the NC, said "there is still a hesitation among male leaders to give leadership responsibilities to women leaders." Another CA member, a central committee member of the UCPN-M, said "women are not given the opportunity for leadership roles" (Jaypuri Gharti Magar). Jaypuri was appointed Minister for Women, Children and Welfare in 2011. Since she was the only one from her party, she refused to participate in the swearing-in ceremony, demanding at least 33 per cent representation of women in the cabinet (see *Kathmandu Post*, 2011). Usha Kala Rai said:

> The practice of male members sitting in the front rows and women members sitting in the back is an indication of gender-based discrimination in the CA. The composition of the cabinet also reveals the gender disparity in the leadership roles . . . men get priority even in the media and women's concerns do not even become news.

Even when women were given the opportunity for leadership roles, acceptance from the male members was an issue. Nabodita Chaudhari, CA member from the RPP who is highly educated and comes from a high-profile family, was nominated as a chairperson of the Committee for Determining the Base of Cultural and Social Solidarity. She said that although it was a great opportunity to work with a diverse group of people, it was very challenging for her to chair this committee because the male members did not take her seriously. She said:

> There were a lot of challenges . . . I didn't get the support from my own committee members . . . Male members were not paying attention in the meeting I coordinated. Maybe because they didn't like working under a woman!

The entrenched power of patriarchy was also observed on 28 May 2011, when the future of the CA was uncertain. It was a chaotic situation. The aim of the

CA was to write a new constitution of Nepal. However, due to disagreement between key political parties, especially about the structure of federalism, the constitution could not be finalized. The only option left was the extension of the CA for another year. However, leaders could not even reach a consensus about the extension. The whole nation was waiting for the decision which seemed to lie in the hands of just four key leaders; everyone else was just waiting to hear from them.

I was with my research participants at Birendra International Convention Centre (BICC) for 24 hours on 28 May 2011. These CA members, who were mandated by their parties to be present at BICC, were just like the public who were waiting outside the BICC. The only difference, according to a women CA member, was that they had the privilege of entering the building. Since I had built a rapport with some of my interviewees, I went to BICC with them as a guest. They said they were not any different from me, waiting to hear from the leaders. Sunita Kumari Mahato (UCPN-M) said, "once the decision is made then we will be invited to clap and that's our role."

Sunita and others said they feel bad about the current political situation. There is nothing that they can do because the key political leaders alone make all the decisions. They said they feel guilty for not fulfilling the promises they had made to the people when they stood in the election. They said, "we do not know how to

Figure 4.1 Protest outside BICC on 28 May 2011

face the public because we are not going to be trusted again and we don't know if they will vote for us again." Sunita said,

> The public don't know that we are not the ones who are not working. We are just like them . . . we wait and watch for the decisions of the key leaders but these leaders are not making the decision. [pointing towards the protest outside the BICC] . . . those people must be scolding us as they think we are getting paid by the state and not doing anything. They don't know it's not us but it is the leaders who are not letting us do anything.

She also shared a bad experience she had when she visited her constituency, Siraha. She said:

> People of my constituency were very angry with me. They thought I was there in Kathmandu enjoying my life and not doing anything for my people. To stop me from visiting my constituency, the locals threw stones and broke the glass of my car. They also tried to set it on fire. It's not me to blame, it's the leaders who need to be blamed.
>
> (Sunita Kumari Mahato, UCPN-M)

In addition to women, male CA members were also waiting for the decision. However, the four key leaders who were in a position to make decisions were all men. The rest of the CA members were just waiting for the decision, as they were not allowed to leave BICC until the decision was made. As a result, the CA members were there at BICC from 7 am till the decision was made at around 4 am the next morning. All this suggests the continuity of a political structure in which decision making was limited to a few key leaders. However, this does not suggest that the rest of the CA members did not have agency or were just passive dupes. The resistance from these CA members, especially the women, was remarkable.

Difficulties in promoting a distinctive women's agenda in the Constituent Assembly

Another challenge which arose repeatedly during my interviews was the difficulties women CA members face in making women's agenda a priority. According to them, there were always other important topics to discuss rather than women's agendas. Shanti Devi Chamar (CPN-UML) said "women's issues are not prioritized. Women CA members are given little time to speak and there is always something else to discuss. Economic and other political agendas get priority over the issues and concerns of women." Shanti and a few other CA members said they became CA members to write the constitution and people had voted for them with high expectations. However, the decision is not in their hands. They therefore feel guilty for not being able to fulfil their expectations and feel sad when people ask questions about the failure of the CA.

Discrimination based on gender and social status

In addition to male domination and the influence of the patriarchal structure, women also faced other challenges including discrimination based on education, class, castes, region, political affiliation and age. While I was sitting with them on 28 May 2011, I observed that women who had been in politics for a long time and had earned a reputation were sitting separately, either with other women leaders (senior) or with their male colleagues, who were perceived to have similar status in terms of seniority in the leadership. However, women who had a low educational level and had recently joined politics were sitting together even though they were representing different political parties. Women who were new to the political field said there was no discrimination. However, one could easily observe clear divisions. Likewise, women from Terai/Madhesh were sitting on one side and women from the hilly regions were sitting separately. Although I saw some mixing, the separation between established leaders and newcomers and between women CA members from various castes, classes and educational backgrounds was obvious.

The CA members had different experiences due to their age as well. Babina Mokhtan Lawati (RPP) said, "it was more challenging for young leaders to establish themselves than the old ones." Some of the newcomers faced other kinds of challenges. Asha Sardar (MJF-Democratic), for example, said it was hard to navigate her way in Kathmandu initially because she had never been there before. She is from the plains of Nepal, and only came to Kathmandu after she became a CA member. Likewise, illiterate women CA members had problems in the beginning understanding the rules and procedures of the CA. They said "even when we had to vote for different bills, they were all in a written form which we couldn't read so someone had to read it for us" (Kalawati Pasman Dushadh, MJF-Democratic).

Women's resistance to patriarchy

Despite all these challenges, women were negotiating with male leaders to include their agendas in the constitution, and as a result they were able to get some bills passed that favour women, as discussed earlier. Deniz Kandiyoti (1988, p. 275) describes "patriarchal bargains," by which she means that "women strategize within a set of concrete constraints . . . (which) open up new areas of struggle and renegotiation of the relations between genders" and use various techniques to have their voices heard. Women in Nepal are now being accepted as leaders and have a better position in politics compared to the past. However, patriarchy has thousands of years of history, which has become the habitus of the people, and the people who have been benefitting from it resist any radical changes. Uneven patterns are seen even in the political field in Nepal, where women are accepted in some roles but not included in others. However, women have been resisting this practice using various means. I will now present some of the strategies women CA members applied to resist patriarchal power.

Refusing cooperation to patriarchy

As mentioned earlier, Jaypuri Gharti Magar was appointed a minister in 2011 but she refused to take the oath. She said:

> I refused to take oath for the Minister because I was the only woman nominated by my party. We sacrificed our lives and fought for ten years just to be able to create a better space for women in our society but our own party does not recognize women's contribution. We need to fight within our own party. If we cannot bring change within our party, we will not be able to fight with others as well.

Although Jaypuri was from the UCPN-M, women from the NC, CPN-UML, MJF and other political parties appreciated her decision. All the women CA members from various political parties came together and showed their solidarity with her. Ram Rati Ram (CPN-UML) said, "we appreciated Gharti's decision as it was not only her concern but it was of concern to all women in the CA. Therefore, we all protested against this decision." This put pressure on the government and parties to include more women in the cabinet. Her refusal was taken seriously by the people and it was also highlighted in the media (see Lamsal, n.d.).

Exercise of power to challenge the patriarchal mindset

Despite being challenged by her own committee members, Nabodita Chaudhari completed her task on time. She finished her report and submitted it to the CA. She was among a few to complete reports on time. She said:

> People were against me when I submitted my report. I was blamed for not having a proper consultation with other members of the committee but I thought people will do it anyway. Even if I took another year, they will still find faults in me. I thought I had put in my best effort. It was difficult but I successfully handled the committee and submitted my report.
>
> (Nabodita Chaudhari, RPP)

Nabodita exercised her power to get things done and proved her capability. Like Nabodita, other CA members also said that they exercise their power when needed, inside or outside the CA.

Collective agency and support from outside

Collective agency of women was an important pattern that was observed during the CA. Despite the ideological, educational, class and caste diversity among the women CA members, they were able to unite and show solidarity when there was something which affected women. They crossed all the boundaries and became one to advocate the women's agenda. Puspa Bhusal (NC) said:

> We have been raising concerns about women's issues such as citizenship rights, children should be given citizenship on the basis of a mother's name as well, and women should be given 50 per cent representations in all state organs.

Another important pattern observed in the CA was the pressure from outside, especially from women's rights activists. They supported women CA members and put pressure on leadership to consider the issues and concerns of women which were neglected or overlooked.

Women's experience of individual transformation

Despite the challenges they face, almost all of my research participants said their lives have been transformed in many ways. Transformation was more significant and visible for women who had just joined politics as compared to the women who had been in politics for many years. However, even those who had chosen politics as a career and had spent their whole life in politics said the situation has become much better now, as they are more easily accepted as leaders now than they had been in the past.

Sunita Kumari Mahato (UCPN-M), who became a CA member after the death of her husband, said despite the loss she feels that her life has been transformed:

> People were just not accepting women doing anything before. They used to point the finger on anything we did . . . like even if when they saw someone talking to a guy they said she is characterless. Women of Madhesh were in veil. Even those who were educated couldn't go in front of the male members of the family. We had to cover our face but things are changing now. My life has totally transformed. As a widow, I was supposed to stay at home and follow some restricting rituals but I don't need to do anything now. I am like other women. Despite my loss, I feel lucky, as I am at the policy making level. I can write people's future. I feel I am lucky and proud of myself. I was only a school teacher and now I am one of the leaders of the country.

Shanti Devi Rajbansi (UCPN-M) also became a CA member due to the death of her husband. She did not have a formal education, but she showed her concerns about discrimination against women in politics. Her journey from housewife to CA member was remarkable. She says:

> Women are 51 per cent of the population but if you see the current cabinet, how many women we have there? Just three! Two state ministers and one full minister . . . even the full minister refused to take the oath because she wanted to have at least 33 per cent representation in the cabinet as well. I want to have all the rights reserved in the constitution.

Another CA member, Pramila Devi Yadav (UCPN-M), said:

> Everyone knows me now. I don't have to cover my face. I have learnt that you won't get anything if you ask for it. You need to snatch it or demand it.

Budhni Devi Mahato (UCPN-M) said that by joining the Maoist movement her life has transformed. She said:

> Before, women were just in four walls. They didn't know anything. If you didn't allow women to go out, how will they see or know what's going on outside? How will she know about her rights? How will she do something for the nation? When she goes out, she learns many things. When I went to my village before, people were backbiting about me and said she became Maoist. Now the same people respect me, greet me and make me feel so special when I go to my village.

The husband of Durga Devi Mahato (MJF-Democratic), was working in a textile factory but after she became a CA member, he left his job and became her personal assistant (PA) – a rare situation in Nepal. However, despite the transformation women have experienced, they complain about the discrimination against women and also the discrimination they still face based on caste/ethnicity, education, region and religion. Pramila Devi Yadav said:

> When there is a movement or fight, women go in the first row and when it comes to giving power and position, women are discriminated against and excluded. I am from a family where there are 5 martyrs. I have been discriminated against because I am from Madhesh.

She mentioned during the interview that it was her turn to be a minister but she was not offered that position because she was from the Madhesh. An interesting point to note is that, although she feels discriminated against, there has still been a significant transformation in her life. Despite the challenges, all of my research participants said they have experienced some level of transformation in their lives. Their experiences of transformation were quite distinct; some felt more liberated than others, but all of them had benefitted from their new roles. They also mentioned that their mobility was not restricted as it had been in the past; they have access to power, knowledge about the outside world, and they feel more confident now.

As Bourdieu argues, "there is a gap between the progress made by women and men therefore the structure of gap is maintained" (Bourdieu & Nice, 2001, p. 91). One of my key informants, who is a human rights activist, said "social transformation has occurred in Nepal but individual transformation is more rapid and radical than the transformation in the social structures." She added, "because of the gap between individual transformation and social transformation, we see all these tensions and protests in the street" (Mandira Sharma, Advocacy Forum

Nepal). Habitus is a "system of generative scheme" which Bourdieu defines as both durable and transposable (Calhoun, LiPuma, & Postone, 1993, p. 4). Habitus is durable because it has a long history, it sits in the cognitive structure and lasts longer. It is transposable as it can be shared by a group of people or a community. However, habitus is visible through the actions of individuals. Since it depends on the action of each individual, which is subjective, there is a possibility of reflexivity which may lead to the continuation of the same habitus and/or reproduction of some with modifications. In the case of Nepal, although some aspects of life have changed, some are still being followed from the traditional culture. Therefore, transformations are seen in some aspects of people's lives and not in others. Moreover, because of differential impacts of the People's War, some people have experienced a significant level of transformation in their lives and some have experienced only a small change. Therefore, because of these varied experiences, although a majority of people may experience a high level of transformation, society still seems to be catching up. However, the movements and resistance against discriminations that are taking place in Nepal will provide opportunities for reflection and therefore will create possibilities for change.

Women's experience of social transformation

When I asked my research participants if they had witnessed or experienced any changes in their society, all said that despite the strong influence of patriarchy, they have witnessed and experienced some level of social transformation in their communities since the People's War. Two different patterns were observed in the interviews with women CA members from *Madhesh* and *Pahad* (the hilly regions). Women CA members from the Madhesh said people seemed to be more aware of aspects of gender discrimination, such as the dowry system and its consequences, the low literacy rate among women, discrimination against girl children, unmatched marriage (i.e. a large age difference between husband and wife) and so on. Women who had never been to school said that even though they themselves did not have the opportunity to go to school, they have sent their daughters to good schools, and there is an increasing number of girls enrolled in their communities. The overall literacy rate has increased since 1996 among both men and women in Nepal, but gender disparity still exists in the overall literacy rate. The *Nepal Living Standards Survey* (2010/2011) suggests there is a less gender disparity among young people. For example, the literacy rate among men under 19 is 94.8 per cent, and 84.1 per cent among girls of the same age. The literacy rate also varies between urban and rural contexts: in urban areas it is 96.3 per cent among boys and 90.9 per cent among girls under 19 years; in rural areas it is 94.4 per cent among boys and 82.5 per cent among girls. The gender disparity is minimal among children under the age of 14 years: 87.3 per cent among boys and 84.3 per cent among girls. This shows that there is an increase in girls' enrolment in school (see *Nepal Living Standards Survey*, 2010/2011, p. 86; Sharma & Donini, 2010, p. 15).

The women CA members also said there is a decrease in child marriage and an increasing number of women in the public sphere. There are even several cases of inter-caste marriage with parental consent, when inter-caste marriage used to be something that people were not even allowed to talk about.

Laxmi Chaudhari (UCPN-M) said:

> There was a lot of discrimination against women in Nepal like the dowry, veil, low literacy rate among women, unmatched marriage etc. But the situation has become better now. People have become more aware because of the Maoist movement. They know about their rights. Women participate in different programs which was never the case before.

Jwala Singh (UCPN-M) says inter-caste marriage was previously restricted, and marriage between *Madhesi* and *Pahade* was out of the question. However, she has seen a lot of inter-caste marriage since she got married. Laxmi Chaudhari and Jwala Singh both had inter-caste marriage. Jwala said:

> I got married when I was still underground. A *Madhesi* girl marrying a Brahmin boy was something one would not even think about in our society but since we both were involved in the Maoist movement . . . we got married. Our parents had no idea about this. Initially my parents were very angry with me but now they have accepted us. After I got married, several other girls from Chaudhari community got married with men from hilly regions. *Madhesi* girls got married with *Pahade* boys and *Pahade* girls got married with *Madhesi* boys which was never the case before.

There were some cases in the past where *Pahade* girls eloped with *Madhesi* boys, but they were never accepted by their families. But now, even though it is not open and free for everybody to choose anyone from any caste and only arranged marriages are recognized as prestigious, this is slowly changing.

Although women from hilly regions had more flexibility than women from Madhesh, they also faced serious gender-based discrimination such as polygamy, the *Chhaupadi Pratha* (having to sleep in a cowshed during menstruation), discrimination against girls and so on. The *Chhaupadi Pratha* is still practiced despite being declared illegal by the Supreme Court of Nepal in 2005 (Harley, 2013). There have been many awareness-raising programs about the impacts of *Chhaupadi*, by both the government and NGOs. Save the Children in collaboration with the Ministry of Women, Children and Social Welfare implemented a *Chhaupadi* elimination program in the Western districts of Nepal. The midterm evaluation of this project suggests some villages have been declared *Chhaupadi*-free (see Chapagain, n.d.; Uprety & Bhandari, 2010). Sharma and Donini (2010) also suggest that the *Chhaupadi* system has been reduced to a great extent in some of the Western districts of Nepal.

CA members also said that there is an increased awareness among people about protecting women's rights. Women have started coming together and forming groups. Women themselves are aware of their rights and they are demanding them. Babina Mokhtan (RPP) says:

Society has transformed now, there is less discrimination compared to before but still people experience unequal treatment. People are flexible about untouchability. Increased participation, increased self-confidence, and learning opportunities have also increased because of increased mobility.

Pampha Bhusal, who is a CA member and one of the top leaders of the UCPN-M, said:

Political transformation is a key to social transformation. When women are in mainstream politics then it's an encouragement for others. When women see their friends or another woman from the same community in the higher level politics, it gives them hope and a 'can do' attitude. They feel that if she can do this then why can't I? We are role models for many women.

In summary, most of the participants said they have experienced some level of transformation in the country. More women are in the public sphere, more girls are going to school and there are more women in politics. Women are also included in various state organs and people are aware about their rights and the rights of others, so there is a general claim that there is less discrimination based on gender, caste and region. Women are more vocal and more confident. Interviewees said more women are reporting domestic violence, they are ambitious now, the veil system is slowly disappearing from *Madhesh* and there is a dramatic decrease in child marriage. The foregoing analysis indicates the unevenness and non-linearity of the social transformation process underway.

Conclusion

All women have the capacity for . . . transformation.
(Butler, Puigvert, & Beck-Gernsheim, 2001, p. 117)

Women's involvement in mainstream politics significantly increased after the CPA. Attaining one-third of women's representation in CA was a historic move towards greater gender equality in Nepal. Although the inclusion of women was political objective, when they were included it did not just transform their lives; they also became role models for their societies which created space for other women to participate in the public sphere.

When women left their homes and took part in the CA, even those who had just joined politics, they got the opportunity to learn new things. It also boosted their confidence because they were counted among the policy makers of the country. They were given a variety of trainings, they participated in the debates, became ministers and took up various responsible roles. All this contributed to their transformation. They were able to reflect on their roles in the past and recognize the discrimination they had suffered. This helped them transform their own lives, but they also became committed to helping other women who were in the same situation.

This kind of rapid change would not have been possible without the collective efforts of individuals. The women's movement against the discrimination within and outside the CA contributed to the continuation of the gains that women had achieved and also helped demand more. Women through their collective agency are changing the whole discourse of womanhood, which would not have been possible by only individuals' efforts. Benhabib (1999, p. 355) argues that "collective identity is a renewed respect for the universal." This new social subject arose from the interaction between women themselves (Puigvert, 2001, p. 111). However, if the social context was not favourable, the achievement that is experienced at this level would not have been possible.

I had asked my research participants about their future plans and where they see themselves after they finish their tenure of CA. All of them said they will continue their career in politics. Even if they did not get the opportunity, they will still be involved in social work. They will not go back to their previous roles. How practical this will be is yet to be seen. It would be misleading to say that there is a complete transformation in Nepal, but it can be argued that Nepal is on the right path towards positive transformation, especially in relation to gender equality. In the next chapter, I will present an in-depth study of a community to examine how one person's involvement in politics has changed the lives of many people in that community and how it has contributed to the transformation of the society.

Notes

1 The conflicting groups/parties included Janatantrik Terai Mukti Morcha (Republic of Terai Liberation Front), Limbuwan Swayatta Sarokar Manch (Limbuwan Autonomous Concerned Forum), Madhesi Mukti Morcha (Madhesi Liberation Front) and Madhesi People's Rights Forum, to name a few (see Hangen, 2007).
2 There is no formal documentation of these groups. I was working in an I/NGO at that time and was responsible to look after safety and security of the staff; therefore, I collected these names with the support from other organizations in Nepal. Some groups are listed by Bogati et al. (2003) and Hangen (2007).
3 For the direct, first-past-the-post seats, the country was divided into 240 electoral constituencies on the basis of population. Likewise, 335 CA members were nominated on the basis of the votes that each political party had received to nominate CA members proportionately on the basis of gender, caste, ethnicity and religion. The third group consisted of 26 persons who were to be nominated by the cabinet from among people who were well known in their fields or had made significant contributions to the country (see *Constitution of Nepal*, 2015; Thapa & Sharma, 2009).
4 Most of the names mentioned in this chapter are real names. I have used pseudonym for Devi and ex-combatants for confidentiality as they did not want to disclose their real names.

References

Benhabib, S. (1999). Sexual Difference and Collective Identities: The New Global Constellation. *Signs, 24*(2), 335–361. doi:10.2307/3175645.
Bogati, S., Carapic, J., & Muggah, R. (2003). The Missing Middle: Examining the Armed Group Phenomenon in Nepal. *Small Arms Survey Issue Brief*. Retrieved 20 October 2015 fromhttp://www.smallarmssurvey.org/fileadmin/docs/G-Issue-briefs/NAVA-IB1-Missing-Middle.pdf

Bourdieu, P., & Nice, R. (2001). *Masculine Domination*. Cambridge: Polity Press.

Butler, J., Puigvert, L., & Beck-Gernsheim, E. (2001). Gender and Social Transformation: A Dialogue (J. Vaida, Trans.). In E. Beck-Gernsheim, J. Butler, & L. Puigvert (Eds.), *Women and Social Transformation* (pp. 116–136). New York: Peter Lang.

Calhoun, C. J., LiPuma, E., & Postone, M. (1993). *Bourdieu: Critical Perspectives*. Cambridge: Polity Press.

Chapagain, B. (n.d.). Shackles of the Chhaupadi System. *Astitwa*. Retrieved 20 October 2015 from http://www.astitwa.com/index.php/shackles-of-the-chhaupadi-system

Constitution of Nepal, 2072. (2015). Retrieved from https://drive.google.com/file/d/0B1EyNP0s1r6JUGhoMHBtYmtvdDA/view

El Bushra, J., & Piza-Lopez, E. (1993). Working on Gender in Conflict Situations: Some Ideas on Strategy. *Focus on Gender, 1*(2), 15–16.

Falch, A. (2010). *Women's Political Participation and Influence in Post-conflict Burundi and Nepal*. Oslo: Peace Research Institute Oslo (PRIO).

Gardam, J., & Charlesworth, H. (2000). Protection of Women in Armed Conflict. *Human Rights Quarterly, 22*(1), 148–166. doi:10.2307/4489270.

Hangen, S. (2007). *Creating a "New Nepal": The Ethnic Dimension*. Washington, DC: East-West Center.

Harley, R. (2013, 30 April). Nepalese Menstruation Ritual Hard to Discontinue. *Globe and Mail*. Retrieved 20 June 2014 from http://www.theglobeandmail.com/news/world/nepalese-menstruation-tradition-dies-hard/article11644844/

IDEA. (2008). *The Constituent Assembly of Nepal: An Agenda for Women*. Lalitpur, Nepal: International Institute for Democracy and Electoral Assistance. Full report retrieved from http://www.capwip.org/readingroom/TopotheShelf.Newsfeeds/2008/The%20Constituent%20Assembly%20of%20Nepal-%20An%20Agenda%20for%20Women%20(2008).pdf

IDEA. (2011). *Women Members of the Constituent Assembly: A Study on Contribution of Women in Constitution Making in Nepal* (p. 905). Kathmandu. Full report retrieved from http://www.idea.int/publications/women-members-of-the-constituent-assembly/index.cfm

Kabir, F. (2003). *Political Participation of Women in South Asia*. DAWN.

Kandiyoti, D. (1988). Bargaining with Patriarchy. *Gender and Society, 2*(3), 374–290.

Kathmandu Post. (2011, 24 July). Maoist CC Meet: Maoists Decide to Reshuffle Their Team in Cabinet. Retrieved 12 July 2013 from http://www.ekantipur.com/the-kathmandu-post/2011/07/24/top-story/maoist-cc-meet-maoists-decide-to-reshuffle-their-team-in-cabinet/224367.html

Lamsal, Y. N. (n.d.). Crisis Is Part of Politics. *Gorkhapatra*. Retrieved from http://www.gorkhapatra.org.np/rising.detail.php?article_id=50757&cat_id=7

Manchanda, R. (2001a). Ambivalent Gains in South Asian Conflicts. In M. Turshen, S. Meintjes, & A. Pillay (Eds.), *The Aftermath: Women in Post-conflict Transformation* (pp. 99–121). London: Zed Books.

Manchanda, R. (2001b). Where Are the Women in South Asian Conflicts? In R. Manchanda (Ed.), *Women, War and Peace: Beyond Victimhood to Agency*. New Delhi: Sage, pp. 9–41.

Nepali, R. K., & Shrestha, P. (2007). *Unfolding the Reality: Silenced Voices of Women in Politics*. Kathmandu: South Asia Partnership.

Nepal Living Standards Survey. (2010/2011). Kathmandu: Government of Nepal, National Planning Commission Secretariat and Central Bureau of Statistics. Retrieved from http://cbs.gov.np/?p=158.

Pankhurst, D. (2007). *Gender Issues in Post-war Contexts: A Review of Analysis and Experience, and Implications for Policies* (Vol. 9). Bradford: Department of Peace Studies, University of Bradford.

Puigvert, L. (2001). Dialogic Feminism: "Other Women's" Contributions of the Social Transformation of Gender Relations (J. Vaida, Trans.). In E. Beck-Gernsheim, J. Butler, & L. Puigvert (Eds.), *Women and Social Transformation* (pp. 29–60). New York: Peter Lang.

Sharma, J. R., & Donini, A. (2010). *Towards a "Great Transformation"? The Maoist Insurgency and Local Perceptions of Social Transformation in Nepal.* Boston, MA: Tufts University.

Thapa, G. B., & Sharma, J. (2009). From Insurgency to Democracy: The Challenges of Peace and Democracy-Building in Nepal. *International Political Science Review, 30*(2), 205–219. doi:10.2307/25652899.

Turshen, M. (2001). Engendering Relations of State to Society in the Aftermath. In M. Turshen, S. Meintjes, & A. Pillay (Eds.), *The Aftermath: Women in Post-conflict Transformation* (pp. 78–96). London: Zed Books.

Turshen, M., Meintjes, S., & Pillay, A. (2001). There Is No Aftermath for Women. In M. Turshen, S. Meintjes, & A. Pillay (Eds.), *The Aftermath: Women in Post-conflict Transformation* (pp. 3–18). London: Zed Books.

UNDP. (2008). *The Interim Constitution of Nepal, 2063 (2007): As Amended by the First to Sixth Amendments.* Kathmandu: UN.

UNDP. (2009). *Nepal Human Development Report 2009: State Transformation and Human Development.* Kathmandu: UN. Retrieved 15 June 2011 from http://hdr.undp.org/en/content/state-transformation-and-human-development

Uprety, A., & Bhandari, R. R. (2010). *Midterm Review of Chhaupadi Elimination Project in Accham.* Kathmandu: Save the Children Country Office Nepal.

5 Tea stall story
The power of one

This chapter presents an in-depth analysis of a small community in Siraha to demonstrate how one woman's involvement in politics has changed the fabric of social relations within a short period of time. Siraha is one of the districts in the Eastern region of Nepal. It is in the plains of Nepal, which is known as Terai/Madhesh. The total population of Siraha district is 637,328 (CBS, 2011) and made up of more than 30 castes and ethnic groups (UNDP, 2008). There is a small town in Siraha district, which is also called Siraha. Although some people from the Hills and the Mountains have migrated here, the majority of people have lived there for hundreds of years. Siraha is close to the Indian border and the culture of the majority is similar to that of Bihar, the neighbouring Indian state. The distance between Siraha and the capital Kathmandu is about 314 kilometres, but it takes one full day to get there because the roads are not good. However, the distance from Siraha to Jayanagar, at the Indian border, is only about 11 kilometres. As a result, local residents travel to Jayanagar to watch films and shop for special occasions, such as marriages and religious festivals, because food and clothes are cheaper there.

I was born in Siraha. About 50 meters from my parents' house there is a small community of about only 75 households of lower caste people (untouchables) called *Tatma*. Although there was not a significant physical distance between the two communities, there was a large social gap. It always felt as if there was a large social fence between the two communities.

The communication between upper and lower caste people was limited to work. Since the lower caste people were poor, their livelihoods depended on upper caste people. Upper caste people could not do without the lower caste people because they were essential to help with the farming. However, in terms of power relations, the lower caste people were subordinate to the upper caste. The daily wage was negotiated between these communities where lower caste people had little say in decision making. Once negotiated, the wage was fixed for years. The wage was given mostly in kind, for instance, 4 kilograms of rice plus breakfast and lunch for that day. Although the wage was fixed, the lower caste people had some favourite landlords depending on who gave good food.

I grew up seeing all this. Although I had to go past that community almost every day, I did not pay much attention to them, and I never thought it was important because they were just workers and did not have any social status. But they knew everything about me. I knew them by their faces but I had no idea about their names or their families. I left Siraha in 1999. I visited my parents every year until 2004 but only a few times after 2005. Although the armed conflict had impacted the whole country, Siraha was less impacted than the western regions of Nepal. However, the Madhesh movement, which started in 2007 after the Comprehensive Peace Agreement (CPA), was strong in Siraha because the majority of the people were Madhesi, who had been discriminated against for hundreds of years by the people from the Hills.

Significance of a tea stall

Devi[1] comes from the lower caste community. She used to work in my neighbour's house as a domestic helper, mainly washing clothes and dishes. In 2008, I heard that Devi had been nominated for the Constituent Assembly (CA). Initially I could not recognize her by name, but later when my brother explained to me about her husband and her family, I was able to figure out who she was. In 2011, I began my fieldwork with the intention of interviewing women CA members. Since I knew Devi from my childhood and I was curious to learn about her life after she had become a CA member, I decided to start my interviews with her. Although she was stationed in Kathmandu after she became a CA member, she happened to be visiting her constituency (Siraha) for some political assignments. I requested an interview and she happily agreed despite her busy schedule. She asked me to come to her house in the morning.

The concept of time is very different in rural Nepal. Morning could mean any time before lunch and it could also mean anytime when she is free. I woke up in the morning and walked towards her house which is just a few metres from my parents' house. When I got there, I could not find her. I asked people where she was. They said she might be in *Pakhair Gachhi*. They directed me towards a usual gathering place for the people of this lower caste community. There is a big tree, near a pond, which is only about 5 minutes' walk from her house. Under this tree, there is a concrete platform where people have both formal and informal community meetings/gatherings. Initially I thought she would be at someone's house near the tree, but when I got there I saw her sitting in one of the tea stalls with many other women. I was surprised because I had never seen women from that community having tea, which was a luxury for them. The sight of women sitting in a tea stall and having tea was something I never had seen or imagined in my life.

A few years ago, it was completely different. Only men used to have tea in the morning with other men from the same community at the tea stall at *Pakhair Gachhi*. It used to be a men's place where men gathered, had tea and talked about different things, mostly about politics as well as issues and concerns of the people of that community, before departing for work. The tea stall used to be run by a man and all the customers were men. I had never seen a single woman having tea with men, not even an older woman. I had never seen women in public participating in those kinds of discussions.

This time what I saw was completely different. Women were sitting and having tea and talking about politics in the same way men used to do. This tea stall was run by a woman and Devi was surrounded by another 10 women. All these women were from the same community, they shared the same language and culture and had similar economic backgrounds. It was not a displacement of men by women from that place. The practice among men still exists. However, it was no longer just a men's space. Certainly this was a big shift in terms of gender relations.

I wanted to keep my conversation going with Devi and wanted to find out more about her life. Therefore, I asked her to share the story of her journey from a housewife to a CA member. She said it was very challenging in the beginning but things have changed now, not just in her life but also in her community. She added:

> I got married when I was 12 or 13 years old. I don't remember the exact age but it was something like that. I was married to a very poor family so we had to work for our daily meal. My husband was alcoholic. He used to beat me up for every little thing. He didn't take any responsibility for the family so I had to work in others' houses to feed my children. I have three children. I don't have a higher education so I couldn't get a decent job. I went to school only for three years and then got married so I had to stop as I had to move to my husband's place. I was fortunate that I was sent to school by my parents but I couldn't continue as daughters-in-law in our community were not supposed to go to school. My husband is illiterate . . . he has never been to school.

Devi is now 40 years old. When I asked her how she got involved in politics, she said she had never imagined she would ever become a CA member. It was not just her; no one from her community had ever imagined that anyone from her community could ever take part in politics because they thought it was out of their reach. She recounted the story of her involvement in public life:

> After marriage, it was very difficult for me to step out of my house except for work. However, since I had done some schooling, I had a better idea about life and about the outside world. I was outspoken as compared to other women of my community . . . I was able to read and write, a little. Therefore, I was picked up by an organization to work as a community health volunteer in 2051 [1994]. Also the Human Rights Commission was looking for a member for its local committee so I became a member of that as well. Though I was involved in these organizations, it was not easy for me. At that time, women's mobility was restricted. Women who went out and got involved in these kinds of programs were considered 'bad women'. That's why people didn't want to do anything because they didn't want to be outcast.

Recalling an incident, she said:

> Once an organization started a literacy program, especially targeting women of my community . . . it was free for all of us. Since we were busy during

the daytime, the literacy class was scheduled for 8 pm so that we all could participate after finishing the household chores. Although the time was set in consultation with us, going out of the house at night was a nightmare for us. Some of us got permission from our families and joined the class. We always went to the class together but still people started talking about us. They blamed us for going out at night even though they knew that we were going to the literacy class. People believed that women will be spoilt if they are educated. We were blamed as 'bad character' women.

Devi explained the consequences of these attitudes towards women:

I was the leader of that group so they blamed me and said I was ruining the community by taking those women out. There are instances when some men of that community followed us to check what we were doing. Some men even came to beat me up. Some women left that program in the middle because of the fear of being discarded by the family and the community. Though some of us were able to convince our family members, society was the barrier . . . we couldn't complete the literacy class.

The structure which defines the body also decides about bad women and virtuous women, chaste or impure (Bourdieu & Nice, 2001, pp. 15–16). Butler (2001) argues that to be able to transform society is not about having the capacity to act differently but about having support from institutions which provides an enabling environment for women to exercise their agency.

It seems to me that when we talk about whether women can act or whether they have agency, we are always asking whether the social condition permits. It is why our personal transformation is dependent on social transformation. So, whether my individual capacity is, it makes no difference unless I am able to live in a world which allows me to realize it.

(Butler, Puigvert and Beck-Gernsheim, 2001, p. 122)

Devi had showed her agency and she was also supported to some extent by her family, but her community was not open to accommodate any changes. Therefore, despite her efforts, she could not achieve much. However, in order to meet her daily needs, she kept trying and finding new ways. It was a matter of survival, so despite the restrictions there was a flexibility amidst the rigid boundary for her. She had the flexibility to go out and look for possibilities for work.

The Madhesh movement[2] led by the Madhesh Janatantrik Forum (MJF) started in 2007. Since she was from a poor family, Devi was asked by the movement organizers to help them with cooking and cleaning for their protesters. She accepted the offer and started helping them. Initially she was not interested in politics, but while she was with them she learned that the protest was to demand the rights of

Madhesi people, including people like her. When she realized that, she started taking part in the protests. She said:

> I needed work and they needed someone to help them with cooking and clean-
> ing so I worked for them with that. Later I got actively involved in protest as
> well. People from my community were against my decision. They even talked
> to my husband and said he should not allow me to go out and take part in such
> activities. My husband tried to stop me but I did not listen to him. I went to
> different villages and created awareness about the rights of *Madhesi* people
> during 18 days of protest. The *Madhesh* movement was successful and later
> in the CA election in 2008, they nominated me for Constituent Assembly
> (CA). This achievement was beyond my imagination. I never had expected
> that I would ever reach to this level but here I am.

A crisis situation not only breaks the relationship between field and habitus, but it also creates unexpected conditions and space for people, which can be liberating. Although initially Devi had not thought that she would get involved in political protests, when she was exposed to the political field, which was new for her, where she was also exposed to the new knowledge, she felt like doing something for her people without expecting anything in return. The crisis in this particular situation can be seen in two ways: the individual crisis and the social crisis. On the one hand, Devi had stepped into another field which did not fit well with her existing habitus and therefore created the possibility for her to be reflexive about her own situation. On the other hand, there was a social crisis created by the Madhesh movement. As a result, not only was Devi open to new ideas, but society was also opening up new space for her.

After the successful Madhesh movement, MJF decided to take part in the election. As mentioned earlier, due to the People's War and also because of ethnic conflict, inclusion of discriminated and under-represented people had become one of the main agenda items for all the political parties. The parties who had more people from discriminated groups were identified as good parties. There was therefore a symbolic competition to become inclusive. Since MJF was one of the parties advocating for the rights of the discriminated, it had to demonstrate its inclusiveness. MJF therefore included people from various castes, ethnic groups and economic backgrounds. Devi was from a lower caste and was therefore a good catch for MJF. Devi was nominated for the CA.

Devi has experienced many changes in her life since she became a CA member. Her experience of transformation is not limited to the individual level – she said there have been many transformations in her community as well. She has been receiving significant support from her community. The same community which had stopped her from going to the literacy class and blamed her for ruining the culture is now taking her as a role model and inspiration for others. They want their daughters and daughters-in-law to become like her.

> People who blamed me for going out and participating in politics are asking
> me to take their daughters and daughters-in-law with me so that one day they
> can learn and become like me.

(Devi)

She says many women of her community have joined different political parties since she became a CA member. She says the challenges are less for women who are joining politics now. She recalls her past and says:

> Even after finishing all the chores we were not allowed to go to the literacy program before, but now there is no need to schedule the classes in the evening. Women can join any programs that are beneficial to them. Women do not have to convince their families because they get encouraged by their families because I have set a good example.

Bourdieu (1989, p. 21) argues that a person's subject position is constructed based on a combination of various social capitals and their value in a particular time and context. Foucault's notion of subject complements Bourdieu's notion of subject position, as he argues, individuals are made subjects through various forms of power (Foucault, 1982, p. 781). Devi's subject position had changed from a housewife to a CA member. This new role, which already comes with a set of powers, puts her on top of everyone else, not only in her community but also in the neighbouring high caste community. Devi's new role certainly has made a significant difference in people's perception.

> As I recall my life before being a CA member, it was all struggles. No one would listen to me before. I was just a woman but now I am always surrounded by people when I come to my constituency. Everyone respects me, even people from the upper caste. People call me by my name now whereas before, I wonder if anyone knew my real name. They used to call me Janakpurwali.[3] I feel like my self-esteem has increased and I am confident that I can do anything.
>
> (Devi)

She feels proud of her achievements and the change that is taking place in the community because of her. She says her society has opened up the door for women to participate in the public sphere only because of her. She also mentioned that her relationship with her husband has improved since she became a CA member.

> My relationship with my family has improved. My husband does not beat me up now. He still drinks but not as much as he used to and more importantly he doesn't say anything to me.
>
> (Devi)

Her status has changed, and so has the status of her family. Her husband was an alcoholic. He used to drink and swear at people even in the street, but he does not do that anymore because he is now a husband of a CA member. During informal conversations with others from that community, they said her husband used to steal goods from people's houses and sell them for alcohol. He does not do that anymore. He dresses nicely and talks to people gently. Devi's children are now going to school. This suggests that her new subject position, which comes with wealth and power, has not only changed her life but there has been much positive transformation in her family as well as in her community.

Foucault (1982, p. 781) argues that the exercise of power is dependent on each individual and their circumstances, meaning not all CA members will exercise the same level of power. It is interesting to note that the CA position itself comes with a set of powers. It is like a given situation. However, how powerful a person can be and what level of power they can exercise depends on each individual and their circumstances, which includes their other social capital which was accumulated prior to the CA, meaning their social status prior to becoming a CA member. On the one hand, Devi's status significantly changed her community as soon as she became a CA member; on the other hand, her previous status influenced her current status when she was among other CA members in the parliament house.

I observed Devi while she was in Kathmandu at her work and in Siraha with her community. She was held in a high regard in her community because she had gained something which was highly valued. Her subject position had put her somewhere high compared to other members of her community. She had become an authoritative/authentic voice of her community. However, when she was with other politicians in Kathmandu, she was seen as a less experienced politician, who was illiterate and belonged to a lower caste. All this social capital she had in the pre-CA period had some level of impact on her current position. And this was not only true for Devi, but it was also the case for all the other women CA members, as they had come from various backgrounds. Therefore, as Bourdieu (1985, p. 724) says, the value of social capital is not always the same. Devi's experience was also different from other women because of her personal circumstances, that is, her lack of formal education and knowledge about politics.

> It was very challenging in the beginning because I couldn't understand legal and political languages and had no idea about political procedures but later with the support from my colleagues, I learnt many things. I raise concerns about tobacco farming in our region . . . I am against that. I also raise concerns about discrimination against women in Madhesh. I did not know anything about politics but now I am one of the decision makers of the country. I encourage women from my community and also all Madhesi women to participate in politics.
>
> (Devi)

However, Foucault (1978, pp. 92–93) argues that "power is not something that is acquired, seized, or shared, something that one holds on to or allows to slip away; power is exercised from innumerable points, in the interplay of non-egalitarian and mobile relations." Despite her individual and structural limitations, she was able to negotiate and exercise her power. Although she, like other women CA members, still faces challenges, she is happy about the new role and transformation she has experienced and the contribution that she has made, both in the parliament as well as in her own community.

Devi's community

One woman from Devi's community emphasized:

> Devi has set up an example for all of us. She is our role model.
>
> (Gaya, FGD participant)

Inspired by Devi's interview and curious to investigate further the status of women in that community, I decided to conduct a focus group discussion (FGD) with women. Ten women participated in the FGD. All were from the same community, belonged to the same caste and had a similar economic status. They ranged in age from 25 to 55 years.

When I asked them to share how their life was earlier, Kamli, an FGD participant, said their life was limited to the household. There was a clear division of labour and women were not allowed to participate in public meetings. She said:

> We used to stay at home. Our main job was to cook and do all the household chores, take care of the elderly and kids. Since we were poor, our livelihood was dependent on wage labour . . . Only during the farming season, we could afford to have good food and also saved a little bit for the rest of the year . . . The wage wasn't enough as we had many members in the family but

Figure 5.1 Women from Siraha participating in a focus group discussion

we still liked farming season because we were able to feed children . . . Men used to plough and we were involved in planting. Women were not allowed to plough.

(Kamli)

Jamuna, another FGD participant, added to that:

During off season, we didn't have much opportunity for wage labour. Some men used to work in the construction site and women sometimes were offered some jobs like helping out with domestic chores . . . such as washing dishes, cleaning the house, washing clothes. We were untouchables so we were not even allowed to enter into their houses. We used to get some leftover food and rice. Though it was too little to feed the family, there was no other alternative . . . Some men from our community use to go to India during the off season but it was very rare. We didn't have this level of awareness about the outside world. That's why we were relying on the work that was available locally.

Another FGD participant, Janki, added that "there was an alcoholism problem among men and as a result we had a high rate of domestic violence." She also said that they did not have any concept of saving. Whatever they earned they spent, but now they do save.

We didn't have money but there was a huge problem of alcoholism among men. Once men were drunk, they used to beat their wives. We had quarrels every day in one family or the other. In the morning, it was within the family or with someone else and at night it was between husband and wife . . . because men used to come home drunk. We had no concept of saving, especially among men . . . When we had money, we ate good food and when we didn't, we slept with empty stomach. That's how our days were like.

(Janki)

This community's role in politics was also subordinate, as Mamata said:

'Politics' was nowhere near to our house. We were given food and clothes and mostly alcohol and meat at night before the election by the candidates and we were asked to vote for them. We had never thought that anyone from our community will ever take part in politics. We had no idea what the politicians were doing. They used to come to our community only during the election and after that we never used to see them . . . they didn't even recognize us so we just voted for whoever gave us more food and money. Though it was never more than what we could eat in one day but even that was coming for free so we wanted that.

They also said that the election meant an opportunity to eat good food for few days, as all the candidates used to come to their community to ask for votes. The

FGD participants said initially they accepted anything that was offered to them but later they started asking for more, and whoever gave them more food, money and alcohol got their votes. However, almost all the FGD participants said their lives have been transformed now. Most of them said they had joined a political party and some of them said they are members of different groups formed by various non-governmental organizations (NGOs). The most popular group was the savings and credit group. Women in the group had started saving. Since they could also take a loan from the group, they had started their own small businesses and some had bought a piece of land with the money.

Women who had been blamed as characterless for attending the literacy class were now encouraged by their families to participate in different programs in the hope that they would become like Devi. During the FGD, they also shared other kinds of transformations that had taken place in their community.

Significance of wearing a blouse: confidence in the public sphere

The *Sari* is the main clothing for married women in this community. *Sari* comes with a *Petikot* (a layer under the *Sari*) and a blouse (top), also called a *Cholo*. I had seen all newlyweds in this community wearing a blouse with a *Sari*, but soon after their marriage they used to wear only a *Sari* and a *Petikot*. This had become inherent in the culture of this community. Roshni said:

> People used to tease us if we wore a blouse. They used to send remarks like, she is acting like a rich woman . . . she is showing off. That's why I never wore a blouse after I had my first child. I only wore one when it was too cold or when I was travelling.

Bourdieu argues, "doing one's duty as a man means conforming to the social order, and this is fundamentally a question of respecting rhythms, keeping pace, not falling out of line" (Bourdieu, 1977, p. 161). Benhabib (1999, p. 350) notes something similar: one "feels secure in maintaining the boundaries of its own identity without being threatened by dissolution into otherness." These women did not want to be strangers in their own community. Another participant Rina said:

> I stopped wearing a blouse after two years of my marriage. People would talk about me behind my back if I wore. . . . I would have been blamed for showing off. I wanted to avoid that situation and also wanted to be part of that community so I stopped wearing it. Only a newly married had to wear it as she had to cover her whole body.

However, during my fieldwork trip, all the women were wearing a blouse. When I asked them about how they started wearing it, one of the FGD participants said, "initially we started wearing it when we started going to different trainings and meetings, now it feels awkward to go anywhere without this" (Namrata).

Figure 5.2 Devi's neighbourhood, Siraha

Another FGD participant said:

> All of us wear blouse now, except few old women (especially grandmothers).
> We need to go out to the public places. Some of us do our own business and we
> also need to participate in trainings that's why we can't go without a blouse.
> (Mamata)

Yuet See Monica Owyong (2009, p. 196) argues that clothes are not only used to fulfil our physical and psychological needs, but have various meanings, such as being used as a marker between the powerful and the weak as well as between the rich and the poor. In the case of this community they were poor, but the custom of not wearing a blouse was not only because they could not afford it. It had become like a norm and the pressure to maintain that norm did not come from outside but from within the community. It is interesting to note that although the dichotomy of rich and poor was used, it was not what women said. It seems to go with the dichotomy that Patrizia Calefato (2010, p. 348) identifies:

> the uniform [clothing] is the emblem of the separation between the inside and the outside of a culture . . ., between the 'normal' and the 'topsy-turvy' world, between the familiar and the unfamiliar, between what is 'ours' and what is 'theirs'.

These women did not want to feel like outsiders in their own community. However, it was interesting to note what women experienced after they started wearing a blouse.

Manhari, an FGD participant, said she did not realize the significance of wearing a blouse until she started wearing one. She stated:

> When I didn't wear a blouse, I felt awkward to go out and speak in the public places. It felt awkward to go where men were gathering. When I started wearing a blouse, I can now confidently take part in any events. I realized this only after I started wearing it.

Another FGD participant, Gaya, said:

> I had to wear a blouse to be able to participate in the training programs, as we were told to dress up properly . . . that's when I started wearing it. When I started wearing a blouse, I felt comfortable sitting with others. I felt confident . . . I can take part in any public event without hesitation now. In fact I now realize that since I wasn't dressed up properly, I felt awkward to participate in any events. However, I didn't realize this until I started wearing it.

Calefato (2010, p. 333) argues that "the clothed body is both a subject and an object of visuality." In this community, the blouse has certainly removed one of the barriers from women's life. Since they are more visible in the public space, men also view them differently now. When I was conducting this FGD, a man who was passing by asked me, "is this program only for women?" This is the same community where women were chastised for participating in a literacy class, but now it seems to have a high level of acceptance of women in different roles. Although there was curiosity about what these women were doing, the restrictions on them have lifted to some extent. Women are now being accepted in public places. Social space has widened for these women, and they are now capable of resisting if they are challenged.

Significance of naming: sense of belonging, respect and recognition

> Questions of identity, self-definition, and recognition are central to many contemporary struggles for freedom and dignity.
>
> (Baum, 2004, p. 1073)

Another interesting change I noticed during the FGD was naming. I started the FGD but introducing myself and asked them to introduce themselves. I was surprised by how they started introducing themselves, and most interestingly almost all of them were able to write their names. Though I had spent 20 years of my life in this village and knew all the women, I had absolutely no idea of their names. Most of these women were known by their nicknames, and I only knew those nicknames. I had never paid attention in the past and I did not feel a need to ask what their real names were. Although all the women had a given name, when they moved to their husband's place they used to have only one identity and that was the name of the place they came from. For instance, if a woman came from a place called Janakpur, she would be called *Janakpurwali*. Likewise, if someone was from Madar, she would become *Madarwali*. And sometimes, if a woman had a slightly different character – if, for example, she was more talkative than others – the community or the family members would give her another nickname such as *Charcharhi* (talkative), and the women were known by that nickname throughout their lives.

This was a general practice for women that no one ever questioned until women started going out and attending trainings. In those trainings, they had to introduce themselves by their names. As Rina puts it:

> We were reluctant to say our full name in the past as we did not have this practice. I was only called by my first name when I was young but after marriage I was called Madarwali as I was from Madar. But now, after attending a literacy program as well as several trainings, we have learnt how to introduce ourselves.

These women, who were scared of speaking or introducing themselves in front of one person, are now able to introduce themselves confidently in front of anyone.

So what? What is the significance of it? Katja Guenther (2009, p. 412) argues that "the act of naming is an act of power . . . naming involves the assertion of authority and control." When these women started introducing themselves, initially they took it as a formality or as a rule of the game, but later it became a vehicle for them to establish their own identity. There were several *Sirahawali*, *Madarwali* and *Janakpurwali* in the same community, because everyone who came from the same place was called by the same name or they had to be introduced by their husband's or father in-law's name. It says nothing about that particular woman. But now they have established their own identities. So choosing to introduce themselves by their given names was reclaiming their own identities, which is a personality transformative act as well as a political act. It transforms their identity in the society. It establishes a place for women in the public sphere as subject, as a separate identity. Announcing the name is also refusing the only identity which is *Janakpurwali*. It is so very important because they want people to know their individual names. They all want to do something for the community, not just for money but for name. All the FGD participants had some kind of affiliation in a political party or in non-political organizations. Devi had set a precedent and all the women of that community wanted to become like her, but it was certainly not a competition for the position; rather they wanted to do something for the name.

Janki said, "Punam, bring some leadership program for us. We know a lot more than what we used to know before but we need more trainings. We need to build our capability. We need leadership trainings." This was a significant and revealing request. Bourdieu argues that "to change the world, one has to change the ways of world-making" (Bourdieu, 1989, p. 23). The group of women we are discussing here still live in poor economic conditions. However, throughout the discussion, they never mentioned money. They did want skills trainings so they can make money, and they do not need to rely on others. These women aspire to achieve something. They have a different world view now.

Moreover, the changes in this community are not limited to this. Now women of this community do not cover their faces and their children are going to school, which was very rare in the past. Likewise, in this community, there was a high rate of child marriage. As soon as they got to 5–7 years old, they were married off. I had seen that since my childhood, but it is no longer the case. It would be wrong to claim that there is no child marriage at all in this community at present. Although 18 years is the legal age of marriage in Nepal, in this community the definition of age is different. If a girl looks grown up and does not look like a child anymore, then she is at marriageable age. Therefore, there may still be some cases of child marriage in this community (meaning girls or boys may be married off before 18 years), but they do not marry their children when they are only 7 years old anymore.

Some of the FGD participants also mentioned that there is a change in their language and how they communicate with others. They used to speak a rough language (not in a decent way) such as "re" "te" (meaning calling someone without respect), but they do not do that anymore. An FGD participant said, "we learnt from the trainings, which were provided by different development agencies" (Namrata). They also mentioned that they now have the capacity to deal with any situation. Roshni said:

> We were scared to go to the police station and talk to them so we used to sort out all the issues within the community. We suffered but never went to the

police but now we can teach them about our rights. We can talk to any big government officials now. We go to the CDO [Chief District Officer] office and any other office when we need to do something but before it wasn't even in my thinking that we can even do such thing. Now we can go to the minister as well, if needed.

In addition, the gap between the upper caste people and this community has decreased. There is increased communication between the two communities. Devi said "people from the upper caste also respect me and listen to me." During my visit this time, I also noticed that men from both communities were talking together about politics and other community matters. Devi, who is from the untouchable caste, was allowed to sit in my parents' lounge which was never the case in the past. Although there is still discrimination against the people from this community, the relationship between the two communities has improved. The durability of habitus was observed in this community. Devi, because of her power relation, has been liberated and is allowed to go to people's houses, but this does not mean that everyone from her caste is allowed to enter upper caste people's houses. On the one hand, there was recognition of these people, and on the other, there was still resistance by the dominant people. As Bourdieu says, doxic practice benefits dominant groups and they therefore try to preserve them. Therefore reflexivity alone is not enough: something more needs to be done (Bourdieu, 1989, p. 21). In this case too, social space has been liberated for people from her caste, but this certainly does not translate into full liberation. It will take many years to eliminate the discriminations against these people as it has a long history. However, one cannot deny the transformation that is taking place in this community.

Conclusion

On the surface it appears that little has changed. The community looks almost the same as it did 10 years ago because there has not been much improvement in infrastructure and economic conditions have not improved significantly. Their houses are almost the same and the street which is in the middle of the community becomes even worse, muddy and slippery, during the rainy season. They still need to do wage labour for their survival. They did not have enough for two meals a day in the past, but now they may be able to feed their family. This may perhaps not be considered a significant change. However, their lived experiences are not the same as before. As Turshen, Meintjes, and Pillay (2001, pp. 7–8) argue, "transformation is not just about conditions or structures, but also about intentional processes of consciousness, of creating words and language that will provide women with a sense of their own agency."

There is improved communication within their own community and between the lower caste and upper caste communities. They are not only able to negotiate their wages with their landlords but also communicate about other social matters. Children of this community, including girls, have started going to school. An FGD participant said, "I didn't get the opportunity to go to the school that's why I am forced to live this kind of life but I will educate my children" (Manhari).

Almost all the women of this community are involved with either political institutions or development organizations or both. They no longer rely on wage labour alone. Men now go to India or the Gulf country as migrant workers and they send money home. Women have started small businesses and also work with different organizations. Their economic status has not been significantly improved but their world view has changed. They did not have a concept of saving but they are members of saving and credit groups now. Some of them have bought a small piece of land with savings. However, it would be wrong to claim that all these transformations have taken place because of Devi's involvement in politics. There are other factors which have contributed to the transformation of this community, including support from NGOs and the government, media, migration and so on. However, the Maoist movement created the space for ethnic movements and then the Madhesh movement created space for these people. Devi's new role accelerated the process of social transformation in this community.

Notes

1 Pseudonyms are given to all my research participants quoted in this chapter to maintain their confidentiality.
2 See *Inclusive Democracy for Madheshis: The Quest for Identity, Rights and Representation* by Farah Cheah, at http://www.isas.nus.edu.sg/Attachments/ResearchAttachment/Report%20-%20Farah.pdf.
3 *Janakpurwali* means a woman from Janakpur, one of the districts of Nepal. Devi comes from Janakpur.

References

Baum, B. (2004). Feminist Politics of Recognition. *Signs: Journal of Women in Culture and Society, 29*(4), 1073–1102. doi:10.1086/382630.

Benhabib, S. (1999). Sexual Difference and Collective Identities: The New Global Constellation. *Signs, 24*(2), 335–361. doi:10.2307/3175645.

Bourdieu, P. (1977). *Outline of a Theory of Practice* (Vol. 16). Cambridge: Cambridge University Press.

Bourdieu, P. (1985). The Social Space and the Genesis of Groups. *Social Science Information, 24*(2), 195–220. doi:10.1177/053901885024002001.

Bourdieu, P. (1989). Social Space and Symbolic Power. *Sociological Theory, 7*(1), 14–25.

Bourdieu, P., & Nice, R. (2001). *Masculine Domination*. Cambridge: Polity Press.

Butler, J. (2001). The Question of Social Transformation (J. Vaida, Trans.). In J. Butler, E. Beck-Gernsheim, & L. Puigvert (Eds.), *Women and Social Transformation* (pp. 1–28). New York: Peter Lang.

Butler, J., Puigvert, L., & Beck-Gernsheim, E. (2001). Gender and Social Transformation: A Dialogue (J. Vaida, Trans.). In E. Beck-Gernsheim, J. Butler, & L. Puigvert (Eds.), *Women and Social Transformation* (pp. 116–136). New York: Peter Lang.

Calefato, P. (2010). Fashion as Cultural Translation: Knowledge, Instructions and Transgressions on/of the Female Body. *Social Semiotic, 20*(2), 343–355.

CBS. (2011). *The Population Census 2011*. Kathmandu: Government of Nepal.

Foucault, M. (1978). *The History of Sexuality, Vol. 1: An Introduction*. London: Penguin Books.

Foucault, M. (1982). The Subject and Power. *Critical Inquiry, 8*(4), 777–795.

Guenther, K. M. (2009). The Politics of Names: Rethinking the Methodological and Ethical Significance of Naming People, Organizations, and Places. *Qualitative Research, 9*(4), 411–421. doi:10.1177/1468794109337872.

Owyong, Y.S.M. (2009). Clothing Semiotic and the Social Construction of Power Relations. *Social Semiotic, 19*(2), 191–211.

Turshen, M., Meintjes, S., & Pillay, A. (2001). There Is No Aftermath for Women. In M. Turshen, S. Meintjes, & A. Pillay (Eds.), *The Aftermath: Women in Post-conflict Transformation* (pp. 3–18). London: Zed Books.

UNDP. (2008). *Siraha District: Distribution of Caste and Ethnic Groups*. Kathmandu: UNDP. Retrieved 30 October 2015 from http://un.org.np/maps/siraha-district-distribution-caste-and-ethnic-groups

6 Women combatants
Challenging habitus

Transformation which would have taken centuries has come within ten years in Nepal due to the revolution.

(Yami, 2007, p. 11)

The Maoists are making us travel in 10 years a path we would have travelled in 50.
(Nepali Congress Youth Leader Gagan Thapa,
cited in Goering, 2008)

In previous chapters, I have argued that the People's War has expedited the processes of social transformation in Nepal. Bourdieu argues that "crises also provoke a redefinition of experience, giving rise to new forms of language" (Moi, 1991, p. 1028). The People's War in Nepal has provided new experiences for women, which have accelerated changes in the traditional image and the dominant discourse about womanhood.

Although the quotations with which this chapter begins are from political leaders, they reflect the reality of radical transformation that has taken place in Nepal within a short period. The first quotation is from a book called *People's War and Women's Liberation in Nepal* by Hishila Yami (Comrade Parvati). Comrade Parvati (her alias) is a Central Committee member of the UCPN-M, a former president of the All Nepal Women's Association (Revolutionary) and wife of Comrade Baburam Bhattarai, who is one of the main leaders of the Maoist movement and ex-prime minister of Nepal.[1] Comrade Parvati was involved in the Maoist movement from the beginning and has closely observed women's participation in the People's War. I consider her view as an insider's perspective.[2] The second quotation is a statement from an influential youth leader of the Nepali Congress.[3] His view can be taken as an outsider's view. However, both of them are in agreement that the Maoist revolution paved the way for the radical transformation of Nepali society.

Despite some differences about whether to give full credit to the Maoist revolution or to include others as contributing factors to the radical transformation in Nepal, there seems to be an agreement among feminist scholars that the Maoist conflict brought a new experience to women's lives. Pettigrew and Shneiderman (2004) argue:

> The 'people's war' has certainly precipitated new experiences for Nepali women of all backgrounds, whether in learning to use guns for combatant women, or negotiating the fine line of safety between state forces and the Maoists for civilian women. While such shifts cannot be claimed entirely as the intentional achievements of Maoist policy, it is clear that on the individual level of embodied practice they have introduced women to potentially transformative possibilities.

Rita Manchanda (2004, p. 255) shares a similar view:

> For disempowered rural women, despite the contradictions of the competing priorities of the 'anti-feudal revolution' and the paradox of the possibility of an emancipatory politics amidst an authoritarian militarized culture, their lives have been changed by the political opportunities offered by the Maoist revolutionary vision.

Taking on board the views of Pettigrew and Shneiderman and Manchanda, I argue that women's participation in the People's War has not only changed women's lives but it has also led Nepal towards a radical social transformation. Despite the criticism that the Maoist revolution has not brought the promised changes to women's lives (Manchanda, 2004; Tamang, 2009), I argue that the Maoist revolution has broadened women's horizons. It has provided women with knowledge and skills to question doxic practices (the gender discriminatory practices which were never questioned before), which have opened up the possibility for women to critically reflect on their own status as well as the status of others. Such critical reflexivity is leading to changing performance among women and, due to the changing performance of women, the dominant image of womanhood is shifting.

This chapter is based on the lived experiences of 21 women who were directly involved and performed various roles in the People's War. Fifteen were CA members at the time I interviewed them, and six were ex-combatants who had just come out of the cantonments and were now living in Kathmandu as civilians. When the People's War started in 1996, I was a university student. I was studying my masters at the Tribhuvan University, the oldest and largest university in Nepal, where I was also involved in student politics. Some of my friends, who shared my vision about life and who wanted to do something to bring about positive change, joined the Maoist movement. Although I was never asked to join and there was no pressure for me to join, I somehow felt like supporting the movement, because I found that the way the movement was going was very promising and convincing. According the Maoist leaders, it was a movement for liberation, from all caste-based, gender-based and class-based discriminations. Their aim was to transform the nation and build a new Nepal where everyone would be equal.

On the one hand, the Maoist movement was on the rise and their message to people was very convincing. On the other hand, people were frustrated because of the behaviour of political leaders who were in power. People's high expectations from the democratic government after the establishment of democracy in 1990 were never met. Instead, the power hunger among political leaders led to unstable government. Moreover, due to some disagreement between two leaders, one of the biggest political parties, the Communist Party Nepal – United Marxist Leninist (CPN-UML), split into two. This was the reason why many people who initially supported CPN-UML joined the Maoist movement, including academics, students, engineers, doctors and others. I was a supporter of CPN-UML then. However, after the split, I did not know whom to support because it was a clash between two leaders instead of a clash in their ideology or approach. I did not feel right to join any of the groups so I stayed ideal for some time, but when two groups united after sorting out their issues, I lost faith in them and left politics. However, a group of my friends, who were unhappy with what was going on in CPN-UML, called for a meeting and invited all interested to join the Maoist movement. I also attended the meeting where around 200 students had gathered, and they all joined the Maoists on the same day.

I also felt like joining, but my friends said it was too risky to join the movement, as the government had given orders to arrest anyone who supported the Maoist movement. All of my friends who joined the Maoists had decided to sacrifice their lives in the name of the nation, but I could not do so as I had two small children. However, I supported my friends by providing a meal, a place to hide for a night, or sending messages to their families that they were safe. It was very risky for them to visit their families, as that was the first place the army would look for them. That is why they always stayed away from their families during the movement and might only have secretly visited a few times. My experience of being a friend of Maoists has certainly influenced my analysis, but in a positive way. It provided me with an opportunity to have an in-depth understanding of their inside story.

Gender-based discrimination: a main reason for significant participation of women in the People's War

A much remarked aspect of the Maoist revolution in Nepal is the high level of participation by women. However, the question of women's liberation was not on their agenda in the beginning. The chairperson of the United CPN-M, Pushpa Kamal Dahal (Comrade Prachanda), in his interview with Li Onesto (2000) said gender was not their main agenda in the beginning of the People's War. Likewise, other top level women leaders such as Comrade Parvati in her book (Yami, 2007) and Pampha Bhusal, in her interview with me in June 2012, also confirmed that gender was not the party's main agenda initially. The revolution was against "feudalism and monarchy and for political and economic change in Nepal" (Hatlebakk, 2010, pp. 99–100). Pampha Bhusal, in her interview with me, said "the question of women's liberation became one of our agendas only after a year." Prachanda said the movement saw overwhelming participation by women after including women's liberation in the agenda (Onesto, 2000). He said although women were there from the beginning of the war, they were not as enthusiastic as they became after the inclusion of the 'women question' (Onesto, 2000).

Although women's liberation became one of the main agendas of the Maoist revolution, it was still defined within an "overarching framework of class revolution" (Pettigrew & Shneiderman, 2004). Maoist leaders, including women leaders such as Parvati, believe that the issue of women cannot be addressed without addressing the issue of class (Yami, 2007, p. 121), which is problematic. Class and gender are two separate categories. Women suffer from various types of discriminations within each class, and this becomes even more complex when class intersects with other social identities such as caste, ethnicity, religion and region. When class gets priority over gender, women's agendas become secondary (Tamang, 2009, p. 74). This trend was evident during the war and it is still observed in current practices.

Despite the mentality of the Maoist leaders, who on the one hand were advocating for the liberation from all kinds of discriminations, and on the other hand were not recognizing women as a separate category, women's participation was overwhelming in the Maoist movement. Although, I have briefly discussed the motivations for joining the People's War in Chapter 4, it is worth shedding some light on why women joined the People's War. First I will consider an insider's perspective, and then I will analyze an outsider's perspective on women's high level of representation in the People's War.

Comrade Parvati, who is an insider, gives two main reasons for women's involvement in the People's War. The first she calls "objective reasons," which include "poverty, male migration, exploitation from landlords, secondary status of women in the family as well as in the society, early marriage and early motherhood in rural areas and victims of consumerism by comprador bourgeois in urban areas" (Yami, 2007, p. 5). The second she calls "subjective reasons":– the "scientific outlook" of the CPN-M, by which she means their ability to locate the oppression of women in relation to class, caste and ethnicity (Yami, 2007, p. 5).

Although she does not categorize this as a third reason, she asserts that the Maoist movement was not like other movements when women were just drawn in as a last resort. The Maoist party encouraged women to join the movement from the beginning. According to her, they were encouraged to join the party because they were more reliable and trustworthy than men. When a woman became a party member, her whole family got involved (Yami, 2007, p. 5). Hence, it seems to be a strategic decision of the Maoist party.

The outsider's view differs slightly from the insider's. A study on women combatants in Nepal suggests that factors such as "socio-economic background, family relation, social discrimination, gendered sexuality (also as victims of sexual violence), forced recruitment and self-defence (a result of brutal state interrogations, and other forms of gross brutality)" were the reasons for women's involvement in the Maoist revolution (Khadka, 2012, p. 57). In addition, "the Maoist ideology in general and specific political agendas for women and poor and discriminated people (based on caste and ethnic discrimination) was also to some degree a central motive for many of them when they joined PLA" (Khadka, 2012, p. 57). Man-chanda (2004, p. 246) argues that women may have joined because of "structural violence" in the public and private sphere, exposing them to the risk of direct violence both in domestic settings and at the hands of the state.

Statements by my research participants on their reasons for taking an active role in the People's War can be illustrated under two general headings. On the one hand, the danger, discrimination and disadvantage they faced in a feudal, deeply patriarchal society gave them something to gain from radical change. On the other, the growing prominence of explicit calls for a transformation of gender relations in the agenda put forward by the CPN-M held out the prospect that their demands would indeed be addressed in the process of winning the People's War. Below these two general headings were several sub-themes. Women recounted experi-ences of oppression such as killing, disappearance and torture of family members by the state forces. On the "subjective side," they named factors drawing them towards active roles in the struggle, including family members' association with the Maoists, interest in politics, peer pressure, poverty and a desire to do something for the country.

Durgi Devi Paswan is a Madhesi woman from the Dalit community who had witnessed the suffering of women since her childhood and wanted to do some-thing for the liberation of the Madhesi women.[4] She said, "I joined the Maoist party because I thought it was the only party that would help liberate the status of women in Madhesh."

Jaypuri Gharti Magar explained why she joined the Maoist movement. She said:

> I was against all sorts of discriminations such as discrimination based on castes and gender, violence against women, polygamy, and regional discrimination.

She added,

> People were living an extremely difficult life under poverty. People from Far Western region were feeling discrimination by the people from Central region. I wanted to do something about that and that's why I joined politics.
>
> (Jaypuri Gharti Magar)

Rupa Chaudhari, who comes from the Mid-western region and belongs to Terai Janajati, said:

> I am from a middle class family. My father joined the Nepal Communist Party (Mashal) and went underground in 2055 [1998]. I got arrested about a year after my father's arrest. I was only in my high school then. My father was killed when I was in custody. Army wanted to kill everyone in my family because we were supporting the Maoists. My mother was arrested several times and my brothers were arrested as well. I was jailed for 20 months but they could have arrested me again therefore I became the whole timer.[5]

Indramati Yadav joined the People's War after her husband was killed by the army in 2003. There were other women like Indramati, who joined the Maoist movement because their husbands or other family members were either killed or disappeared by the state.

Saru, who is an ex-combatant, joined the Maoist party because of poverty:

> My father died when I was little. All my brothers and sisters joined the Maoists. My sister in-law is also Maoist. Only my mother is at home. We were poor so my mother couldn't afford to pay for my education. My eldest brother joined Maoist first and then my sister as well and then I joined.

Some of my research participants mentioned that they joined the Maoist movement as artists, such as singers and dancers, and performed motivating revolutionary songs and dances during the war. The revolutionary songs were used as a tool to motivate people to join the revolution and also to boost the confidence of their cadres during the People's War.[6]

Some people said they were members of the Student Union of the CPN (Maoist) party. There appear to be two reasons for the overwhelming participation by women in the Maoist revolution: (1) the agenda of women's liberation from all kinds of discrimination and promise from the Maoist for equal and just society; and (2) the Maoists' own strategic interest as Yami (2007) has pointed out that women were more trustworthy.

The numbers game

Women's participation in the Maoist revolution was significant, but estimates of the exact number of women involved in the People's War vary. As discussed in Chapter 3, women's participation in politics was minimal (about 5–7 per cent) prior to the People's War (Yami, 2007, p. 6). Although there are no exact details about how many women were involved in the People's War, the most commonly used number is 30–50 per cent (see Tamang; Yami, 2007). However, some people do not agree with this data. Manjushree Thapa, a journalist and writer, asserts that this was an exaggeration by the Maoists and that female participation was in fact far lower (as cited in Pettigrew & Shneiderman, 2004).

A study carried out in 2001 by the non-governmental organization (NGO) called the Institute of Human Rights Communication Nepal suggests a significant level of participation by women in the Maoist movement. This study was carried out in Rolpa, Rukum and Jajarkot – three districts highly affected by the Maoist movement. It reveals that nearly half (40–50 per cent) of the Maoist militia were women and among them, more than a third (35 per cent) were at squad level and more than a fifth (20–30 per cent) were at platoon level; and nine women were at the highest leadership levels (Gautam, 2001, as cited in Manchanda, 2004, p. 242).

Moreover, after the Comprehensive Peace Agreement (CPA) in 2006, the reintegration of Maoist combatants into the Nepalese Army became one of the main agendas in post–People's War Nepal. The responsibility of the verification of Maoist combatants was given to the United Nations Mission in Nepal (UNMIN), who verified 15,756 combatants, of whom 3,846 were women, which is about 24 per cent of the total People's Liberation Army (PLA).[7] Certainly these numbers do not match the proportion of women combatants that the Maoists claimed initially. However, not all women who were involved in the People's War were militants. As discussed earlier, there were women supporting this movement from wherever they were, including intellectuals, leaders, artists, engineers and doctors. Only counting the number of militants would not give the actual figure of women involved in the People's War.

Moreover, it hardly matters if they were 30 or 50 per cent – women's significant participation in the People's War was historic in itself. Women's involvement in combat roles was almost nil until the Maoists started their movement in 1996. Although there were women in the Nepal Army, their representation was limited to nurses, doctors and in other supporting roles. The Maoist movement introduced a new image of women. As the conflict escalated and women proved to be effective fighters, the Nepal army started recruiting women in combat roles to counter the women in the Maoists (Yami, 2007, p. 6). There is currently a quota for women at all levels in the armed force. Recent vacancy announcements for both the Nepal army and Nepal police illustrate the inclusion of women as a priority.[8] However, who gets included and whether women from the Hills get priority over women from Madhesh is a question (Labh, 2013). It is clear, however, that women's increasing participation in combat roles is new. This could never have been imagined in the past. Whatever the reasons for both the Maoists and the Nepal army to recruit women for combat roles, the inclusion of women in politics and armies has challenged the doxic image of womanhood and must be seen as both an effect of, and a contributory factor to, radical social transformation.

Whose representation? Homogenization of women in the People's War

> The most visible face of the Nepalese People's War is that of women dressed in combat dress with guns slung over their shoulders.
>
> (Yami, 2007)

The quotation with which this section starts suggests the image of women in the Maoist revolution. The images of young women combatants carrying guns are not just found on the Maoist's website (Pettigrew & Shneiderman, 2004, p. 1) but also in the writing of national and international journalists (Tamang, 2009, p. 73) including on the websites of various organizations, such as Integrated Regional Information Networks (IRIN).[9] These powerful and influential images of young guerrillas have contributed to an understanding that women's representation in the Maoist movement was a remarkable step in Nepali society.

Women's participation as combatants in the Maoist movement has been represented differently, perhaps to further different agendas by insiders and outsiders.

These representations contain some significant contradictions. For example, an insider, Comrade Parvati (an alias) presents a highly essentialized image of Nepali women by saying, "Today the image of a tired malnourished woman carrying children with one hand and rearing cattle with the other has been transformed into an image of a dignified fighting women with a gun" (Yami, 2007, p. 11). Those who took up the gun included poor rural women, but the comment downplays the heterogeneity among Nepali women who joined the Maoist cause. Not all women in Nepal are – or even were – 'tired [and] malnourished' and confined to domestic drudgery and child-rearing. Maoist activists include women who were highly educated, economically well-off and leaders in their own fields, such as Comrade Parvati herself.

A sympathetic outsider, Li Onesto, a journalist for the *Revolutionary Worker*, offers an extended analysis which is similar to that of Comrade Parvati. In her article titled, "Red Flag Flying on the Roof of the World," she claims that the People's War liberated Nepali women from oppression. She states that when the People's War started in 1996 it was like opening the "prison gate" for women as they rushed to participate in the revolution, to fight against discrimination and to achieve equality (as cited in Manchanda, 2004, p. 224, and Pettigrew & Shneiderman, 2004). But does a desire to claim success for the Maoist revolution lead such accounts to gloss over fault lines and contradictions which warrant closer attention in any detailed consideration of the nature and extent of social transformation in Nepal and its effect on women?

Manjushree Thapa offers a more critical perspective on women's involvement in the Maoist movement. She argues that the Maoist conflict has been more notable for altering the form and image of gendered relations, than for any substantive change. She quotes a teenage girl to argue her point: "You see, there used to only be sickles and grass in the hands of girls like us. And now there are automatic rifles" (as cited in Manchanda, 2004, p. 224). Although Thapa has apparently given more agency to one of her respondents, her generalized view of overall women's participation in the Maoist movement is not dissimilar to that of Comrade Parvati or Li Onesto.

Pettigrew and Shneiderman (2004) and Tamang (2009) strongly oppose the essentialization of women expressed in such representations. Tamang (2009) argues that the diversity among Nepalese was compromised in the name of creating national identity. She calls it "strategic essentialism," which was an outcome of the unification of Nepal. The 1962 constitution declared Nepal a Hindu state, compromising and silencing the diversity of many cultural and religious groups (Tamang, 2009, p. 64). As discussed in Chapter 3, about one-fifth of the population follow other religious beliefs, including Buddhism, Islam and Christianity.

Tamang (2009, p. 64) argues that women have been presented as a single category in the Maoist revolution, which overlaps with this essentialism. Not all women are Hindu or from impoverished rural communities. Even women who fit the stereotype may have a range of different cultural values and experiences of womanhood. Tamang further argues that representations of women joining the People's War that tend towards essentialized images, such as those evoked by Comrade Parvati and Li Onesto, serve to obscure or minimize the heterogeneous experiences of Nepali women. Janajati women, for example, she contends, do not face as much discrimination as other Hindu women. Janajati women are, in Tamang's view, comparatively more liberated than women from other castes/ethnic groups (Tamang, 2009, p. 64). Gender inequality varies among women from different socio-religious groups in Nepal. Upper caste (Indo-Aryan) women have more restrictive cultural regulations than Tibeto-Burman (Janajati) women.

Even within the Janajati, there are various caste groups with different cultures. Gurung may have distinctive cultural features different from Limbu. Since values are culturally constructed, such differences may exert significant influence on women's capabilities "to achieve outcomes that they value and have reason to value" (Sen, 1999, p. 291). Any attempt to assess the degree of transformation brought about in women's lives by social upheavals associated with the People's War must also attend to cultural diversity, and therefore take account of the lived experiences of Nepalese women from different sections of society.

The nature of representation must also come under critical scrutiny. Representations of women in struggle, such as those furnished by participants in that struggle, for example, Comrade Parvati and Li Onesto, clearly focus on aspects of the object being represented that suit their own agenda. But I do not attempt to counterpose a corresponding theory of representation, or any claim that reality can be accessed 'as it is' or retrieved 'as it was'. Rita Felski (1997, p. 17) argues that "depending on the criteria used, it is clearly possible in principle to demonstrate that any two randomly chosen objects in the world are either similar to or different from each other." Where I have organized interview data into themes and sub-themes, for instance, I am conscious that the categories so formed are not 'natural' or incontestable. Felski (1997, p. 17) further argues:

> There is no reality-in-itself that can provide ultimate proof of the significance or value of either difference or similarity. Both the construction of commonality among subjects and the assertion of difference between subjects are rhetorical and political acts, gestures of affiliation and disaffiliation that emphasize some properties and obscure others.

My research reveals that, based on their own values and views of significant capabilities, the experiences of Janajati women can be represented in common stories, or themes of suppression and oppression in feudal Nepali society. Despite Tamang's (2009) claims that women in the Janajati community enjoyed a greater degree of equality, this shared experience still motivated many of them to join the People's War (Pettigrew & Shneiderman, 2004).

In these and other accounts, however, the tendency to homogenize the experience of women remains in all the writing about women in the People's War. They were not only combatants or militia but, as discussed earlier, some of them were leaders, artists, students, intellectuals and cadres of the CPN-M's sister organizations. Therefore, an analysis of women as combatants versus women as civilians will not give a complete picture of the contributions women made in the Maoist revolution, neither will it be helpful for an overall understanding of women's involvement in the People's War.

The women question – women's liberation: rhetoric or reality?

> Patriarchal exploitation and discrimination against women should be stopped. Daughters should be allowed access to paternal property.
>
> (No. 19 of 40 Point Demand)[10]

The 'women question' (women's liberation) in the Maoist revolution has received significant attention from journalists, human rights activists and academics, both within and outside the country (see Adhikari, 2007; Ariño, 2008; Bhattarai, 2012; *eKantipur*, 2011; IRIN, 2010; Khadka, 2012; Pettigrew & Shneiderman, 2004; Shakhya, 2003; Tamang, 2009; Yami, 2007). As mentioned in Chapter 3, just a week before the Maoists announced their People's War, they submitted a 40-point demand to the government on 4 February 1996. Number 19 of the demands was about women's subordination within the patriarchal structure, with particular focus on women's access to inherited paternal property as an important step towards gender equality. Later, as the Maoists set up 'people's courts', Pathak (2005, pp. 106–107) records that, in their own law enforcement, they provided specifically for women's rights to be considered and respected: "If a case is filed by a woman against a man, the punishment is often decided by women," on the explicit rationale that "only a woman can understand the . . . degrading treatment suffered by another woman."

Women's liberation was not the main agenda when the Maoists started their movement. For the reasons discussed earlier, women's liberation became one of their main agendas to achieve their ultimate goal: reconstruction of Nepali society through radical social transformation (Pettigrew & Shneiderman, 2004). However, the question remains whether the Maoists have been able to fulfil their promise of gender equality (Logan, 2006; Manchanda, 2004; Pettigrew & Shneiderman, 2004; Tamang, 2009). Tamang (2009, p. 74) notes:

> Criticism about the gap between rhetoric and actual gender equality within the Maoists have been made time and again. This includes not just the number of women in the CPN-M, but the claims of equality within the movement.

She further argues that within the Maoist movement women mostly played traditional roles such as cooking, cleaning and child rearing. She calls it "differently structured gendered relations" (Tamang, 2009, p. 74).

Felski (1997, p. 19) argues that neither equality nor history is stable. They are reproduced, changed and articulated differently in different contexts. Considering the complexity within the Maoist structure and the crisis situation during the war, when they could not stay in one place for more than one day, Tamang's claim warrants close scrutiny, lest the stirrings of a deeper transformation of gender roles be too easily missed.

Nepal and India had outlawed the party. An Interpol Red Notice labelled the 14 top Maoist leaders terrorists (*Kathmandu Post*, 2003; *Times of India*, 2005) and the United States put the Maoists on its list of terrorist groups. The state ordered the Nepali army to kill Maoists anywhere they saw them. 'Price tags' for the heads of several Maoist leaders were announced by the state, including NRs 5 million for Comrade Prachanda (*Himalayan Times*, 2003). The *Guardian* reported:

> Deuba (then Prime Minister) has ruled out all negotiation with the Maoists and appears determined to crush them. The most recent attack took place when government troops apparently spotted a high-level meeting at the training base and pounded it from attack helicopters.
>
> (Harding, 2002)

All this gives an indication of how difficult the situation was for Maoists at that time.

Rupa Chaudhari, a former commander of the Maoists who became a CA member by winning the direct election in 2008, shared her experience:

> [The] situation was very difficult for us. Army had order from the government to shoot us anywhere they see us. They killed hundreds of civilians based on their suspicion that they were Maoists or the supporter of the Maoist movement. Many of my friends were raped and killed. Luckily, I survived.

Another example is Jaypuri Gharti Magar. In her short biography published by International Institute for Democracy and Electoral Assistance (IDEA) in 2011, she says she prioritized her work over her family:

> While being taken uphill in Dang, her two month old daughter caught pneumonia and stopped breathing. Jaypuri lost all hope of her baby surviving. Since neither time nor circumstance allowed her to take care of her baby, she left her with a Women's Association in the village saying, "Foster her if she survives, and throw her away if she dies." The women cared for the little baby girl and saved her from dying through the use of local medicines. Although she was fortunate to have her daughter live, her husband Bibek KC who was working as a political commissar in the party was killed by the police in 2003.
>
> (IDEA, 2011, p. 327)

When I interviewed Jaypuri in June 2011, she also said she had devoted her life to the movement and that was her priority at all times.

Returning to the question of gender equality, Tamang's (2009, p. 74) claim about "differently structured gender relations" within the Maoist movement does not seem to fit with reality. Women performed various roles within the Maoist movement. Moreover, questions may arise here: Equality of what? Whose equality?

Women come from various background and they have different views about the world. Who is going to decide whether I have achieved my gender equality? Is equality static? Can our needs always be the same? One may want to fight for the freedom of their clan and feel satisfied, and others may find satisfaction if their business is growing. Hence, equality could mean different things to different people. Pettigrew & Shneiderman (2004) argue one can engage in the debate of agency and victimization but realities for Nepali women lie in the lived experiences of those who have experienced both victimization and empowerment at various times. Hence, bringing women's lived experience to the front would give us a clear picture of the situation and how far behind we are (Pettigrew & Shneiderman, 2004).

I have discussed changes in laws and policies in regards to gender equality in Chapter 3. In the following section, I will present stories of combatants about their lived experiences and what they feel about their own status at present.

Lived experiences of women during the People's War

> I was an artist. I worked with Magarat Cultural Organization.
>
> (Moon, ex-combatant)

> I was a Platoon Commander.
>
> (Samita, ex-combatant)

> I was a District President of All Nepal Women's Association – Revolutionary.
>
> (Shanti Devi Rajbansi, CA member)

Preeti is an ex-Maoist combatant. I have chosen to present her story in this chapter because her story is typical of the stories of other women combatants. The government of Nepal announced a voluntary retirement package for the combatants who were verified by the UNMIN and were living in cantonments. Preeti was living with other combatants in one of the cantonments after the CPA. She was forced to take a voluntary retirement package as her right hand and right leg were badly injured during the war, when she was involved in an attack on a police post. Preeti was only 28 years old when I interviewed her in May 2012. She lives in Kathmandu after her voluntary retirement and wants to start a new life. I will present her story in her own words:

> I was 7 years old when I got involved in politics. I was inspired by my father. My father was also in politics. He always encouraged me to serve for the nation . . . I was only 13 year old when I joined the Maoist party in 1998. I was very active so the party (Maoist party) nominated me for the chairperson of Women's Area Committee. I was only 14 when I first time got arrested. I was tortured by the Royal Army.[11] They put me into a sack and beat me up and didn't give me anything to eat. When I asked for water, they said drink *Prachanda ko mut* (Prachanda's urine).[12] They also verbally abused me. They called me *Prachanda ko Ghoda* (Horse of Prachanda). I was released after

10 days but they came to arrest me again within a week but I was able to escape . . . I got arrested again in 2001 but they released me after a few days.

Preeti married a comrade from the same party during the war. There was no respect for traditional marriage:

> I met my husband during the party's meeting (of the Maoist party). He was also a Maoist cadre like me. We both had big responsibilities within the party. His name was Prabhat and he is the one who gave me my name, Preeti. I had a different name before. I had no idea that he liked me. I only came to know about it when the proposal of my marriage came through my party. People in our party were very disciplined at that time. Everyone would show respect to women cadres and whatever our party decided we had to follow. Since the Party brought the proposal of marriage, I accepted it. It was a *Janabadi Bibah* (revolutionary marriage). We exchanged the garland and vows and then committed ourselves to each other. This is how all marriages within the Party were done at that time. None of us had traditional marriage.
>
> Although we got married, due to our responsibilities as both of us were commanders, we couldn't stay together. We might have met a few times but we didn't have any complaints about our lives. We both had devoted our lives for the nation and we had bigger goal to achieve than our personal happiness. We wanted to bring happiness to everyone's life. We knew that we might die any minute. That's why we always understood each other. He always encouraged me and respected me. And I did as well.

They could not live together like a normal couple because of the war and their responsibilities:

> One night we ended up in a same village. He was with his friends (other combatants) and I was with my friends. We decided to stay together that night. We never stayed in one place for two days. We had to move from one place to another because the army were everywhere and they had orders from the government to kill us wherever they see us. But luckily we ended in the same village that night. We had a good conversation that night. My husband said, "if I die before you, make sure you move on with your life. Don't cry, be strong because you need to lead your team. I will do the same if you die." He gave me a flag of our party and said if I die before you, please put this flag on my body. Since we both had to depart early in the morning with our teams so we went to sleep.

Despite having the same role as combatants, when she was with her husband, she performed like a normal housewife who wakes up and does household chores:

> We got up early in the morning. I went to make tea for my husband and our friends. My husband was very sharp and clever, somehow he got an idea that Army were coming towards the village. He asked all his friends including me

to leave that place as soon as possible. And he went to check if they really were army. We had to rush from that place because we couldn't take any risk and I had my group with me . . . they were my responsibility so I went with them.

Since we were in two different teams, I had no idea if he returned or not. The next day, I was in another village. I was tired so I sat there and asked for a tea. The tea stall owner started talking to me. She was asking me all sorts of questions like . . . where are you from? who is your father? etc. It was risky to tell her that I was a Maoist so I lied. She then started talking about what had happened last night in that village. She said, "army came and killed a Maoist just there. His body is lying there since last night but no one dares to go there because people are scared." She emphasized, "no one has come to claim that body, even the Maoists! I wonder what will happen to his family if they come to know about this?" I was curious. I asked her what he looked like. She explained a bit. I was losing my consciousness as I had a doubt that it might be my husband. But somehow I gathered courage and went to that place. It was him. I sat there and cried a lot. I put the party's flag on his body and went back to that tea stall. That tea stall owner was asking me "who was that?" I said "may be a Maoist." I couldn't reveal my identity, neither could I show my pain to anyone. I called my friends and informed them about my husband . . . they came at night and we buried him.

She said she was not supposed to show her sorrow as her husband had made a big contribution to the movement by giving his life. He had become a martyr and she could not be weak as her responsibility lay in front of her:

I was very sad but I wasn't meant to show any emotion. I needed to be strong as I was a leader. I had to lead my group. I wanted to be a source of inspiration to my juniors. That's why I couldn't show my emotions and I couldn't be weak in front of them. I knew everyone has to go one day, it could be me anytime . . . but I was proud to have him as my husband as he sacrificed his life for the people.

Her story gives us a glimpse of the lived experiences of women who were involved in the People's War. The complexities within the roles she was playing, as commander, as guerrilla and as wife, gives us an insight into gender dynamics and women's experience of liberation within the Maoist revolution. Four sub-themes – gender equality, marriage and family, special needs and leadership – emerged during my interview with her.

Gender equality

Women are able to compete with men in equal footing.

(Yami, 2007, p. 6)

Yami's claim seems to be true to some extent but there was a limit to it. Preeti said she never felt any kind of discrimination by any member of the party during the war. She said she was always treated equally and there was a strong sense of unity: "we were united for a cause." Lata, ex-commander, also shared a similar view:

> There was no difference between us . . . we had different responsibilities . . . we all performed our roles depending on the situation. There was no difference between men and women. We all were equal. There was no hierarchy between us. Even if I was a commander, I was just like others . . . As a commander I had to take care of my group. Other than that we didn't have any difference. It was an ideological movement and a class struggle. Since we all were from the same class, we were just like brothers and sisters and followers of the same ideological beliefs.

Similar views were presented by other research participants. Four main reasons for this high level of cooperation by each member of the Maoist party were mentioned:

1   A shared goal: whoever joined the Maoist revolution had one goal, and that was to establish a discrimination-free society.
2   Strict rules and disciplinary actions: the Maoist party had imposed strict rules on their cadres. There were certain rules each member had to follow, such as outlawing polygamy or polyandry. Anyone who was found to have been in a relationship other than with their spouse was suspended from the party and punished for their behaviour. Other misconducts were cheating on the party and spying on their own friends.
3   The Maoist party operated in accordance with Maoist ideology, which opposed the class and caste system. Therefore, there was no discrimination between people from upper and lower castes, and as a result there were several cases of marriage between upper caste and lower caste.
4   Cooperation between each other was extremely important. Without trust and cooperation, it would not have been possible to operate in such difficult situation where they were considered terrorists, and would have been killed at any time if the state force found them.

Despite this high level of cooperation and discipline within the party, it was not as simple and straightforward as it may appear. Preeti faced lots of challenges when she wanted to be promoted to a leadership role. Although Maoists claimed that there was no hierarchy within the Maoist party, various roles and responsibilities were given to people. Even among commanders, there were various levels, such as section commander, platoon commander, company commander, battalion commander, brigade commander and division commander. Preeti said she always felt supported and appreciated in her work when she started, but it all became challenging for her when she proved herself and wanted a higher level of responsibility. She said when she demanded her right to higher responsibilities, she was not only denied this but was not given any responsibilities afterwards. This suggests that while gender equality was promoted within the Maoist party during the war, it was limited until women reached certain levels.

Comrade Parvati argues that women's political participation is rooted in patriarchal economic and social relations (Yami, 2007, p. 16). In spite of women's major participation in the People's War, they are still not easily accepted in or promoted to leadership roles due to the patriarchal mindset among men within the party (Yami, 2007, p. 7). Comrade Parvati claims that although there is recognition of women's contribution and there are systems in place within the party to educate women, that is not enough. There has to be an enabling environment for women to be able to take up leadership roles. Comrade Parvati sees the challenges facing women in leadership roles as twofold. The first challenge is the patriarchal mindset among males within the party: "conservatism in the party expressed by relegating women cadres to women related work, thereby robbing them of the chance to develop skills in party polity matters and other fields" (Yami, 2007, p. 10). The second challenge is women themselves. Yami writes:

> In regards to their position in Party, they exhibit plenty of proletarian spirit and sacrifice but their ideological acumen has yet to mature. They still tend to see things in persons, in parts, in intentions rather than in trend, pattern, totality and in end result. Conscious effort by women themselves and the party has to be made to bridge this gap.
>
> (Yami, 2007, p. 10)

She also emphasizes:

> Women still need to work hard to exercise their authority so that masses accept them as leaders. They need to know that merely working hard, being simple and practical is not enough: they need to win the minds of the masses for which ideology and political acumen is necessary.
>
> (Yami, 2007, p. 10)

Although Yami is critical of the Maoist male leadership, her observation about women (where she excludes herself from the 'other' women) is an indication of deep-seated sexist and classist assumptions among top-level women in the Maoist movement.

Marriage and family

Marriage was another debated issue within the Maoist movement. Drawing from Pettigrew and Shneiderman, Rita Manchanda (2004, p. 251) argues that although the Maoist movement was a 'cultural revolution' to remove all discrimination in the name of marriage, love and family, it has actually done nothing more than reproduce the same traditional gender relations. Quoting Pettigrew and Shneiderman, she argues that marriage was nothing other than "controlling female cadres and making it difficult for them to leave the party" (Manchanda, 2004, p. 250).

However, none of my research participants said they were forced to get married. All of them said the proposals came through the party and the party played the role of a guardian for *Janabadi Bibah*.[13] But they also said the party was everything to them at that time so they did not say no to anything that the party brought to them. Preeti said:

> People were very disciplined in our party at that time. Everyone would show respect to women cadres. If someone liked someone within the party then Party would facilitate it by bringing the proposal for marriage.

Another research participant shared a similar story of being approached by the party. She said there were several proposals but she accepted the one she wanted:

> As a guardian, my party brought a proposal for my marriage in a meeting . . . and then we got married. My parents were not aware about that. Our party gave us leave for four days to convince our families. Two days for me to convince my family and two days for him to convince his family. We went to our parents but it was very difficult to convince them because we had an inter-caste marriage. They were angry in the beginning but now everything is fine.
> (Jwala Singh, CA member)

The concept of traditional family was not possible for couples during the war when both were involved in the movement. There was a high level of awareness about gender equality among people within the Maoists. However, what should we understand from the performance of Preeti when she wakes up and starts making tea like a normal wife? There are at least two ways of looking at this which may be applicable to other relations as well: intrasubjectivity, which is the psyche of the self, and intersubjectivity, which is the political world of the individuals (Benhabib, 1999, p. 352). Borrowing Benjamin, Benhabib argues that "the psychological relations that constitute the self" cannot be collapsed "into the epistemological and political positions that constitutes the subject of knowledge or history" (Benjamin, 1994, as cited in Benhabib, 1999, p. 352). She elaborates:

> For each individual, the process of 'splitting', as an ongoing active process of idealization and defence performed with respect to the other, has a unique trajectory and logic . . . Whether the political other is conceived as the enemy or the liberator, as the oppressor or the redeemer, as the purifier or the seducer – to play with only some permutations – will depend not only on the cultural codes of the public world but on the individual psychic history of the self as well.
> (Benhabib, 1999, p. 352)

Preeti's action of making tea is a reflection of her intrasubjectivity which could not be collapsed into her political world which was different. "All negotiation of difference involved negation, partial breakdowns. Breakdown is only catastrophic when the possibility of re-establishing the tension between negation and recognition is foreclosed, when the survival of the other self, of self for other, is definitely over" (Benjamin, 1994, as cited in Benhabib, 1999, p. 352). Although she was not like other housewives because she was equally involved in pursuing her dream, she still chose to perform her gender role, at least at that particular time. Certainly there was a negation of her traditionally defined roles but not a complete breakdown because there was no threat to her survival. This can also be a good of example of how the habitus has a lasting impact on individuals and society. Despite not having to follow any traditional norms, Preeti still held her traditional image of a wife in her practice, though it was rare.

Consequences of taking men and women as absolute equals

> Often it is seen that the party does not actively intervene in the existing traditional division of labor between men and women whereby men take to mental work while women are left to do physical labor. This is also manifested in taking men and women as absolute equals by not being sensitive to women's special condition and their special needs. This becomes all more apparent when women are menstruating or are in the reproductive period.
>
> (Yami, 2007, pp. 38–39)

Although it appears that women had a much better position in the Maoist party, equality was experienced within the patriarchal structure. The way equality was perceived as counterproductive because it was understood in relation to men's capabilities. Most of my research participants said that although they did not feel discrimination based on gender in their day-to-day life, women's special needs were not taken seriously. Tika, a 22-year-old ex-combatant, shared her experience:

> I hadn't got my period when I join Maoist so it was easy for the first year but after I got my period, it was tough. We had to walk for long hours even during the time of menstruation. I could have said, I can't do or can't walk but I didn't. I didn't want to feel weaker than men, that's why I walked and did all that I needed to.

Comrade Prachanda said in his interview with Li Onesto that the Maoist party discouraged women from becoming pregnant for 7–10 years during the revolution. He said there were two main reasons for this. First, there was the question of taking care of the baby: who would take care of the baby if the woman wanted to actively contribute to the revolution? Second, abortion was not available, and even if a woman did go through this process, it would affect her health (Onesto, 2000). However, he also added, if women did get pregnant, they were put in safe places with other comrades for 6 months (Onesto, 2000). They could not go home and to other places because they might be arrested (Onesto, 2000). He emphasized that there were several cases when women were arrested when they went outside the safe zone during delivery (Onesto, 2000). Despite Prachanda's claim about special provisions for women cadres, women had different experiences. Jwala Singh shared her experience of giving a birth to her first child:

> I gave birth to my first child in 2004. I had to face several difficulties at that time. It was a heightened conflict period. We were hiding ourselves from the security forces. Government had announced emergency in the country so army was deployed everywhere. I couldn't stay in one place even when I was pregnant. I had to walk every day for several hours . . . When I was in my last month of pregnancy, my party asked me to go to India for some time, at least for a month. I didn't want to go as I wanted to be with the public but Party insisted and it was a kind of order from the party that's why I went to India with my mom.

However, she found herself surrounded by security forces on the second day of her delivery:

> I didn't know who gave information to the Indian security. I had no choice than to run away from there. It was only the second day of my delivery. I was able to escape from there with my baby and my mom. I walked for 24 hours and reached the border. Luckily my Aunty was married to an Indian guy and she was living at the India-Nepal border. She was my mother's elder sister. We went to her place. Everyone started crying when they saw us like that. My baby's health wasn't good. We stayed there for one day and then came to Nepal. When we came to *Churebhabar* area, we were stuck in cross firing. There was cross firing between our friends (Maoists) and army. Army was firing from the helicopter. We were trapped. I thought my son is going to be deaf because of the noise . . . I went with my son everywhere I went. We couldn't stay in one place because it was risky. I was very upset because of my son's situation. I was worried he won't survive but I had no choice than to keep moving from one place to another to escape from the security forces.

Despite having a little baby, she said, she never stopped working. She did not want to be seen as weaker than a man, which is why she kept working for the party even when her baby was little. However, she also said she had lots of support from her male colleagues:

> When my son was six months old, we had to cross a river to get to a village. It was a rainy season so the river was swollen. Water was up to the neck. I was with my friends. My male friends helped me but the water was up to the neck so my son was all wet. Everyone got wet and had nothing to wear. We went to a village and stayed in a house. That woman, wife of the landlord, was very helpful. She gave me her son's clothes for my son and also gave her own clothes for me. We got changed but my son was serious and he got pneumonia. Luckily there was a health post so they admitted him for two days. Finally, he recovered. I never got to rest. I took my son with me for 11 months wherever I went. I worked for the Maoist party for a good cause. I didn't want to stay

home. First, I knew that security force will arrest me, second I wanted to contribute to the movement. When my son became 11 months old, I asked my mother to look after him and then I fully got involved in the Maoist movement.

There are multiple situations which do not lend themselves to simple analysis. The Maoists provided doctors, but this may not have always been the case. The party had arranged leave for her, but the situation did not allow her to live in safety. Women already had proved themselves as equal to men by fighting with them, but they did not want to feel weaker by bringing their special needs into the discussion. Within the party, gender equality not only meant treating women as equals but also meant not recognizing women's special needs.

Performing agency with guns: is it about gun power?

The Maoist movement was not only fighting against the state but was also creating awareness among people about different kinds of discrimination. The awareness-raising campaign was part of their policy to motivate more people to join their movement. The sister organization of the Maoists started a popular anti-alcohol campaign, which was one of the most successful campaigns in the history of Nepal. The All Nepal Women's Association –Revolutionary (ANWA-R) launched this campaign in 2001. However, the campaign was supported by the whole party. Other campaigns against gender-based discrimination included preventing child marriage; polygamy; unmatched marriage; dowry; domestic violence; *Chhaupadi Pratha*, the segregation of girls/women during menstruation (see Manchanda, 2004; Tamang, 2009; Yami, 2007); and gambling. Each campaign had a different focus in different regions. The anti-alcohol campaign and the campaigns against polygamy, gambling, *Chhaupadi Pratha* and domestic violence were targeted at the hilly regions, while in the Terai (Madhesh) regions the focus was on campaigns against dowry, unmatched marriage, and domestic violence. These campaigns were very successful during the war, but after the 2006 CPA, their effects slowly disappeared. Two questions arise here. First, did the situation revert to its previous state, and did people start to drink and beat their wives again? Second, how did a campaign led by women become so successful in a male-dominated society? Part of the answer lies in Yami's use of Chairman Mao's famous slogan. She said:

Power flows through the barrel of gun.

(Yami, 2007, p. 6)

The ex-district head of ANWA-R, Jwala Singh, said "people wouldn't have listened to us otherwise but during the conflict they did because we were carrying the guns." She elaborated on the context:

I know it is not only because of the fear from the guns but our campaign was divided into two parts. On the one hand we were creating awareness among the people about why discrimination is inhuman acts and how it affects the individuals, the families, the communities as well as the nation and on the other hand we were punishing the people who were committing such crimes. Therefore, people stopped gambling, there was no alcohol sale in rural villages, which reduced the cases of domestic violence so drastically.

There was no policy for the sale, consumption and distribution of alcohol until August 2001 (Dhital, 2000). Rita Dhital, who is the local contact person for the Action against Alcohol and Drug project in Nepal, wrote before the government passed legislation about the sale of alcohol:

> Nepal is perhaps the only country in the world where liquor is available at any time, any place, to any age group without any restriction whatsoever. It's absolutely necessary for social security and to protect our children that there is restriction in sale, distribution and consumption of alcohol. It has been proved that control on three factors as: Accessibility, Availability and Affordability will automatically bring down the consumption volume.
>
> (Dhital, 2001, n. p.)

As a result of the massive anti-alcohol campaign by the Maoists banning the sale of alcohol in villages and shutting down breweries and distilleries, the government of Nepal was forced to introduce legislation to regulate the sale of alcohol (Thapa, 2003, as cited in Manchanda, 2004; Tamang, 2009). During the height of the war, many districts, especially in hilly regions, were declared alcohol-free zones. Later the campaign was supported by the youth wing of CPN-M called YCL (Youth Communist League), who carried out parallel "police" patrols against "social crimes" and the sale and consumption of alcohol (OHCHR, 2007, p. 14). The consumption of alcohol was undoubtedly reduced but it is questionable whether there was a complete end to alcohol consumption. The 2005 report of Child Workers in Nepal says the Maoist campaign was more focused on stopping the use of alcohol than thinking about its religious, cultural and social values. If they had invited the community to participate in the anti-alcohol movement, it would have been sustainable and effective (CWIN, 2005). Some anecdotal evidence suggests that alcohol was still sold illegally, but people could neither drink it in public nor put it on sale.

Lata, an ex-combatant, said:

> Alcohol was the main reason for domestic violence. Men used to drink a lot and beat their wives but this campaign had controlled that. It was not just the banning of alcohol, they also had fear that if they beat their wives, they will be in trouble. That's why although there is no exact estimation, the domestic violence case had reduced dramatically.

Although the campaign ended with the end of the People's War in 2006 and people had freedom to drink if they wanted to, due to government regulation as well as increasing awareness among people the impact of the anti-alcohol movement can still be seen. Several NGOs recognize this as a social problem and are working with local people on this issue (see Sharma & Donini, 2010).

Comrade Parvati argued that "it [Civil War] has unleased the medieval oppression that women have been carrying ideologically, physically, psychologically, sociologically and economically in various forms" (Yami, 2007, p. 5). This has happened in two ways. First, women have been educated about superstitious religious beliefs which have taken over women's psychology and made them insecure. Second, it destroyed the feudal image of women as impure, diseased and helpless souls. She said women were using the theoretical teaching of the Maoists applied to practical experiences (Yami, 2007, p. 6). The situation was not as Comrade Parvati described, that "women are able to compete with men in equal footing" (Yami, 2007, p. 6), but it is certainly much better than it was. All of the women I interviewed said they struggled a lot but were also provided with opportunities for empowerment.

Women's lived experience in the post-conflict

Life after the CPA was different for women who were involved in the war. The combatants were sent to cantonments, student leaders were freed and started living like normal people, and the Maoist party leaders started to live like leaders of other mainstream political parties. Depending on their status within the party, their experiences also varied.

Among combatants, experiences varied between those who were physically fit and those who were injured during the war. Many young combatants, under 18 years, were sent off from their homes after the verification by UNMIN. The post-war experience was liberating for some women while for others it led to uncertainty and insecurity. For example, a woman who became a CA member said she had never imagined such a day would ever come and was very happy with her achievements. Preeti's experience was different. She neither got the opportunity to become a CA member nor was eligible to be integrated in the army because of her injury. She was, therefore, forced to take voluntarily retirement from the cantonment. She said she did not know what would happen to her. She was still in touch with the Maoist leaders but she said, it was not like what she used to be. People were disciplined and committed during the war and we had one goal to achieve, but now everyone is after power and position.

One of the ex-combatants said she made an inter-caste marriage during the war which was arranged by the party. However, after the CPA, when the situation went back to normal and everyone went home, she was not accepted by her husband's family because she belonged to a lower caste. As a result of pressure from his family, her husband did not take her home. Now she is living with her child and her husband is married to another woman from his own caste. This was certainly not the case with everyone. At least three of my research participants who had inter-caste marriages said they have very good relations with their families. One of them was a Madhesi Janajati woman married to a Yadav family. This would never have been accepted under any circumstances before the war but now she is not only accepted but is allowed to be involved in politics.

Individuals' experiences differed depending on their status in post-conflict Nepal. Women who got better opportunities, such as becoming CA members, had higher status than women who did not have any position in the post-conflict context. However, wherever they were and whatever they were doing, almost all the women said they were happy about their new identity. Jwala Singh said, "if I hadn't joined Maoist movement, I would have been married to a man in the village and would have been raising my kids." An ex-combatant said, "my life has changed. If I hadn't joined the Maoist movement, I wouldn't have any idea about the outside world. I wouldn't have known about the politics. I am confident and I feel like I can do anything now."

During the conflict, the Maoists opposed the bourgeois education system and many women therefore left school and joined the Maoist movement. However, after the CPA, they realized the value of education. They realized that it was those who were educated who had the opportunity to become leaders. Some of them started their education again. At least four of my research participants (two CA members and two ex-combatants) said they had gone back to school. Two of them were sitting intermediate level exams and two were sitting School Leaving Certificate exams.

Conclusion

> The insurgency was instrumental, although not solely responsible, in bringing monumental transformation to Nepal's social and political sphere. It was driven primarily by the quest for a more just and equitable society, but its rapid growth over a short period of time would not have been possible had it not been for a number of factors at play at the same time.
>
> (Thapa, 2012, p 55)

Despite some challenges, women who were directly involved in the war as combatants have not just experienced transformation in their own lives but have also made a great contribution to the changing discourse of womanhood in Nepal. Women were never considered for combat roles because they were seen as weak and emotional beings. Their involvement in the Maoist movement challenged this doxic notion, leading to change in the habitus of people. As a result, the government of Nepal has already recruited hundreds of women into the army.

Because of the crisis situation during the war, women were forced to do things that they had never done in the past. Toril Moi (1991, p. 1028) argues that "when the everyday order is challenged by an insurgent group, hitherto unspoken or private experience suddenly finds itself expressed in public, with dramatic consequences." Women who were not involved in the Maoist conflict also experienced dramatic changes in their lives. On the one hand, women were forced to go into the public sphere because men were absent and they started doing things which had been culturally restricted, like ploughing. On the other hand, the Maoist awareness campaign played an important role in increasing political consciousness among people, which included consciousness about their rights and responsibilities. Although the anti-alcohol campaign could not continue after the CPA, society became aware of the violence caused by alcohol. There are still various women's groups who have made anti-alcohol campaigns part of their campaign. The government of Nepal also introduced several policies to regulate alcohol sale, distribution and consumption after 2001. There are civil society organizations which are working as watchdogs to monitor the regulation of alcohol.

Due to the history of male domination in Nepal, it will take many years for women to experience equal treatment at home as well as in the wider society. But there is certainly a significant shift in women's lives in Nepal. In the past, the subordination of women was taken for granted. However, because of the increased political awareness and awareness about their rights and responsibilities, people including men have started speaking about discrimination against women. One recent example is Parbati Thapa, who was supposed to be promoted as deputy inspector general. Instead her junior officer was appointed. In the past, she would either have kept quiet or no one would have listened to her appeal, but now she has formally filed a writ against the government's decision to promote her junior and has criticized the government for being biased against women. She put her concerns in writing, saying it was against the law and that she was not promoted because she was a woman (see *eKantipur*, 2013; *Setopati*, 2013). Parbati Thapa's action has been appreciated by both men and women.

Reintegration of women combatants is not as challenging as Comrade Parvati initially expected because people's perception of the Maoists changed as a result of the changing political context. Perceptions of the people involved in the Maoist movement also changed. However, there are still diverse challenges faced by women. Their status in pre-conflict times also affects their experiences in post-conflict situations.

Notes

1   United CPN (Maoist) was previously known as CPN (Maoist). The name changed after the formal unification of the CPN-M with the Communist Party Nepal (Unity Centre-Masal) in January 2009. Baburam Bhattarai recently resigned from the UCPN-M to support ethnic movement. He formed a new party called Naya Shakti Nepal (New Force Nepal) in January 2016.
2   In this chapter, 'insider' means one who was directly involved in the Maoist movement, and 'outsider' means anyone other than the Maoist leaders or the people who were not involved in the Maoist movement.
3   The Nepali Congress is one of the main political parties in Nepal.
4   Women suffer greater discrimination in the Terai/Madhesh (the Plains of Nepal) than women in the Hills and the Mountains.
5   'Whole timer' means full-time commitment in the Maoist movement. There were many people who supported the Maoist movement but not all supporters were full timers.
6   See for example https://www.youtube.com/watch?v=DNq7a7YhT7g and https://www.youtube.com/watch?v=Z2kvqnO9FQs.
7   For more details about the verification process, see http://un.org.np/unmin-archive/?d=activities&p=arms.
8   Some recent vacancy announcements by the Nepal Army and Nepal police where priority is given to women candidates. See http://www.nepalarmy.mil.np/vacancy.php? and http://www.nepalpolice.gov.np/global-vacancy-2071–01–03.html.

9 United Communist Party Nepal (Maoist), see http://ucpnmaoist.org/Album. aspx?id=1; IRIN, see http://www.irinnews.org/in-depth/33611/11/between-two-stones-nepal-s-decade-of-conflict.

10 For details, see http://www.satp.org/satporgtp/countries/nepal/document/papers/40points.htm.

11 The Royal Army was renamed the Nepal Army when the country moved from a monarchy to a republic.

12 Pushpa Kamal Dahal (Prachanda) is the chairperson of United CPN (Maoist).

13 Revolutionary marriage, which did not have any of the features of traditional marriage. It just involved exchanging garlands, lighting candles and then giving a speech.

References

Adhikari, S. (2007, 26 June). Nepal: Women Combatants in Cantonments: Where Next? *Telegraph Nepal*. Retrieved on 16 July 2013 from http://www.telegraphnepal.com/opinion/2007–06–26/nepal:-women-combatants-in-cantonments:-where-next-

Ariño, M. V. (2008). *Nepal: A Gender View of the Armed Conflict and the Peace Process*. Retrieved on 6 May 2012 from http://escolapau.uab.cat/img/qcp/nepal_conflict_peace.pdf

Benhabib, S. (1999). Sexual Difference and Collective Identities: The New Global Constellation. *Signs, 24*(2), 335–361. doi:10.2307/3175645.

Benjamin, J. (1994). The Shadow of the Other (Subject): Intersubjectivity and Feminist Theory. *Constellations: An International Journal of Critical & Democratic Theory, 1*(2).

Bhattarai, T. (2012). Female Former Combatants Struggle to Re-adjust to Civilian Life in Nepal. *Global Press Journal*. Retrieved on 9 November 2013 from http://www.globalpressjournal.com/asia/nepal/female-former-combatants-struggle-readjust-civilian-life-nepal

CWIN. (2005). *Anti-Alcohol Campaign and Its Impact on Children: A Study in Rukum, Rolpa and Salyan Districts of Nepal*. Kathmandu: CWIN-Nepal.

Dhital, R. (2000). *Alcohol and Young People in Nepal*. Kathmandu: Child Workers in Nepal (CWIN).

Dhital, R. (2001). *Alcohol Control in Nepal: Challenges and Opportunities*. Kathmandu: Alcohol, Drugs and Development Organization.

eKantipur. (2011, 23 November). Unmarried Female Combatants to Join Nepal Army. Retrieved 17 November 2013 from http://www.ekantipur.com/2011/11/23/editors-pick/unmarried-female-combatants-to-join-nepal-army/344268.html

eKantipur. (2013, 7 November). DIG Files Writ against Aryal Promotion, eKantipur. Retrieved 15 November 2014 from http://www.ekantipur.com/2013/11/07/headlines/DIG-Thapa-moves-SC-against-AIG-promotion/380440/

Felski, R. (1997). The Doxa of Difference. *Signs, 23*(1), 1–21. doi:10.2307/3175148.

Gautam, S. (2001). *Women and Children in the Periphery of the People's War*. Kathmandu: IHRICON.

Goering, L. (2008). Women Put on Hold in Nepal. *Chicago Tribune*. Retrieved from http://articles.chicagotribune.com/2008–01–24/news/0801240080_1_maoist-nepali-congress-rural-areas

Harding, L. (2002). Nepal Army Kills 390 Maoists. *Guardian*. Retrieved 26 September 2015 from http://www.theguardian.com/world/2002/may/05/nepal

Hatlebakk, M. (2010). Maoist Control and Level of Civil Conflict in Nepal. *South Asian Economic Journal, 11*(1), 99–110.

Himalayan Times. (2003, 30 October). THT 10 YEARS AGO. SC Backs Removal of Price Tag on Maoists. Retrieved 12 November 2014 from http://www.thehimalayantimes.com/fullNews.php?headline=THT+10+YEARS+AGO%3A+SC+backs+removal+of+price+tag+on+Maoists&NewsID=395474

IDEA. (2011). *Women Members of the Constituent Assembly: A Study on Contribution of Women in Constitution Making in Nepal* (p. 905). Kathmandu. Full report retrieved on 14 August 2013 from http://www.idea.int/publications/women-members-of-the-constituent-assembly/index.cfm

IRIN. (2010, 14 April). *Nepal: Reintegration Challenges for Maoist Female Ex-combatants*. Kailali, Nepal. Retrieved 16 June 2014 from http://www.irinnews.org/report/88806/nepal-reintegration-challenges-for-maoist-female-ex-combatants

Kathmandu Post. (2003, 30 September). Interpol Red Corners for 14 Maoist Leaders. Retrieved 30 September 2012 from http://www.ekantipur.com/the-kathmandu-post/2012/09/30/business/plan-to-let-foreigners-to-buy-apartments-in-nepal/3609/

Khadka, S. (2012). *Female Combatants and Ex-combatants in Maoist Revolution and Their Struggle for Reintegration in Post-war, Nepal* (Masters), University of Tromsø, Norway. Retrieved on 12 September 2013 from http://munin.uit.no/bitstream/handle/10037/3980/thesis.pdf?sequence=2

Labh, B.K. (2013, 25 July). A Few Good Women. *Kathmandu Post*. Retrieved on 15 July 2015 from http://www.ekantipur.com/the-kathmandu-post/2013/07/25/oped/a-few-good-women/251599.html#.UfIiKjcJYqs.facebook

Logan, M. (2006, 10 July). Nepal: Despite Promises, Women Left Out of Building 'New Nepal'. *Global Information Network* (p. 1). Retrieved on 12 June 2012 from http://ezproxy.library.usyd.edu.au/login?url=http://search.proquest.com/docview/457558394?accountid=14757

Manchanda, R. (2004). Maoist Insurgency in Nepal: Radicalizing Gendered Narratives. *Cultural Dynamics, 16*(2–3), 237–258. doi:10.1177/0921374004047750.

Moi, T. (1991). Appropriating Bourdieu: Feminist Theory and Pierre Bourdieu's Sociology of Culture. *New Literary History, 22*(4), 1017–1049.

OHCHR. (2007). *Human Rights in Nepal: One Year after the Comprehensive Peace Agreement*. Kathmandu: OHCHR. Retrieved 6 July 2010 from http://nepal.ohchr.org/en/resources/Documents/English/reports/HCR/CPA%20Report.pdf

Onesto, L. (2000). *Red Flag Flying on the Roof of the World – Inside the Revolution in Nepal: Interview with Comrade Prachanda*. Retrieved 15 September 2011 from http://www.revcom.us/a/v21/1040–049/1043/interv.htm

Pathak, B. (2005). *Politics of People's War and Human Rights in Nepal*. Kathmandu: BIMIPA.

Pettigrew, J., & Shneiderman, S. (2004). Ideology and Agency in Nepal's Maoist Movement. *Himal Magazine*. Retrieved 20 October 2015 from http://www.himalmag.com/component/content/article/4272-women-in-the-maobaadi-ideology-and-agency-in-nepals-maoist-movement.html

Sen, A. (1999). *Development as Freedom*. Oxford: Oxford University Press.

Setopati. (2013, 7 November). DIG Parbati Thapa Aryan Ko Badhuwa Rokna Sarbochha. Retrieved 8 November 2013 from http://setopati.com/raajneeti/5227/?utm_source=twitterfeed&utm_medium=facebook

Shakhya, S. (2003). The Maoist Movement in Nepal: An Analysis from Women's Perspectives. In A. Karki & D. Seddon (Eds.), *People's War in Nepal: Left Perspectives* (pp. 375–404). Delhi: Adroit.

Sharma, J.R., & Donini, A. (2010). *Towards a "Great Transformation"? The Maoist Insurgency and Local Perceptions of Social Transformation in Nepal*. Boston, MA: Tufts University.

Tamang, S. (2009). The Politics of Conflict and Difference or the Difference of Conflict in Politics: The Women's Movement in Nepal. *Feminist Review, 91*, 61–80.

Thapa, D. (2012). The Making of the Maoist Insurgency. In S. v. Einsiedel, D.M. Malone, & S. Pradhan (Eds.), *Nepal in Transition: From People's War to Fragile Peace* (pp. 37–57). New York: Cambridge University Press.

Thapa, M. (2003). *The Tutor of History*. India: Penguin Books.

Times of India. (2005, 13 September). Face to Face, with Maoist Leader Prachanda. Retrieved 20 September 2015 from http://articles.timesofindia.indiatimes.com/2005–09–13/india/27862936_1_prachanda-nepal-king-pushpakamal-dahal

Yami, H. (2007). *People's War and Women's Liberation in Nepal*. Kathmandu: Janadhwani.

7 White sari

Transforming widowhood in Nepal[1]

> While a wife is her husband's "half-body" (*ardhangini*), one can almost say that on
> · his death she becomes 'half-corpse'. She must henceforth dress in a white shroud-
> like sari and is excluded from any significant ritual role.
>
> (Banerjee & Miller, 2003, p. 140)

The People's War in Nepal, which lasted for 10 years (1996–2006), led to a large number of young widows (WHR, 2010). There is no exact estimate of the total number of war widows in Nepal. However, the Nepal Demographic Health Survey shows that there are more widows than widowers (NDHS, 2012, p. 65). This data is also supported by a recent census in 2011, which suggests that out of 659,837 who have been widowed, 75 per cent are widows and only 25 per cent are widowers. Similarly, a study carried out by the Women for Human Rights, single women group (WHR), one of the few organizations closely working with single women in Nepal, suggests that many households in rural areas, especially in western parts of Nepal, are headed by single women (WHR, 2010, p. 27).[2] Among these single women, most are widows and some are wives of missing people (WHR, 2010, p. 27). WHR also observes that more than half of these widows (52 per cent) are young women under 40 years of age and the majority (77 per cent) of the widows cannot read and write (WHR, 2010, pp. 30–31).

Widow is *bidhawa* in Nepali; the direct translation is 'woman without a husband'. Prior the People's War (1996) in Nepal, widows were not allowed to wear anything other than the white sari, especially in Hindu families. It was a common practice even among highly educated women. Although this practice varied as to how many days or years the widows should wear a white sari, it was widely practiced among all the castes/ethnic groups in Nepal.

There are various explanations for the white sari practice. The most common understanding of the white sari is that it signifies purity. Traditionally widows were expected to withdraw from normal life and live a life of celibacy, almost like a *shanyasi* (saint). This chapter seeks to examine and provide explanations of how widowhood works in practice in Nepal. Widows are on the one hand expected to be pure, to give up their family and social life, but on the other hand they are called also *Randi* (also pronounced as *Radi*), which is a synonym for 'prostitutes' (see Bennett, 1976, p. 17; Doherty, 1974, p. 27). This double meaning reveals the precarious nature of 'performing' widowhood in Nepal, which is also observed in other Hindu societies such as India (see Lamb, 2000).

This chapter argues that traditionally the white sari operated as a powerful symbol in Nepalese social discourse, one that was "socially constitutive as well as socially conditioned" (Fairclough & Wodak, 1997, p. 258). It served to reproduce, in public spaces, multiple forms of discrimination against widows – social, political and economic. This chapter explores how the liberation of widows from wearing the white sari is transforming the whole experience of widowhood and at the same time changing the habitus of people as well as social behaviour towards widows in Nepal.

This chapter considers the practice of the white sari from two different perspectives. First, it does not ignore the individualized experiences of widows (which were often mediated by complex social dynamics of caste, class, cultural context, religion and so on), but projects these experiences onto a wider social canvas to visualize the collective suffering of widowhood imposed in the name of religion, tradition or honour (of the family, society or the country).[3] Second, this chapter explores the transformative performative agency through women's resistance, including the explicit resistance of widows to the white sari in post-conflict Nepal.

The white sari

The sari is a common dress among married women in Nepal. Like other dresses, a sari comes in various colours, designs and patterns. Women wear saris of different colours and patterns depending on their age and marital status. There are plenty of choices for young women, but as women age or become more senior in the family (as mothers or grandmothers), their choices become limited (Banerjee & Miller, 2003, p. 138). However, the notion of 'choice' must be interpreted critically. In considering the implications for feminism of Foucauldian concepts of social structure, Carolyn Ells (2003, p. 224) remarks, "a choice must be understood in explicitly relational terms that include social relationships. It is a decision or authorization situated within a set of practices." In most cases, a woman's relationship with her husband exerts the primary influence over what colour she wears (Banerjee & Miller, 2003, p. 140). A bride is supposed to be dressed in red, a colour that indicates she is connected to the world and has desires, and symbolizes that she is sexually active. As women get older they are supposed to wear 'cooler' colours, which indicate that they are distant from such desires (Banerjee & Miller, 2003, p. 139). Likewise, a woman's relationship with her children within the family cycle also influences their choice of the colour. For instance, an older woman with married children and grandchildren will begin to wear subdued colours like off-white, cream, grey and so forth.

In widowhood, women are expected to completely abandon the colour of desire (Banerjee & Miller, 2003, p. 140). Hence, colour is very much linked to the sexual state of people in Hindu society. Beck argues that "red substances symbolize 'heated' states [sexually active] and white substances 'cooled' ones [sexually inactive]" (Beck, 1969, p. 553). Coolness signifies a state of sexual inactivity (Philips,

2004, p. 259). White is regarded as a 'cool' (*thanda*) colour, symbolic of infertility, asexuality, asceticism, old age, widowhood and death (Lamb, 2000, p. 214). White is also a ritual colour of mourning for both genders. White is therefore given to widows to mark the end of their sexual and social life.

When the white sari turns red

In 2005, I attended an event organized by an international non-governmental organization (NGO) in Nepal. This particular organization had been working in Nepal for several years and had various programs supporting women and discriminated groups. It was a district level event where the chief district officer, district heads and regional political figures were invited. The purpose of the event was to distribute red saris and red *tika* (small red mark on forehead) to widows. The aim of the program was to create awareness about discrimination against widows, especially the stigma associated with wearing a white sari. The majority of the women who participated in the event were war widows under 30 years old, and only a small percentage (less than 5 per cent) were around 50. The young widows cried when they received the red sari and red tika, which was overwhelming to watch, but the older widows looked shy and embarrassed, as if they were doing something wrong.

According to the organizers, the event was very successful. However, as I left the hall, I saw most of the widows hiding the red saris they had received and wiping off their red tika. I also observed some men outside the hall, standing on the sidelines and talking about the widows. They were criticizing both the NGO and the widows for attending such a program, which conflicted with Nepalese culture. The widows were criticized: I overheard one man commenting that 'they were characterless women'. In Nepal, character is associated with an individual's sexual behaviour, which determines whether a person is good or bad.

Culturally, for both men and women in Nepal, it is only within marriage that sexual expression is allowed. In practice, however, these social mores are flexible for widowers, who are permitted to remarry within 'socially accepted circumstances'. The program offering red saris and red tika to widows challenged the status quo and led people to raise doubts about the character of the widows taking part in the program.

The following day, the NGO was criticized in national and local media for hosting such a program as it was perceived to be challenging the cultural values. There was also speculation about the widows who had received a red sari. Although it looked as if the program was a failure, it now seems to have planted a seed for the transformation of widowhood in Nepal.

I left Nepal in May 2005 and returned in August 2007 to find that the practice of wearing a white sari had become less common among widows. I started to see female leaders, who were widows and had long been wearing a white sari, appearing on television and in public spaces wearing saris of all colours. It had only been about three years since I had attended the event, but now widows everywhere in Nepal appeared liberated from the confines of a social status inflicted on them through the white sari. It would have been unimaginable a few years ago, but in 2012, on the occasion of International Women's Day, widows collectively celebrated *Holi*, a festival of colour.[4] This made me ask: how was this social transformation or massive "step change" (Castles, 2010) for women enabled in Nepalese society in such a short time frame? To address this question, it is necessary to highlight the lived experiences of widows.

This chapter is based on in-depth interviews with 17 women, 15 of whom were widows and 2 were wives of missing men. In addition, a focus group discussion (FGD) with 6 widows and interviews with 5 key informants were carried out to explore the collective understanding of widowhood and the women's perception about the transformation of widowhood in Nepal. Among the 17 'single women', 8 women were under 30 years old; 6 were between 36 and 45; and 3 were 49 or older. Out of the 17 women interviewed, 5 were from high caste (Brahmin/Chhetri), 2 were indigenous (Janajati), 1 was from lower caste and 9 were from other Madhesi castes. A majority of the single women (15) came from Hindu families; 1 came from a Muslim family and 1 from a Buddhist family.

Experience of widowhood in the recent past

> Entering widowhood is painful and traumatic for most women, who simultaneously lose their husbands and are transformed into other, alien beings.
>
> (Lamb, 2000, p. 217)

Losing one's husband is a traumatic event in a woman's life, but the trauma can be heightened by the social and cultural restrictions placed on them afterwards. In Nepal, women have to follow some strict rituals upon the disclosure of their husbands' deaths.[5] For instance, neighbours or members of the family break the marriage bangles and wipe the red tika from her forehead and the vermilion (*sindhur*) from the parting in her hair. This ritual removes all the signs of marriage immediately after the death of the husband and from that moment, the widow avoids wearing red (Lamb, 2000, p. 214). Further, widows have to follow certain rules and regulations throughout their lives, which includes restrictions on food, mobility and participation in community activities. As widows are considered inauspicious, they are prohibited from attending any propitious events such as religious ceremonies or weddings. However, the experience of widows can differ depending on their personal circumstances.

Nisha,[6] the chair of a district level single women's group in Rolpa, explained the problems faced by widows in the recent past:

> Women were blamed for their widowhood. They were not allowed to go to any of the ceremonies or celebrations, especially marriage ceremonies and religious *poojas*. No one wanted to start their day by seeing a widow. There was a fear that if they wore colourful dresses, or if they dressed like other normal women, bad desires [sexual desires] would come to their mind or men might be attracted to them . . . In the case of young widows, there was a fear in the

family that she might elope with someone or might re-marry. Therefore, the rules were even stricter for them.

This discriminatory culture associated with widowhood has a long history. As discussed in earlier chapters, the root of Hindu tradition comes from the Vedic period, which is believed to be between 1500 B.C. and 600 B.C. (Embree, 1966, p. 3). According to the *Manusmriti*, women should always obey their husbands:

> When her father, or her brother with her father's permission, gives her to someone, she should obey that man while he is alive and not violate her vow to him when he is dead.
>
> (*Manusmriti*, Chapter 4, trans. Doniger & Smith, 1991, p. 115)

Marriage is still extremely important for Hindu families in Nepal, and everyone is expected to participate in this tradition when they reach a certain age (Allendorf & Ghimire, 2012; Bajracharya & Amin, 2010; Thapa, 1996). As described in the *Manusmriti*, giving away a daughter (Kanyadan) at the right age is still perceived as a significant religious event. Moreover, marriage is considered a lifetime commitment (Allendorf & Ghimire, 2012) and divorce is still taboo in Nepal. Embree suggests that, although there has been some transformation within cultural practices, "there is an unquestionable continuity linking the remote past in an unbroken line with the present" (1966, p. 69). Many aspects of marriage still reveal the continuity of traditional patterns in Nepal (Choe, Thapa, & Mishra, 2005, p. 159).

Nepal has also witnessed the practice of *Sati* (WHR, 2010, p. 7). The word Sati means a "virtuous woman" (Embree, 1966, p. 98; Major, 2007, p. xv) or a "good wife" (Spivak, 1988), and the practice involves burning the widow alive on her husband's funeral pyre. The origin of the Sati system remains obscure. In 465, Lichchhavi King Mandev persuaded his mother not to end her own life when his father died, which was the first reference to Sati in any South Asian inscription (Whelpton, 2005, p. 19). Although the British government banned the Sati system in India in 1829 (Spivak, 1988, p. 93), it was practiced in Nepal into the twentieth century. It is important to note that Sati was not practiced among all castes and ethnic groups in Nepal. Even though Sati was practiced predominantly among the upper caste (Mani, 1998, p. 1), it had a significant impact on Nepalese society. While there has been some resistance against the practice in the past, it did not bring the level of transformation that we observe at present.

Yogmaya Neupane (1860–1941), who was the first women's rights activist in Nepal, was married to a boy when she was between 5 and 9 years old. Her husband died within 3 years of their marriage. She was considered inauspicious and faced extreme forms of discrimination. After few years of struggle, she managed to flee from her in-laws to her family home. Later, she eloped with another man to Assam in India. She returned to Nepal in 1903 and got involved in religious activities. In 1906, she formed the first *Nari Samiti*, or women's committee. With her 2,000 followers, she started protesting against discriminatory practices, including polygamy, widow marriage and child marriage. She submitted 24 demands, which included abolition of the Sati system, to Prime Minister Chandra Shamsher Rana (1901–1929), who formally abolished slavery and the Sati system in Nepal (see Dhungana, 2014; Sangraula, 2011; Whelpton, 2005). After Chandra Shamsher Rana died, Yogmaya went to new Prime Minister Juddha Shamsher Rana with her remaining demands, but they were not fulfilled. Instead, she was jailed with her followers for 4 months. After her release, as a final rebellion, she committed suicide with 68 of her followers by leaping into the Arun River on 14 July 1941 (see *Kathmandu Post*, 2011; Sangraula, 2011). The work of the women's committee ceased with Yogmaya's death; however, her contributions are now being recognized by both activists and academics (see Aziz, 2001; Dhungana, 2014; *Freenepal News Network*, n.d.; Sangraula, 2011). Women's rights activists are demanding that the government celebrate Yogmaya as a national luminary (see *Aankha.com*, 2013; *Freenepal News Network*, n.d.).

Performance of widowhood in the white sari

Simone de Beauvoir argues that the "female body is marked within masculine discourse" (as cited in Butler, 1990, p. 17), thus the construction of widowhood is undoubtedly a masculine construction of femininity. Religion is used as a tool to discipline widows' sexual desires. Michel Foucault refers to this as "disciplinary power" (Mills, 2003, p. 43). According to him, "disciplinary power is exercised on the body and soul of individuals" (Sawicki, 1986, p. 25). Discipline is an individual's internalized behaviours, a person's habitus that contains concern about control. It originates within society and aims to control each individual within a particular set of cultural norms (Mills, 2003, p. 43). An example of this phenomena is widows internalizing the stigma associated with their social position and thus disciplining their own bodies or participating in their own suppression.

Rupa explained that she felt awkward participating in wedding ceremonies as a widow, as she was scared that something would happen to her family:

> I went to my husband's home when my youngest brother in-law was getting married. I did all the preparation but I was afraid to go out when there was a pooja [worshipping ceremony] as we [widows] are thought to bring misfortune. I was scared that something might happen to the couple. I didn't want to see any bad things happening to my family, that's why I was hiding.

In the dominant religious and cultural narrative, widows were considered inauspicious and as carriers of bad luck. It was believed that if widows participated in religious ceremonies, the ceremony would become impure. During a wedding ceremony, the presence of a widow was believed to bring bad luck to the new couple. This belief system is a manifestation of a gendered social discourse of suppression and domination. Bourdieu argues that when people's thoughts are structured by the dominant discourse, in this instance male domination, the act of cognition becomes an act of recognition or submission (Bourdieu & Nice, 2001,

p. 13). This is evident in Rupa's story of not participating in the religious ceremony at a wedding. She was worried that if she participated in the ceremony, god will get angry and something bad might happen to her family.

Foucault argues that "all subjects are equally unfree," as their actions and choices are constructed by a particular discourse and thus their thoughts or decisions may not truly be their own (Foucault, as cited in Heller, 1996, p. 91). The discourse of widowhood, much like other discourses around moral values, is constructed around ideas and taboos concerning sexuality. Patton (1994) argues that an agent's capacity is constrained in two ways: by external and internal limits. He suggests internal limits are created by agents themselves, in that they perceive themselves as incapable of performing a specific act or in other ways create internal restrictions (Patton, 1994, p. 352). External limits, on the other hand, may be created by family or society, which influences the internal limits perceived by the individual. Their internal limits are also affected by a person's knowledge of their external reality. For example, women are often afraid to deviate from rules stipulated or visualized in religious ceremonies imposing stigmatizing practices because of the fear imposed by sacred rituals.

The dominant religious narrative within Hindu ideology positions the husband as a god in relationship to his partner. The wife has to be devoted to her husband when he is alive and when he is dead. A widow's disciplined lifestyle shows her continued devotion to her husband. Girls are raised within this religious narrative. The religious narrative of widowhood has been adopted by illiterate women in rural villages as well as educated urban women. This does not mean that women do not have agency and that they only operate in conformity with a set of cultural diktats. The performance of widowhood varies among women from different educational and cultural backgrounds. However, there are certain core principles that are assumed to be obligatory for all women.

In this chapter, I am referring to the white sari as a signifier of widowhood. Although historically not all widows had to wear a white sari, it was rare and the option to reject the white sari was, in practice, only available to a few women. In the past, the link between signifier (the white sari) and signified (the widow) has been so deeply entrenched in cultural, religious and historical locations that up until about 2003 it was unimaginable that this performance of widowhood could change. I asked my respondents how they felt when they wore a white sari; the majority said they felt vulnerable and insecure. In addition, they also experienced restrictions on their mobility, symbolic as well as systematic denial from public spaces, and they said they were exposed to increased level of violence. Sumedha shared her experience:

> I felt vulnerable when I was wearing a white sari. People could easily recognize . . . from [a] distance that I was a widow. We [widows] were often targeted by people with bad intentions.

Rusa, who is 29 years old, had similar experiences. Widows, especially young widows, felt vulnerable because 'woman in white sari' also meant 'woman without a man', and they were therefore understood as weak and vulnerable. The white sari did not just make women feel insecure; it also exposed them to violence. Many widows feared going outside the home when they were wearing the white sari. Sita shares her experience:

> We do not have a toilet in our house. I had to walk for a few minutes to go out to the field but I was scared to go out alone, especially in the evening. Either I had to go with someone or I had to wait until morning.

In 2011, only 62 per cent of Nepalese households had access to a toilet (CBS, 2011). In rural areas, that percentage is much lower (Bhattarai, 2013).

Widows in white sari also suffered emotionally. Sabina explained that the white sari served as a constant reminder of her tragic loss:

> I felt very bad about being in a white sari. I was suffering from my husband's sudden death and the white sari never let me forget the incident. It kept reminding me that I had lost my husband and that I was no longer like other women; which made me emotionally very weak. I didn't feel like I was part of the family or part of the community. I thought I was left alone in this world.

The white sari functioned as a symbolic denial of existence in both private and public spaces. While marriage makes women socially visible (Philips, 2004, p. 269), widowhood makes them invisible in social life. Nisha and Rusa, aged 28 and 29 respectively, were from Rolpa and said they had had no roles to play in social life when wearing a white sari.

> We were not allowed to participate in any public or community events. Our existence was not even recognized; as if we didn't exist.
>
> (Nisha)

> It was highly restricted for us to participate in any of the events, especially wedding ceremonies.
>
> (Rusa)

In theory, the symbolic meaning of a white sari is to 'discipline' widows, to keep them 'pure' in memory of the deceased husband. White is also considered a colour of purity, spirituality and asceticism as well as a symbol of peace. However, by wearing a white sari, widows become targets for the unwanted advances of men, particularly by their own family members. This vulnerability was intensified by their financial dependence on the family. Kala, who is 28 years old and a mother of two children, stated:

> After my husband's death, I thought my family will support me but instead my brother in-law wanted to take advantage of the situation. He wanted me

to sleep with him. He threatened me to kick me out of the house with my children, if I didn't sleep with him.

As discussed earlier, women did not have any inheritance rights until the 12th Amendment of the National Law in 2005. In the past, only unmarried daughters who were over the age of 35 were able to claim their ancestral property, which they had to return to their family if they decided to get married. The purpose of the law was not to protect a daughter's right to her inheritance, but to provide her with some financial security if she decides not to get married. Before the amendment, a widow had to wait until the age of 35 to be able to claim property – even if she was widowed at the age of 16 – and like all women, she had to return the property if she remarried. Widows did not have rights to property; with few exceptions under special circumstances, they were provided with small parcels of land to ensure their survival if they remained widows for the rest of their lives.

A study on single women carried out by Linda Weiss in one of the villages of Nepal shows that as women often lack productive skills, the death of a husband condemns women to economic hardship. Since childhood, women are trained for domestic chores such as cooking, cleaning and taking care of the house and family. Thus, their lives become difficult if their husbands die (Weiss, 1999, pp. 253–254). Economic hardship, social restrictions and personal loss are factors that affect how widows were able to interact in social spaces, they were perceived as 'ghosts, 'invisible' in their visually distinct white saris.

'Unwearing' white saris

I asked the participants in this study, especially those who had lived under strict rules, how they felt when the white sari was no longer compulsory for them. They responded:

> After we [widows] started wearing other colours, we felt comfortable. We feel like we are part of the family and society. I feel comfortable talking with other people and other people also behave normally with me now. I can go anywhere now like other women.
>
> (Rusa)

> When I was wearing a white sari I was not invited to community meetings. I also excluded myself as I didn't feel part of them. But now I am welcomed as a member of society to participate in those kinds of forums.
>
> (Namita)

Through their collective struggle and resistance, which was supported by various NGOs and civil society organizations, widows have not only been able to change their own lives and experiences, but they have also been able to influence key policy changes.

Since 2002, the Nepalese government has made some legislative changes, mostly through the 11th and 12th Amendments of the Civil Code (also known as the Gender Equality Bill). These changes specifically address the rights of widows, for example, a widow does not have to return property of her deceased husband to his family if she decides to remarry, and widows receive a monthly allowance from the state. Further, widows no longer require the consent of a male family member to obtain a passport, nor do they need permission from their children (a son or unmarried daughter) to sell or share their property (see Gender Equality Act 2063 [2006]). The new constitution, which was promulgated on 20 September 2015, also ensures the widow's rights to inheritance and entitlement to social security (see Constitution of Nepal, 2072, 2015). Moreover, widows are now active in all sectors of society. They are not only participating in politics on a national level, but they are also taking part in international forums and have formed alliances with other groups globally. In the next section I will demonstrate how these radical social transformations were made possible in a short period of time.

Key reasons for radical social transformation

> No one wears a white sari now and no one even questions this.
>
> (Sumedha)

There have been cases of widows' resistance to discriminatory practices in the past (for example, Yogmaya Neupane, discussed earlier). However, the transformation of widowhood currently taking place is having a far more significant impact on Nepalese society than any earlier movements.

Nepal is far from the only society where the impact of war on traditional social structures has prompted a transformation in the symbolic construction of gender roles. The Maoist People's War in Nepal opened up various previously restricted avenues for women (Manchanda, 2004, p. 244). Along with the wartime experience, the intervention from NGOs is another component I have identified to be a source of influence that affects the radical transformation of gender roles and widowhood in Nepal. These influences can be divided in to five primary categories: crisis tendencies; collective agency and changing performance; advocacy interventions and support from governments and I/NGOs; role models; and cultural limbo. Each of these categories will be discussed in the following sections.

Crisis tendencies

Crisis is understood as a situation where the normal system is disrupted or destroyed as a result of a catastrophic event (Connell, 2003, p. 260). Raewyn Connell (1987, 2002, 2003) borrows the term 'crisis tendency' from Jürgen Habermas and applied this theory to gender. She argues that the analysis of crisis tendencies allows us to visualize the process of change (Connell, 2002, p. 71). According to Connell, there are two types of crisis tendencies that lead to social change: internal tendencies and external tendencies. A crisis can erupt internally or externally, impacting the whole social structure (Connell, 2002). Connell (2002, p. 70) argues that "the social forces can produce change in gender relations." Internal tendencies towards change, when individuals themselves want change, are triggered by various factors, such as exposure to new ideas through education and travel (Connell, 2002, p. 70). However, change can also be affected by the need for survival.

Connell argues that gendered division of labour and gender roles become less rigid during a crisis situation (Connell, 2002, p. 71). This is relevant in the Nepalese context as the crisis following the People's War influenced social changes. This was especially true for women who were forced to perform duties traditionally associated with men in order to survive. When they stepped out of the traditionally defined gender relations, they did not just learn to cope with the new situation but also had time to reflect back on their past. When analyzing this particular set of circumstances, Bourdieu's notion of reflexivity can be fruitfully applied. When women leave their usual fields or roles, they are distanced from their usual habitus or way of thinking, which creates space to reflect on their own positions, which in turn leads to change.

Due to the dislocation of traditional cultural and religious narratives during the decade-long People's War in Nepal, new spaces for social interaction opened up. As people were generally sympathetic towards young widows, the social norms were less rigid for them.

In addition, due to the absence of male members of the family, women had to undertake men's jobs as well as their own, which interrupted the entire social structure. A women's rights activist said:

> All of a sudden, the number of young widows increased during the People's War. People didn't know how to respond to this situation and how strict they could be with young widows. There was confusion but also sympathy for the widows.

> (Sabita)

Likewise, a widow shared her experience:

> It was very difficult during the heightened conflict. When the Maoists bombed the police beats in the villages, all the police started coming to the district headquarters. There were more police than the general population. We had a curfew every night. Most of the male members of the community had gone. They had either died, were displaced, had migrated, or had joined the Maoists, so mostly women were left in the villages. Since men were not there, women had to do everything, even the jobs they were not allowed to do in the past such as ploughing.

> (Nisha)

The changes to the performance of gender involved the complex dynamics of the disruption of doxa, norms taken for granted, and habitus, the way of thinking (Bourdieu, 1977, 1989; Bourdieu & Eagleton, 1992). In certain situations, such as widows joining the police force, the widows were still expected to perform traditional rituals, but due to the nature of their professional roles these expectations were much lower for them than they had previously been.

Moreover, some widows who were housewives started organizing and working together with other widows outside the home in order to earn an income. Radhika, an FGD participant, explained that "widows are also working in construction sites." Women had never previously been seen at construction sites as labourers, and it was once unimaginable for widows to work there, but now it is seen as normal. Because of widows' increasing presence in the public sphere, they are accepted as regular members of society. These widows also described this social transformation as an internal experience:

> I had never imagined that I would be able to manage my family on my own but I am confident that I can handle any situation, if I have to.
>
> (Kakulti)

María Villellas Ariño (2008) argues that armed conflict can transform the social structure as gender roles and norms are questioned during a crisis. Anderlini (2007) argues that conflict brings women to the fore of public life. When women are exposed in the public sphere, they are able to see how their roles in the family and society can be different. She also argues that conflict may also increase men's reliance on women, causing them to respect women for their abilities to cope, survive, protect and recover. Thus, conflict plants seeds of social transformation (Anderlini, 2007). Widows' exposure to new roles was a starting point for the transformation of widowhood in Nepal.

Collective agency and changing performance

Historically, discriminatory sociocultural norms have been effective because social institutions have actively worked to maintain them (Puigvert, 2001, p. 30). Puigvert (2001) uses a case of rural Spanish women, who have never attended university, to discuss how collective agency can bring transformation within a society. She argues that when these women, who had grown up within a patriarchal society, came together, they started questioning assumptions about their roles and developed alternative ways of dealing with oppression. She also argues:

> Together they reflected on the nature of their role, questioned their experiences, and planned strategies for change. They turned from being women without any alternatives or mere observers of change into active protagonists of social transformation with regard to gender relations.
>
> (Puigvert, 2001, p. 43)

Similarly, when widows in Nepal came together and shared their painful experiences, they stopped blaming themselves for not being able to perform according to the expectations of their families and society. Instead of blaming themselves or blaming their own fate, they started thinking critically about the social norms that affected them and as a result, they began questioning discriminatory practices and social expectations (Brooks, 2007, p. 61). As they realized these were common problems for all widows, the issues were no longer conceived as individual concerns. One widow explained:

> Our problems are similar. We have all been victims of the old traditions therefore we are always sympathetic to each other and we support each other in any way we can. Widow marriage was not even talked about in the past, but we talk about it openly in our group.
>
> (Mira)

If one widow had refused the white sari it would have been unacceptable, but since it was a collective resistance to discrimination against widows, it did not take much time to transform society.

When widows stopped wearing the white sari, they looked 'normal' like other women, although they were still widows. Their changed appearance increased the opportunities for widows to act in the public sphere, and slowly the discriminatory practices against widows (such as restrictions on food and mobility) were questioned, challenged and removed. This transformation in social attitude towards widows did not only benefit widows from higher castes or widows wearing the white sari, it also liberated widows from other castes/ethnicity groups who might not have worn a white sari but had faced other kinds of discrimination due to their widowhood.

Advocacy interventions and support from government and I/NGOs

Lily Thapa, who herself became widow at young age, established an organization, Women's Human Rights (WHR), for single women in 1994 (Thapa, 2010; WHR, 2010). Due to the lack of funding to support their initiatives, WHR struggled in the early years of its existence. However, during the People's War, a lot of international funding was supplied to support the victims of the conflict. WHR was thus able to secure some funding and expand its program to support widows. A field coordinator for WHR, said:

> We started forming single women's groups in various districts of Nepal. Initially it started with a monthly meeting. The aim of that meeting was to provide a common forum for widows to come and share their problems. It took a while for them to open up but when they started sharing their problems, they realized that it was not only their problem, all the widows were going through

similar pain. When they realized that, they stopped blaming their own fate and started getting together.

The field coordinator further shared her experience of working with widows:

> WHR organized a first national level workshop for widows in 2001, which was part of the 'Red Colour Movement'. We distributed red thread for the name tags. Widows were excited about the red thread but at the same time they were nervous because they were afraid of being questioned since 'culturally' they were not supposed to wear anything red. They put their name tags on, but took them off when taking pictures as they did not want to be seen in the pictures with the red thread. Although it was a good initiative, the women were too scared.

As a result of this experience, a new approach was developed by WHR. They decided to step back and started creating awareness among widows involving their family members. They invited religious leaders to speak about myths around widowhood and the white sari. Slowly the movement grew with increased participation from widows and the public started accepting widows dressed in other colours.

Today there are many other organizations, including the Department of International Development, UK and Care Nepal, that support widows. WHR itself has expanded its scope and has various programs supporting widows and their children in Nepal.[7] Some of the widows have returned to education and some were able to start small businesses. Most importantly, widows provide each other with support. Nisha said:

> We always thought that it was against the culture and that god will do something to us and our family if we wore any other colour than white and did not follow the rituals, but now we are aware of our religious values. I can support myself. We support each in our group so no one dares to say anything against us.

Scholars have theorized and explained this phenomenon. Puigvert wrote: "when reason is applied to the past, tradition, and history, we begin to suspect that we do not necessarily need to be their victims, that we can modify our relation to them, and that social transformation is possible" (Puigvert, 2001, p. 35). Bourdieu argues that "awakening of consciousness" brings the possibility of transformation (see Jenkins, 2002, pp. 82–83). When these women were educated about discriminatory practices, they were able to reflect on their past experiences and tradition. The intervention of different NGOs has contributed to raising awareness and has supported women through establishing income-generating activities. Equipped with economic independence and increased knowledge, widows were increasingly able to resist discriminatory practices.

Role models

> Personal agency has transformative possibilities.
>
> (Butler, 1986, p. 41)

WHR now has formed single women's groups in 73 (out of 75) districts and 1,050 (out of 3,913) Village Development Committees. Ninety-eight per cent of the members of this organization are widows. A field coordinator at WHR explained that "widows who were members of the committee were criticized in the beginning for not wearing white saris, but now they have become role models for others." Widows who were members of the groups got the opportunity to learn new knowledge and their knowledge became power to subvert the pre-existing discrimination against widowhood. In other communities, where WHR did not have a program, women also learned from role models. Since there was no negative consequences for families or society, members of widows' families and the public gradually accepted the transformation of widowhood.

> Those were the same widows who were considered bad luck and were not allowed to attend weddings. They have now become beauticians, take part in weddings and do brides' make up.
>
> (Sumedha)

The media has also played an important part in transforming the stigma of widowhood. In 2012, a famous comedian married a widow after his wife died. His marriage was covered by most of the print media (see *eKantipur*, 2012; Gurung, 2012). The event was portrayed positively and accepted as a step towards transformation.

Cultural limbo

One of my friends was disappeared in 2003 by the army, and while he was killed within a few months of his arrest, his death still has not been confirmed. His status and the status of more than 1,200 other people are still unknown.[8] His family believes he may come back one day, and his wife still dresses like a married woman.

Like my friend's wife, wives of missing people in Nepal live a dual life: the life of a married person and a life of a widow. Rita Manchanda (2004) argues that wives of missing persons exist in a cultural limbo. They are stuck between the states of marriage and widowhood. They have not seen their husband's dead body, and so although their husbands are almost certainly dead, they still perform the roles of married women (Manchanda, 2004, p. 246). In such a situation, blurred boundaries are socially acceptable and the public can be more considerate of transgressive behaviour. Thus, during the People's War, even in cases when it was almost certain that a husband was dead, the wife was not forced to partake in any rituals associated with widowhood, because they had not seen the dead body. This was a phenomenon that neither the individual nor society had control over, which in turn meant that both individuals and social groups were forced to adapt to the situation. This inadvertently created a safe space for widows.

Conclusion

> Whatever an agent does is reflexive of social structure.
>
> (Butler, 1986, p. 41)

The wearing of a white sari in Nepal had a long history. It is a symbolic representation of the 'gender performativity' of widowhood. A doxic practice that was in place for thousands of years become a norm in society and was assumed by widows to be normal.

During the decade-long People's War, when thousands of young women became widows, their presence in the public sphere particularly challenged the doxic habitus: the way of thinking that was accepted as normal behaviour. As evidenced in the empirical data in this chapter, the unexpected, sudden and profound social transformation of women's lived experiences as widows bear witness to the preceding quotation by Butler, starting with the transformation of individual lives as women, collective lives as widows and societal lives as equal human beings under policy and law.

These changes have not occurred in a linear manner nor are they all-encompassing. As circumstances that affect the experience of widowhood vary, such as age, geographical location, economic and educational status, there may be some widows who still experience extreme discrimination within the family. However, the shift accounted for in this chapter reflects a dominant practice in Nepalese society regarding widowhood. The current Nepalese society is more flexible, considerate and understanding towards widows than it was before the People's War.

Notes

1 This chapter (with a slight modification) has been published in *Gender, Technology and Development Journal*, *20*(1), March 2016, 1–14.
2 Widows are now called single women in Nepal. I have used the terms single women and widows interchangeably in this book. However, the term single woman, in this book, refers to women with missing husbands and widows only and it does not include unmarried girls/women.
3 For the purpose of this book, widowhood refers to the experience of widows only.
4 A project funded by the Department for International Development (DFID), 'Enabling State Program (ESP) – Nepal', organized a Holi program for widows in Nepal on the occasion of International Women's Day in 2012. Photos of women celebrating Holi can be found at http://www.edgroup.com.au/nepal-enabling-state-programme/.
5 See Lamb (2000, p. 214) for more detailed explanation about rituals in India.
6 All my research participants are given a pseudonym to maintain their confidentiality.
7 See details about WHR and its initiatives to support single women in Nepal at http://whr.org.np/our-pillars/pillar-i-opportunity-fund-2/#.U0ndlqIk75k.
8 The details about disappearance in Nepal can be found at http://www.amnesty.org/en/for-media/press-releases/nepal-deliver-justice-disappeared-2014–08–29.

References

Aankha.com. (2013, 10 August). Yogmaya – A National Luminary. Retrieved 12 December 2014 from http://aankha.com/newsdetails.php?news_id=1436.

Allendorf, K., & Ghimire, D. (2012). *Determinants of Marital Quality in an Arranged Marriage Society.* Ann Arbor: Population Studies Center, University of Michigan.

Anderlini, S. N. (2007). *Women Building Peace: What They Do, Why It Matters.* Boulder: Lynne Rienner.

Ariño, M. V. (2008). *Nepal: A Gender View of the Armed Conflict and the Peace Process.* Retrieved 18 August 2014 from http://escolapau.uab.cat/img/qcp/nepal_conflict_peace. pdf

Aziz, B. N. (2001). *Heir to a Silent Song: Two Rebel Women of Nepal.* Kritipur, Kathmandu: Centre for Nepal and Asian Studies.

Bajracharya, A., & Amin, S. (2010). *Poverty, Marriage Timing, and Transitions to Adulthood in Nepal: A Longitudinal Analysis Using the Nepal Living Standards Survey.* Working Paper No. 19. Retrieved 5 July 2013 from http://www.popcouncil.org/pdfs/wp/pgy/019.pdf

Banerjee, M., & Miller, D. (2003). *The Sari.* Oxford: Berg.

Beck, B.E.F. (1969). Colour and Heat in South Indian Ritual. *Man, 4*(4), 553–572.

Bennett, L. (1976). Sex and Motherhood among the Brahmins and Chhetris of East-Central Nepal. *Contributions to Nepalese Studies, Journal of the Institute of Nepal and Asian Studies (INAS), 3,* 1–52. Kathmandu: Tribhuvan University Press. Retrieved 15 September 2015 from http://pitweb.pitzer.edu/study-abroad/wp-content/uploads/sites/41/2014/12/02-Bennett-Sex-and-Motherhood.pdf

Bhattarai, T. (2013, 10 July). Nepalese Villagers Embrace Toilets to Eradicate Open Defecation. *UPI.* Retrieved 12 November 2014 from http://www.upi.com/Top_News/World-News/2013/07/10/Nepalese-villagers-embrace-toilets-to-eradicate-open-defecation/PC-4291373490084/

Bourdieu, P. (1977). *Outline of a Theory of Practice* (Vol. 16). Cambridge: Cambridge University Press.

Bourdieu, P. (1989). Social Space and Symbolic Power. *Sociological Theory, 7*(1), 14–25.

Bourdieu, P., & Eagleton, T. (1992). Doxa and Common Life. *New Left Review, 191,* 111–121.

Bourdieu, P., & Nice, R. (2001). *Masculine Domination.* Cambridge: Polity Press.

Brooks, A. (2007). Feminist Standpoint Epistemology. In S. N. Hesse-Biber & P. L. Leavy (Eds.), *Feminist Research Practice: A Primer* (pp. 53–82). Thousand Oaks, CA: Sage.

Butler, J. (1986). Sex and Gender in Simone de Beauvoir's *Second Sex. Yale French Studies, 72*(72), 35–49. doi:10.2307/2930225.

Butler, J. (1990). *Gender Trouble: Feminism and the Subversion of Identity.* New York: Routledge.

Castles, S. (2010). Understanding Global Migration: A Social Transformation Perspective. *Journal of Ethnic and Migration Studies, 36*(10), 1–22.

Choe, M. K., Thapa, S., & Mishra, V. (2005). Early Marriage and Early Motherhood in Nepal. *Journal of Biosocial Science, 37*(2), 143–162.

Connell, R. (1987). *Gender and Power: Society, the Person and Sexual Politics.* Cambridge: Polity Press.

Connell, R. (2002). *Gender.* Malden, MA: Blackwell.

Connell, R. (2003). The Social Organization of Masculinity. In C. R. McCann & S.-K. Kim (Eds.), *Feminist Theory Reader: Local and Global Perspectives* (pp. 252–263). New York: Routledge.

Constitution of Nepal, 2072. (2015). Retrieved from https://drive.google.com/file/d/0B1EyNP0s1r6JUGhoMHBtYmtvdDA/view

Dhungana, R. K. (2014). Nepali Hindu Women's Thorny Path to Liberation. *Journal of Education and Research, 4*(1), 39–57.

Doherty, V. S. (1974). The Organizing Principles of Brahmin-Chetri Kinship. *Contributions to Nepalese Studies, Journal of the Institute of Nepal and Asian Studies (INAS), 1*(2), 25–41. Retrieved 15 August 2014 from http://www.thlib.org/static/reprints/contributions/CNAS_01_02_03.pdf

Doniger, W., & Smith, B. K. (1991). *The Laws of Manu.* London: Penguin Books.

eKantipur. (2012, 22 June). Actor Hari Bansha Acharya Remarries. Retrieved 12 January 2014 from http://www.ekantipur.com/2012/06/22/top-story/actor-hari-bansha-acharya-remarries/355981.html

Ells, C. (2003). Foucault, Feminism, and Informed Choice. *Journal of Medical Humanities, 24*(3/4), 213–228.

Embree, A. T. (Ed.). (1966). *The Hindu Tradition.* New York: Random House.

Fairclough, N., & Wodak, R. (1997). Critical Discourse Analysis. In T.A.V. Dijk (Ed.), *Discourse Studies: A Multidisciplinary Introduction* (Vol. 2, pp. 258–284). London: Sage.

Freenepal News Network. (n.d.). Need to Announce Yogmaya a National Luminary. Retrieved 15 August 2014 from http://www.freenepal.com.np/?p=29819

Gender Equality Act. (2006). Retrieved from http://www.lawcommission.gov.np/index.php?option=com_remository&Itemid=2&func=fileinfo&id=459&lang=en

Gurung, A. (2012, 22 June). Comedian Hari Bansha Gets Hitched for Second Time. *Nepalnews.* Retrieved 18 July 2014 from http://www.nepalnews.com/index.php/international/19-news/general/19654-comedian-hari-bansha-gets-hitched-for-second-time

Heller, K. J. (1996). Power, Subjectification and Resistance in Foucault. *SubStance, 25*(1), 78–110.

Jenkins, R. (2002). *Pierre Bourdieu.* London: Routledge.

The Kathmandu Post. (2011, 1 May). In Focus: Yogmaya, Who Gave Her Life Fighting Rana Atrocities. Retrieved 12 February 2014 from http://kathmandupost.ekantipur.com/news/2011-05-01/in-focus-yogmaya-who-gave-her-life-fighting-rana-atrocities.html

Lamb, S. (2000). *White Saris and Sweet Mangoes: Aging, Gender, and Body in North India.* Berkeley: University of California Press.

Major, A. (Ed.). (2007). *Sati: A Historical Anthology.* New Delhi: Oxford University Press.

Manchanda, R. (2004). Maoist Insurgency in Nepal: Radicalizing Gendered Narratives. *Cultural Dynamics, 16*(2–3), 237–250.

Mani, L. (1998). *Contentious Traditions: The Debate on Sati in Colonial India.* Berkeley: University of California Press.

Mills, S. (2003). *Michel Foucault.* New York: Routledge.

NDHS. (2012). *Nepal Demographic and Health Survey 2011.* Nepal: Government of Nepal, New ERA Nepal and ICF International, Calverton, MD.

Owyong, Y.S.M. (2009). Clothing Semiotic and the Social Construction of Power Relations. *Social Semiotic, 19*(2), 191–211.

Patton, P. (1994). Taylor and Foucault on Power and Freedom. In B. Smart (Ed.), *Michel Foucault (2): Critical Assessments* (pp. 352–370). London: Routledge.

Philips, A. (2004). Gendering Colour: Identity, Femininity and Marriage in Kerala. *Anthropologica, 46*(2), 253–272.

Puigvert, Lidia. (2001). Dialogic Feminism: "Other Women's" Contributions to the Social Transformation of Gender Relations. In E. Beck-Gernsheim, J. Butler, & L. Puigvert (Eds.), *Women and Social Transformation* (pp. 29–60). New York: Peter Lang.

Sangraula, B. (2011, 4 May). Yogmaya Neupane: Nepal's First Female Revolutionary. *MyRepublica*. Retrieved 19 April 2013 from http://archives.myrepublica.com/portal/index.php?action=news_details&news_id=30910

Sawicki, J. (1986). Foucault and Feminism: Toward a Politics of Difference. *Hypatia, 1*(2), 23–36.

Spivak, G. (1988). Can the Subaltern Speak? In C. Nelson & L. Grossberg (Eds.), *Marxism and the Interpretation of Culture* (pp. 271–313). Basingstoke: Macmillan Education.

Thapa, L. (2010). Single Women – Agents of Change. In WHR (Ed.), *A Journey towards Empowerment & the Status of Single Women in Nepal* (pp. 70–72). Kathmandu: WHR.

Thapa, S. (1996). Girl Child Marriage in Nepal: Its Prevalence and Correlates. *CNAS Journal, 23*(2), 361–375.

Weiss, L. (1999). Single Women in Nepal: Familial Support, Familial Neglect. *Journal of Comparative Family Studies, 30*(2), 243–256.

Whelpton, J. (2005). *A History of Nepal*. Cambridge: Cambridge University Press.

WHR. (2010). *A Journey towards Empowerment and the Status of Single Women in Nepal*. Baluwatar, Kathmandu: WHR.

8 Women tempo drivers
Challenging doxa

> The social world doesn't work in terms of consciousness; it works in terms of practices, mechanisms and so forth. By using doxa we accept many things without knowing them, and that is what is called ideology.
>
> (Bourdieu & Eagleton, 1992, p. 113)

Safa tempo is one of the main forms of public transport in Nepal.[1] There are around 700 tempos in the capital city, Kathmandu. Every day, an estimated 127,000 people use tempos to reach their destinations (Cabrido, 2012). Tempo driving was a male-dominated occupation until recently. Sumitra Dangal was the first female tempo driver. She started driving tempo in 1996, despite being severely criticized by people (Limbu, 2000). However, the demography of this occupation has changed significantly within a short period of time. There are now hundreds of women tempo drivers (an estimated 300 out of 700) who have taken this job as their main occupation (KC, 2014). A member of the Association of Safa Tempo said there are many trained women drivers but they do not get to drive because there are only 700 tempos in Kathmandu. There are also some part-time women drivers.

Prior to women's involvement in this profession, although there were no legal or social restrictions on women driving and they were allowed to drive their private vehicles, driving as a profession was not something that women were expected to do. It was solely a man's domain. It was something like a doxa, that people, including women themselves, had accepted as a given without ever questioning it. It certainly does not mean that women did not have the capacity to question or that they tolerated this because of their subordinate position. Bourdieu argues that the doxic attitude is "much more than we believe and much more than they know" (Bourdieu & Eagleton, 1992, p. 114). Even "the most intolerable conditions of existence can so often be perceived as acceptable and even natural" (Bourdieu & Nice, 2001, p. 1). One of the reasons for the acceptance of this doxic norm could be a perception of the condition as normal. Sumitra was the first person to challenge this doxic state of mind by becoming a driver. Bourdieu's concept of doxa is relevant in this case to articulate how women were able to break the gender barriers. This chapter argues that women's participation in this non-traditional role has not only changed the lives of the women themselves but has also enabled them to become agents for social change. This chapter is based on my interviews with 10 women tempo drivers in Kathmandu. A number of stories published in the national and international newspapers about women tempo drivers in Nepal have also informed my analysis.

Women in non-traditional roles: challenging the doxa

Barbara Bagilhole (2002, p. 3), who wrote a book called *Women in Non-traditional Occupations: Challenging Men* argues that any occupation that has been tradition-ally undertaken by men can be considered non-traditional for women. Bagilhole (2002, p. 3) asserts that there is no universal definition of what jobs are to be considered men's and what jobs to be considered women's, as it depends on the culture and history of a particular society. For instance, in the UK and Europe it is uncommon for women to work in the construction industry, whereas this is common practice in India (Bagilhole, 2002, p. 3) and in Nepal.

Gender segregation in occupations is an established discourse. It is widely prac-ticed in every sector of society, from economics to politics, from religion to culture (see Anker, 1997; Cross & Bagilhole, 2002). This stereotyping of occupational roles, as well as decisions about who can do what, is shaped by the "learned cul-tural and social values" which are often discriminatory against women (Anker, 1997, p. 316). As a result, occupational segregation by gender has negative con-sequences for women because it affects their status in the family as well as in society, and it also has impacts on how men and women view themselves, which reinforces gender inequality (Anker, 1997, p. 315). For instance, women's role as caregiver and men's role as breadwinner have enormous impacts on how women view themselves and how others view them. While both caregivers and breadwin-ners are important, male professions are valued more. The perception and the importance of one type of work over another not only influences relations in the family but it also shapes social relations.

Women in non-traditional roles have received significant attention from scholars (e.g. Barbara & Denise, 2005; Cross & Bagilhole, 2002; Lewis, 1982; Nermo, 1996; Potter & Hill, 2009; Sappleton, 2009; Whittock, 2000), indicating that women are increasingly participating in jobs traditionally dominated by men (Bagilhole, 2002, p. 4). However, the attention remains on women in white-collar or pink-collar jobs (Cross & Bagilhole, 2002, p. 204) rather than on women in blue-collar or manual jobs. Margaret Whittock (2000) argues that there has been little attention paid to women working in blue-collar or manual jobs. Tempo driv-ing can be identified as a blue collar job. Apart from some newspaper articles about how women are breaking the gender barriers (Limbu, 2000; Nilima, 2011; Sapkota, 2006), to date there has been no academic research or publication about women tempo drivers in Nepal.

Margaret Whittock (2000), whose study looks at women in blue collar jobs such as drivers and car mechanics in Northern Ireland, argues that women's participa-tion in non-traditional jobs can play an important role in breaking gender barriers which may lead to structural changes. Likewise, women do not have to be passive victims of occupational discrimination as they have the capacity to transform their gender relations within the occupational system (Whittock, 2000). Whittock (2000) shares this view with Bagilhole (2002, p. 189), who argues that just as women take part in maintaining gender relations, the same women through their different performance can change their gender relations. This is similar to Judith Butler's notion of gender performativity. Through gender performance, we not only recognize how gender norms are governed but also how they are reproduced and transformed (Butler, 2001, p. 14). Butler (2001) further argues that one has to understand the norms to be able to transform them. However, how much one can transform depends on the context (Butler, 2001, p. 12).

For women in Nepal, tempo driving is a non-traditional occupation and it was not an option for them until recently. However, increased women's presence in this profession has changed this discourse.

Women tempo drivers: pioneering a new doxa

Nepalese women started driving tempo after 1996. Here I provide a background to the introduction of women tempo drivers in Nepal. I focus in particular on the pioneering women, the first to challenge the doxa, who paved the way for other women to enter this profession.

Some people claim that Laxmi Sharma was the first tempo driver in Nepal (Samriddhi, n.d.). Others point out that while Sharma was in the tempo business from 1984, and owned three tempos and a workshop, she never took up tempo driving as a profession (see Pant, 2006; Sapkota, 2006). Sumitra Dangal is generally known as the first actual woman tempo driver in Nepal (Sapkota, 2006). Sumitra Dangal is a law graduate whose dream was to become a police officer. She went to Kathmandu, but failed to realize her dream and instead tried various other jobs based on her educational qualification, but without success (Burathoki, 2010; Sapkota, 2006). She then decided to do something that no woman had done in the past. In 1996, at the age of 24, she started driving a Safa tempo (Burathoki, 2010). This was something new to Nepali society, and so when she started driving it drew massive public attention, including significant attention from the media.

I was in Nepal at that time. Like others, I was surprised when I heard about Sumitra. As a woman, my first concern was for her safety and security. I wondered if it was safe for her to work in this male-dominated profession. The most common criticism people were making about her was about her character. People said she must be a woman of 'bad character' to think of taking such a job. Sumitra, in later interviews with different media, revealed that it was very difficult for her in the beginning because there was no support from people, only criticism (Sapkota, 2006).

The political context started changing in Nepal after 1996. The People's War had already started and the security situation was getting tighter and tougher every day. People started fleeing from their villages, afraid of being caught between the two sides. The capital city was perceived as a safer place. Therefore many internally displaced people (IDP) came to Kathmandu to save their lives and also in search of ways to earn a living, as opportunities in villages were dwindling due to the war

Figure 8.1 Safa tempo parked at Sahidgate Kathmandu

(Yadav, 2007). Due to the IDP influx into Kathmandu, the city's annual population growth rate increased to 4.71 per cent in 2001. The total population of Kathmandu was only 3.6 per cent of Nepal's population in 1991; it increased to 4.6 per cent in 2001 (CBS, 2001).

As mentioned earlier, there are various estimates about the country's IDP population. An estimated 150,000–200,000 were internally displaced during the People's War and the majority of them went to Kathmandu (IDMC, 2006). About 80 per cent of these IDPs were women and children (Caritas Nepal, 2005). Since there were no IDP camps in Kathmandu, they lived like other internal migrants in the capital city, needing work to survive. On the one hand, there was uncertainty in the country because of the growing People's War. On the other hand, a significant number of women joined tempo driving as they sought ways of making a living. As time passed and with the increasing number of women in the tempo driving occupation, the curiosity and concerns of people slowly faded. Moreover, due to the crisis situation after the announcement of the state of emergency in 2002, attention slowly shifted from women tempo drivers to the Maoists – attacks and killing of people from both sides.

It would be misleading to divide developments into a sequential order because many things were happening at the same time, including the People's War, displacement, price hikes, increasing unemployment, the crisis situation. In addition, support was coming from various parties such as non-governmental organizations (NGOs), the UN and bilateral organizations. All of these events opened the space for women to have greater flexibility in their gender roles.

Sumitra, amidst all the criticism and challenges, was determined to bring more women into this profession (Sapkota, 2006). She took loans from her relatives and started a driving school to train women from poor economic backgrounds (Limbu, 2000). However, she says it was not easy because women who were trained needed to find work, but none of the tempo owners was ready to give tempos to women drivers. Women tempo drivers had not established trust yet (Burathoki, 2010). Finally Sumitra was able to negotiate with owners on the condition that the tempos had to be returned without any scratches (Burathoki, 2010). Slowly, other women started joining this occupation because by then it had become an acceptable job for women. Moreover, driving tempo provided a good income, and it was perceived to be safer than driving a taxi or a bus.

As the number of women tempo drivers grew, they started to be recognized and trusted. Some of the articles published in the national and international media reveal this shifting discourse about women as tempo drivers. Some of the headings of the articles published in 2000 also suggest a positive discourse around women tempo drivers. For example, one of Nepal's top magazine, the *Nepali Times*, published an article entitled "Women in the Driver's Seat," which had a quote in bold saying that "Kathmandu may soon become famous not only for its electric tempos, but also for the women who drive them" (Limbu, 2000, p. 5). Another article published by *BBC News* (2000) at around the same time, "Nepal's Women Breaking Barriers," covered stories of women tempo drivers. Another article appeared in the *Asia Times*, "Women Up the Tempo for Equality in Nepal" (Limbu, 2000). These women tempo drivers had been catching the media's attention since the beginning, but their language and focus had shifted. In 2006 the article "Women Tempo Drivers Taking Control in Nepal" presented Sumitra's story as well as the progress made in the driving profession since she started (Sapkota, 2006). Another article published in 2011, "Women on the Road: Driving with Dignity" (Nilima, 2011), stating that driving had become a dignified profession for women. This was a significant shift in attitudes of the media towards women tempo drivers.

Women tempo drivers were not merely being accepted on the streets. They were also supported by different organizations such as Danida, the United Nations Development Programme (UNDP), the Department for International Development (DFID), the International Transport Worker's Federation and Laxmi Pratisthan, a memorial foundation working for social transformation through capacity building. These organizations help women by providing training in such fields as driving skills; traffic rules and regulations; coping with emergency situations (vehicle breakdowns, tire blowouts, lubricants check-up), and even martial arts training for self-defence.[2]

Now women drivers are given priority by the governmental and non-governmental organizations in Nepal; as a result UNDP, the Swiss Embassy in Nepal and Sajha Yatayat (public transport run by the government of Nepal) already have recruited women drivers. These are historic steps in terms of women's empowerment. Sumitra, who started first, has now acquired licenses not only for tempo but for bus, truck and train, and her only remaining unfulfilled ambition is to become a pilot (Burathoki, 2010). Like Sumitra, other women who started with Safa tempo have started driving microbus, taxi and other office vehicles (Burathoki, 2010).

Motivation to join the tempo driving profession: questioning doxa

As in other professions, women had various reasons arising from their personal circumstances for wanting to become tempo drivers. They also had in common living in poverty, the crisis caused by the People's War, the need to survive in the capital city, concerns about their children's future and so on. Initially it was mostly for economic reasons that women joined this profession. Later, when this profession was taken as normal for women and they had proven to be good drivers, others joined; their reasons included earning extra income, the influence of family and friends already in the profession, free driving training for women provided by various organizations and so on.

Two of my research participants were wives of Nepal army soldiers. Both of them came to Kathmandu with their children because they did not feel safe staying in their villages; because they were army wives, they were potential targets for the Maoists. Narbada, who has been driving tempo since 2001, looked for various jobs when she first came to Kathmandu, but she could not make living from them. She shared her story:

> I came to Kathmandu with my husband twelve years ago. When we came here, we found everything so expensive. His income wasn't enough so I started looking for alternatives. I started a little restaurant . . . I had few permanent customers . . . but it was a very difficult business. People ate but never paid so I closed my restaurant . . . I needed to do something to support my family so I started sewing training hoping to get into the tailoring business . . . while I was doing that training, I saw an advertisement by UNDP (United Nations Development Fund) about free driving training for women. It was free (she smiles) that's why I thought of trying my luck . . . I never had taken any driving lesson before but I thought I can do it . . . The vacancy was only for 50 women but there were more than 150 applications. We had to meet certain criteria to be eligible to get the opportunity such as one should be able to read

and write, physically fit, good eye sight etc. There were two types of tests; a written test and an interview. Many women failed in the written test because they were illiterate. I had completed 10th grade . . . I passed the written test and also got through the interview. It was a tough process. Even people who had passed written test couldn't pass the interview because they did not know about traffic rules. I got through somehow.

Narbada's story is different from Sumitra's because Narbada did not mention anything about hurdles to joining this profession. The only hurdle for her was to pass the test and earn the opportunity for free training. Although the training was provided by UNDP, women had to obtain their driving licences by themselves. They were given only 35 days to obtain the licence after they completed their training. Narbada said she hired a tempo, practiced on her own and obtained her licence. A point to note here is that although UNDP provided free driving training for many women, it was only open to literate women. But women who do not know how to read and write are also in this occupation. Kabita, who had never been to school, got into this profession through her sister-in-law. She said she had never imagined that she would ever become a tempo driver:

> One day my sister in-law (who is a tempo driver) came to see me and she insisted that I learn driving. I didn't agree in the beginning because I was scared. I never had thought or imagined about driving and I didn't know if I could . . . because my sister-in-law kept insisting me, I took some driving lessons, practiced a lot and then started driving. Initially I wasn't confident . . . I had to stop wherever passengers said and then collect money and then drive . . . they all had to be done so quickly . . . I found it very difficult in the beginning but later got used to it and now I find it easy.

Nilima, who wrote an article for *World Pulse* magazine about women tempo drivers entitled 'Women on the Road: Driving with Dignity', claims that women who are in this profession are breaking the gender stereotype. She published a story about a tempo driver, Sita KC. Sita tried various jobs when she came to Kathmandu from "filtering sand, working at a noodles factory, and later at a plastic factory." Eventually she found her path to this profession and has been driving tempo for more than a decade now (Nilima, 2011). Although KC (2014) reports that there are 300 women in this profession, my research participants said that there are more women than men in this profession. Since there are only 700 Safa tempos in Kathmandu now, even though more women are trained and want to drive, they do not have the opportunity. Sunita, a member of EVAN (Electric Vehicle Association Nepal) said that not all women are working full time. Some are part-time drivers and some want to drive but opportunities are not available.

When I asked them why they chose to be tempo drivers – not taxi drivers or anything else – all of my respondents said they prefer tempo because it is safe for women. They only drive a fixed route and they have control over their time, Narbada said:

Taxi is not good at all for us because we need to take passengers anywhere they want. We can't say no and you never know what kind of people they are and where they are taking you. You might be abused . . . they might do anything to you that's why taxi driving is very risky for women.

Kabita, another tempo driver, said:

Tempo driving is a good profession for women because you know exactly where you are going. You can start whenever you want to and finish whenever you like to. If you are driving a taxi, you need to go anywhere, if the passenger asks. It is risky for women taxi drivers, that's why only two women are driving taxi and hundreds of women are tempo drivers.

Tempo driving is considered safe for women and therefore women prefer tempos to taxis. On the one hand, women are accepted as professional drivers; on the other hand, the risk for them has not fallen as they still do not feel safe driving a taxi. This is due to what Bourdieu calls "the inertia of habitus" (Bourdieu & Nice, 2001, p. 89), which tends to perpetuate the dominant image of women as subordinate and sexual objects, even after these shifts. Due to the durable and diffuse nature of habitus, it is not only men but women themselves who have not come out of their perception of vulnerability. It seems, in the case of tempo drivers in Nepal, people's perceptions of different issues are changing at different speeds.

A level up from tempo driving in Nepal is to be at the controls of a four wheeler, the kind favoured by international NGOs. It is considered a respectable job and is sought after by some tempo drivers, including women drivers, as a better position. Most of my research participants said their goal now is to learn and drive four wheelers.

I have a desire to drive four wheelers. I am very much inspired by Mumta Tamang who is now working for the UN. There were few taxi drivers who have now joined UN or other organizations. I also wanted to do that.

(Narbada)

When Sumitra started driving tempo, it was her personal battle, but now women tempo drivers have started coming together. They have realized the need for and the benefits of a collective voice. They have registered a union of women tempo drivers called Nepal Yatayat Mahila Chalak Shramik Sangh (Nepal Transportation Women Driver's Labour Union). Narbada said: "There are many women in this profession but 50 of us came together and registered the union. The aim of this union is to get organized and support each other." Narbada emphasized the benefits of getting organized. Binita Shrestha, who is 29, has joined the Swiss Embassy in Kathmandu as a driver (Nilima, 2011). Like others, Narbada is also inspired by Binita, and she wants to join the UN or some other organization, which is considered a respectable job and has a good salary. She said:

One of the main aims of the union is to have a record of all the capable women drivers who can drive a four wheeler, a kind of a pool of a human resource so that if someone needs a driver, they can contact the union and the union then sends qualified candidates.

Another aim of the union she described is the capacity building of women drivers. Most of the women tempo drivers are only driving three wheelers. All of them, says Narbada, have the desire to drive four wheelers, so they are seeking funding from NGOs for the appropriate training. She emphasizes, "it is not something that can be done alone, one has to get organized, that's why we are coming together to make our voice stronger."

The experience of coming together and getting organized for their rights has enabled women to revisit and transform their assumptions about their societal role, and the scope for changing it. When they were housewives, they had no idea about how to seek help from various organizations; their exposure in the public sphere has not just given them money, but it has also exposed them to different knowledge. In the following section, I will shed light on some of the challenges that women tempo drivers are facing and how they are able to negotiate their space within those challenges.

Negotiating the space amidst the challenges: shifting the doxa

Although the story of women breaking the gender tradition by entering the driving profession looks fascinating and encouraging, it certainly was not an easy job for those who started first. My research participant Kabita, who was one of the first tempo drivers, says women who joined this profession in the earlier days faced lots of criticism and allegations from people, mostly about their character. Kabita says:

> We do get awkward remarks from people even now but initially it was worst . . . they thought we can sleep with anyone. They said women drivers don't have a good character . . . especially male drivers and traffic police used to think like that.

Kabita recalls her days when she quit driving:

> Once I stopped working because a guy came and asked me if I wanted to go (sleep) with him. I felt very bad . . . I don't know what he thought about me. I shared this with my husband . . . I felt embarrassed . . . I felt so bad that I stopped working for some time. I thought I will never get back to this profession but we have a union of tempo drivers and the president is a woman . . . she consoled me and said "if you stop working then people will say that's your fault . . . you need to be courageous . . . these kinds of people will come and go . . . you need to be strong . . . no one will do anything to you" . . . after three months I started again.

The challenges that women tempo drivers were facing can be seen in two ways. The first challenge was to get started with something that they had never done in the past. Women were unsure if they could do it. The second challenge was to establish themselves in this male-dominated space. The lack of trust for women tempo drivers, assumptions and allegations about their character, domination by traffic police and male drivers were among the issues that arose as they engaged with this second, multi-layered challenge. An article published by Sukriti Raut in a national newspaper argues that "female drivers are stereotyped as being slow, hesitant, unpredictable, poor in spatial orientation, unappreciative of distances" (Raut, 2011). Narbada says the situation has become much better and favourable for women since she first started. When she started 11 years ago, it was very difficult for women. Now people trust them as good drivers, and there is an acceptance of women tempo drivers but they still face some challenges:

> There is still discrimination in this field as we are not considered as good drivers . . . not by passengers, actually passengers like us . . . they feel safe with us but traffic police and other male drivers don't behave with us properly . . . traffic police are always rude to us. They are mostly men and they think that we can't drive properly that's why they try to dominate us and harass anytime. Similarly, if a taxi is passing by, the driver sends funny remarks. I don't know what do they think about themselves but they do it purposefully to hurt us . . . to dominate us because we are women.
>
> (Narbada)

Women tempo drivers are facing challenges, but they have also learned skills to deal with such challenges. Kabita says she had no idea about city life as she comes from a rural village. She had never dealt with police and would have been too nervous to speak to any policeman if she were in the village. She had always seen them as very powerful people and not her concern. But she has been dealing with them every day. She shares one of the incidents where she got involved in a dispute with the Kathmandu traffic police:

> Once I was driving . . . it wasn't my mistake . . . a car in-front of me pulled his brake all of a sudden so even I had to stop. Because I stopped, a car behind me was hit . . . traffic policeman came . . . I tried explaining to him but he didn't even listen to me . . . not even a word. He asked me to pay for the damage and also took my license . . . it wasn't my mistake . . . all the passengers who were on my tempo knew that it wasn't my fault so they supported me . . . and I was also bold and debated with this traffic policeman . . . It was intentional from his side . . . I had noticed that this policeman who was watching me for a long time. Not sure why he was angry with me . . . maybe because I was a woman driver . . . maybe he wanted something else from me, I don't know!!! There was a traffic jam for about 45 minutes but I was standing on my point . . . finally, he let me go. He might have thought that he can do anything to me because I was a woman but I didn't let him do that. One day when I was walking through the same street, he came and wanted to talk to me. I didn't want to talk to him but he stopped me and said, hey sister, you are a driver and I am a traffic policeman so we will have this kind of tussle every now and then . . . why are

you angry with me? Let's go for a coffee. I didn't go because I knew what his intention was!

(Kabita)

Kabita's experience with the traffic policeman, although it was complex, can be explained in two ways. On the one hand, she has full acceptance from the public who use her service and will speak out on her behalf. The increasing number of women in this profession gives a clue that this has become an acceptable role for women in Nepal, but an incident like this also indicates continuing resistance to women drivers, especially by men such as traffic policemen and male drivers. Habitus is a "durable yet transposable set of embodied dispositions and competencies which (consciously) shape perceptions and actions" (Adkins, 2003, p. 25). Since male domination in this profession has a long history, it will take time to totally change the habitus of people.

On the other hand, however, women as professional tempo drivers seem more confident and demonstrate a high level of skill in dealing with such issues. As Foucault argues, where there is power, there is resistance (Foucault, 1978, p 95). Women have learned to resist this power; this learning is coming from their exposure to the same world which is dominated by men. They have learned to create their own space. Kabita, who had never faced any police in her life, now has to face them every day. She makes four to five trips on the same route and sees the same traffic police several times a day. In my conversation with her, she said she didn't know how to deal with such situations in the beginning but now she knows and has the confidence to deal with them. Similar experiences were shared by other interviewees. This does not mean that Kabita did not have agency when she started, but her silence at the time was also her strategic decision because she was still learning about the rules and regulations, both written and unwritten. The exertion of agency cannot be 'read back' from a social situation solely by considering overt actions. Strategic inaction can also be a method of conscious self-care as actors gain a sufficient foothold before taking action.

Like Kabita, Narbada also says that her level of confidence has increased. She now believes that she can deal with any situation she might encounter on the roads. She says: "I know about my rights. If I am right, I don't get scared of anyone even if there is a big official. I try not to make mistakes."

Shifting discourse: from individual to social

Working outside the home and earning an independent income tend to have a clear impact on enhancing the social standing of a woman in the household and the society. Her contribution to the prosperity of the family is more visible, and she also has more voice because of being less dependent on others.

(Sen, 1999, p. 194)

Despite the challenges that these women drivers face, all of my research participants said their relations with their husbands and family members have improved.

In the case of Kabita and Narbada, both came from hilly regions, but Kabita was from a Brahmin family and Narbada from a Janajati family. In general conversation, Narbada presented herself more liberal than Kabita in terms of gender relations. Both said they share good relations with their family, and such relations have improved since they started working outside the home. Narbada and Kabita both have two children. They work seven days a week. Their daily routine starts at 5 am and ends at around 8.30 or 9 pm. They have their lunch in a restaurant like other drivers. Both of them have someone who helps them look after their children, as their husbands are stationed outside Kathmandu. Their husbands come and visit them once a month. Both Kabita and Narbada said they can decide what to do with the money they earn.

> I earn enough to run my family, that's why I don't have to ask my husband. I also don't have to give all the details to him about how much I earn and where I am spending. I can take my own decisions.
>
> (Narbada)

Kabita also shares her experience of being able to make her own decision since she started earning:

> I only have to pay the tempo owner NRs 160 per trip. I make four to five trips every day. I get more than NRs 160 in most of the trips but I don't have to give all the money to him (the owner). On top of that, I also get monthly salary of NRs 10,000 . . . I am able to manage my costs with this money. We both (husband and wife) are earning . . . we have decided to save one person's income for future. Both our children are studying . . . We are saving up for our kids' future.

Blanc argues that gender-based power inequality affects decision making about family planning. It is usually the men who decide on the number of children, the gap between the children and the choice of family planning methods (Blanc, 2001, p. 196). Nepal Demographic and Health Survey 2001 suggests that just over 50 per cent of women said that the "final decisions about their own health care were made by their husbands alone" (Mullany, Hindin, & Becker, 2005, p. 1995). Another study in Nepal, where "women's participation either alone or jointly in household decisions on their own health care was considered as an indicator of women's autonomy in decision making," revealed that 72.7 per cent of the women said the decision making regarding their health care was made without their participation (Senarath & Gunawardena, 2009, p. 137). Sen (1999, p. 193) argues that women's increased access to income influences their status in the family as well as in society, which seemed to be true in the case of women tempo drivers. All of my research participants said they now have more say in decisions about family matters than in the past. They control their income and they participate in decision making about family matters. I also asked them how decisions were made about family planning. Both said the ideal number of children is two because everything is so expensive, that they cannot afford to have more than two children. They also mentioned that there was a gap in ages between their two children. Kalyani said:

> I was too busy since I started this job. I couldn't plan for more kids. I start work early in the morning and finish late that's why it was very hard to plan for another child. I take a break only once in a month. Once I felt I was settled and can plan another child, then only decided on having my second child. I was working until I was 7 months pregnant.

She further added:

> I am sharing a good relation with my husband. He had to manage all the expenses when I was pregnant. He then realized that it was hard to manage all the expenses with one person's income that's why he asked me to start the work as soon as I can.
>
> (Kalyani)

The need for survival also played an important role in the acceptance of women at the household level who are performing different roles in the public sphere. As Sen (1999, p. 198) argues, women's empowerment can reduce maternal mortality, control the birth rate and influence children's education. The second and third of these effects applied to both my interviewees. Women tempo drivers have greater say in family planning, and they are saving up for the better future of their children, which involves better education.

Despite the challenges women face in this profession, they seemed to give greater value to the achievements they have gained. They feel empowered and in a better position as compared to the past. Sourya said:

> My life has changed a lot. I was a village girl . . . just in the village, doing household stuff. I was a typical traditional wife and a daughter in-law but after coming to Kathmandu and especially after I started earning, my life has changed. I can spend my money the way I want to. I had no say in decision-making when I was in the village but now my husband and I, we both discuss and then decide about our property, about kids' future and everything really.

When I asked my research participants if they had experienced any changes in people's attitude towards them, both said there had been extensive change. Mahili said:

> Our society has changed a lot as well. This profession wasn't women's profession before. When we saw women driving tempo, we thought if she can, why not us. It was a courageous step for the person who started first but certainly a lot of women have benefited from this.

Because of women's increasing involvement in this profession, tempo driving has become a shared space for both women and men in Kathmandu. There were restrictions on women's mobility, and coming home at night was something one could not even imagine in the past, but women tempo drivers come home late after they finish work. Was this social licence, to stay out later, solely connected to their work commitments, or did it indicate a greater degree of choice, or agency, which women can now 'spend' as they wish – that is, to stay out for other purposes of their own choosing? None of my research participants felt any restrictions, even though they said they have to go home as soon as they finish their work because of their children.

When I asked my research participants about their future plans, Narbada said:

> Once you start earning, you don't feel like sitting at home and doing nothing. I am now used to this life . . . I get up early in the morning, work all day and then get back home. I can't stay idle. I have become independent and more confident since I took up this job.

Sourya shares similar opinions, but she adds that the cost of living in Kathmandu is so high that her husband's income alone would not be enough to support the family.

Moreover, these women who have already established themselves desire to do more. Narbada mentioned that there are women who want to become four wheeler drivers. She emphasized:

> It is not easy for us but women want to take challenges. Just to learn four wheel driving, some women became conductors, collect money from the passengers on the bus, just to learn driving. Some of them already have started driving taxis and microbuses. . . . Women who work as a conductor (which was never the case before), they are not aiming just to be a conductor for money but they want to learn driving. They can't afford to go to a driving school so this is a cheapest way for them. They won't need to pay for driving and they also have a vehicle to practice on in spare time.

Initially, although Sumitra, who started first, wanted to challenge the social norms, not all women who joined this profession wanted to challenge the social structure, nor did they have any idea what their experience would be. Since it was something new for them and it provided good money, more women were attracted to this profession. Some came by seeing others, some joined because of peer influence and some joined because of the support and free training they were getting from various organizations such as the UN. Women are now not just earning good money, but they are also learning new skills – skills to deal with complex circumstances that they never had to deal with in the past. They want to do more now. They are aiming to drive four wheelers one day and their aims are not limited to just that. They want to join various organizations as drivers where there is a better salary, stable jobs and more respect. Lastly, through their own lived experience, they have also realized the power of collective agency and so they have started coming together to strengthen their network and express their demands.

It would be too simplistic to say that conflict has contributed to all these changes. But conflict cannot be dissociated from the emergence of a set of consequent and overlapping factors, such as the need for survival by families displaced by the violence, or threat of it, to the capital city; the entry of more women into the profession following the pioneers who first broke down the barrier; help from NGOs established in Kathmandu to support efforts at social transformation in the post-conflict space, and the readiness of the population at large to accept changes in a society emerging from the shadow of war. Bagilhole (2002, p. 188) argues that "there are moments of transition, when the conditions of practice alter fast; there are periods of more or less steady shift in a given direction; and there are periods when a particular balance of forces is stabilised." The People's War in Nepal played a catalytic role, triggering these changes as it created a crisis situation, which forced people to do things that they would never have done under normal circumstances.

The research so far suggests that increased women's participation in non-traditional occupations does not automatically change the organizational culture, because people usually have vested interests in maintaining it (Andrew, 1994, p. 11). However, the idea that women must give up some of their femininity and behave more like men if they are working in non-traditional jobs (Cross & Bagilhole, 2002, p. 223) does not seem to apply in the context of Nepal. Women tempo drivers still dress in their saris and salwar suits and still perform their roles as women. There has certainly been a slight modification in how they dress now, in that a woman, who would only have worn a sari if she was in the village, can make her own choice. However, there has not been any dramatic change in clothing among women tempo drivers.

Women's participation in non-traditional occupations is evidence that women are capable of doing what men can do. When women can participate in maintaining gender relations, they are also capable of changing them by performing differently (Bagilhole, 2002, p. 188). However, the non-traditional professions have a long history of male domination and, Bagilhole (2002, p. 189) argues, "men's resistance to women's success should not be underestimated." As with the experience in the UK and Europe, despite attempts to reduce segregation in the workplace by encouraging more women to take up men's jobs, and despite women's participation in male-dominated jobs over a long time, gender segregation still exists (Cross & Bagilhole, 2002, p. 205). Women tempo drivers also face various challenges which appear to confirm that a transformation of gender norms is still at an interim stage. Lisa Adkins (2000, p. 261) argues that "the destabilization of the traditional structures of . . . workplaces . . . is the disembedding of individuals, not only from rules, expectations and norms in relation to gender, but also from a range of social categories and identifications." Women tempo drivers have successfully established themselves as a separate category. This changed performance has certainly lifted them out of some rigid gender barriers. However, it does not mean that they do not face gender based discrimination, at home or in society, because "autonomy in economy does not necessarily translate into the transformation of male domination" as the male domination is maintained through various social institutions which "legitimatize the authority to control their women" (Bourdieu & Nice, 2001, p. 96). Women tempo drivers' exertion of agency depends on their personal circumstances and individual context. By challenging doxic practices, these women tempo drivers have certainly contributed to transforming the discourse about womanhood in Nepal.

Conclusion

Social change is "a succession of events which produce over time a modification or replacement of particular patterns or units by other novel ones" (Smith, 1976, p. 13). Only a few years ago when one woman started driving tempo, it was represented – in media reports, for example – as a 'concern' for the whole nation. Now, however, although it often becomes a newspaper headline, the discourse has shifted from questioning women's presence in this profession to recognition and appreciation of their contribution. It appears that questioning of doxa is a difficult task, but once it is questioned, it provides space for critical reflexivity and therefore change starts taking place (Adkins, 2003, p. 21). Radical changes tend to take place if their performance is within an acceptable boundary of gender norms. If tempo drivers were seen to have done something 'wrong', perhaps to confirm their portrayal as being of 'bad character', it would have been less successful in creating a favourable space for other women to join this profession. Julie McLeod (2005, p. 22) argues, "women experience degrees of both autonomy and subordination as they move across social fields such as the labour market, domestic life and the intimate." In their experience as tempo drivers women have experienced both autonomy and challenges, however their participation in a non-traditional role certainly has expanded the space for women more generally, and it is contributing to the changing discourse of womanhood in Nepal.

Notes

1 Safa tempo is a battery-operated three wheeler vehicle which was introduced in Nepal in 1996 when the government of Nepal banned diesel-operated tempos from Kathmandu. It is called *Safa*, which means clean, because it is an environmentally friendly vehicle. See the master's thesis by Maharjan (2002) and the paper by Roy, Gurung, and Bam (2001) for more details about the development of Safa tempos in Nepal.
2 More details about Laxmi Pratisthan and their initiatives can be found at http://laxmi pratisthan.org/Women-in-Driving.html.

References

Adkins, L. (2000). Objects of Innovation: Post-occupational Reflexivity and Re-traditionalisations of Gender. In S. Ahmad, J. Kilby, C. Lury, M. McNeil, & B. Skeggs (Eds.), *Transformations: Thinking through Feminism* (pp. 259–272). London: Routledge.
Adkins, L. (2003). Reflexivity: Freedom or Habit of Gender? *Theory, Culture & Society, 20*(6), 21–42. doi:10.1177/0263276403206002.

Andrew, W. G. (1994). Women in Non-traditional Occupations. *Women in Management Review, 9*(2), 3–14.

Anker, R. B. (1997). Theories of Occupational Segregation by Sex: An Overview. *International Labour Review, 136*(3), 315–339.

Bagilhole, B. (2002). *Women in Non-traditional Occupations: Challenging Men.* New York: Palgrave Macmillan.

Barbara, F. R., & Denise, D. B. (2005). A Sociological Perspective on Gender and Career Outcomes. *Journal of Economic Perspectives, 19*(1), 71.

BBC News. (2000, 3 December). Nepal's Women Breaking Barriers. Retrieved from http:// news.bbc.co.uk/2/hi/south_asia/1052910.stm

Blanc, A. K. (2001). The Effect of Power in Sexual Relationships on Sexual and Reproductive Health: An Examination of the Evidence. *Studies in Family Planning, 32*(3), 189–213. doi:10.1111/j.1728-4465.2001.00189.x.

Bourdieu, P., & Eagleton, T. (1992). Doxa and Common Life. *New Left Review, 191*, 111–121.

Bourdieu, P., & Nice, R. (2001). *Masculine Domination.* Cambridge: Polity Press.

Burathoki, K. G. (2010, 14 May). Motormaniac Mom: From Driving to Flying. *MyRepublica.* Retrieved on 5 October 2014 from http://archives.myrepublica.com/portal/ index.php?action=news_details&news_id=18605

Butler, J. (2001). The Question of Social Transformation (J. Vaida, Trans.). In J. Butler, E. Beck-Gernsheim, & L. Puigvert (Eds.), *Women and Social Transformation* (pp. 1–28). New York: Peter Lang.

Cabrido, C. (2012, 20 January). Charina Cabrido Reports on Safa Tempos (Electric Three-Wheelers) in Nepal. *The Streets of India; Voices of Sustainable Transport, Sustainable Cities and Sustainable Lives.* Retrieved 31 May 2014 from http://indiastreets.wordpress. com/2012/01/20/charina-cabrido-reports-on-safa-tempos-evs-in-nepal/

Caritas Nepal. (2005). *Caravan of Conflict: A Study of Dynamics of Conflict-Induced Displacement in Nepal.* Kathmandu: Caritas Nepal.

CBS. (2001). *Population Census Results in Gender Perspective.* Kathmandu: Government of Nepal. Retrieved on 16 May 2014 from http://www.cbs.gov.np/nada/index.php/catalog/12.

Cross, S., & Bagilhole, B. (2002). Girls' Jobs for the Boys? Men, Masculinity and Non-traditional Occupations. *Gender, Work & Organization, 9*(2), 204–226. doi:10.1111/ 1468-0432.00156.

Foucault, M. (1978). *The History of Sexuality, Vol. 1: An Introduction.* London: Penguin Books.

IDMC. (2006). *Nepal: IDP Return Still a Trickle Despite Ceasefire.* Geneva: Norwegian Refugee Council.

KC, U. (2014, 18 May). First Female Tempo Driver Is Trailblazer. *Global Press News Service.* Retrieved on 3 July 2014 from http://themediaproject.org/article/first-femal-tempo-driver-trailblazer?page=0,0

Lewis, D. E. (1982). The Measurement of the Occupational and Industrial Segregation of Women. *Journal of Industrial Relations, 24*(3), 406–423.

Limbu, R. (2000, 30 August). Women up the Tempo for Equality in Nepal. *Asia Times: Online.* Retrieved on 6 May 2014 from http://www.atimes.com/ind-pak/BH30Df02.html

Maharjan, S. (2002). *Electric Vehicle Technology in Kathmandu, Nepal: A Closer Look at Its Development* (Masters), Massachusetts Institute of Technology, Cambridge. Retrieved on 12 December 2014 from http://dspace.mit.edu/bitstream/handle/1721.1/8169/ 51895154-MIT.pdf?sequence=2

McLeod, J. (2005). Feminists Re-reading Bourdieu: Old Debates and New Questions about Gender Habitus and Gender Change. *Theory and Research in Education, 3*(1), 11–30. doi:10.1177/1477878505049832.

Mullany, B.C., Hindin, M.J., & Becker, S. (2005). Can Women's Autonomy Impede Male Involvement in Pregnancy Health in Katmandu, Nepal? *Social Science & Medicine, 61*(9), 1993–2006. doi:10.1016/j.socscimed.2005.04.006.

Nermo, M. (1996). Occupational Sex Segregation in Sweden, 1968–1991. *Work and Occupations, 23*(3), 319–332. doi:10.1177/0730888496023003005.

Nilima. (2011, 29 March). Women on the Road: Driving with Dignity. *World Pulse*. Retrieved 14 August 2012 from https://worldpulse.com/node/36204

Pant, S.K. (2006). Laxmi Sharma: A Women's Adventure in Entrepreneurial World. *Journal of Nepalese Business Studies, 3*(1), 111–113.

Potter, M., & Hill, M. (2009). Women into Non-traditional Sectors: Addressing Gender Segregation in the Northern Ireland Workplace. *Journal of Vocational Education and Training, 61*(2), 133–150. doi:10.1080/13636820902933239.

Raut, S. (2011, 11 March). Women Behind the Wheel. *Kathmandu Post*. Retrieved on 15 May 2014 from http://www.ekantipur.com/the-kathmandu-post/2011/03/11/related_articles/women-behind-the-wheel/219340.html

Roy, R., Gurung, S., & Bam, P. (2001). A Social Dynamics on Launching Safa Tempos in Kathmandu Valley: A Campaign against the Air Pollution. *Journal of the Environment, 6*(7), 89–95.

Samriddhi. (n.d.). Last Thursdays with Laxmi Sharma. Retrieved 1 December 2013 from http://samriddhi.org/article_details.php?article_id=473

Sapkota, R.H. (2006, 26 January). Women Tempo Drivers Taking Control in Nepal: In the Struggle for Economic Independence, Women Are Creating Own Opportunities. *OhmyNews*. Retrieved from http://english.ohmynews.com/articleview/article_view.asp?no=270893&rel_no=1

Sappleton, N. (2009). Women Non-traditional Entrepreneurs and Social Capital. *International Journal of Gender and Entrepreneurship, 1*(3), 192–218. doi:10.1108/17566260910990892.

Sen, A. (1999). *Development as Freedom*. Oxford: Oxford University Press.

Senarath, U., & Gunawardena, N.S. (2009). Women's Autonomy in Decision Making for Health Care in South Asia. *Asia-Pacific Journal of Public Health, 21*(2), 137–143.

Smith, A.D. (1976). *Social Change: Social Theory and Historical Processes*. New York: Longman.

Whittock, M. (2000). *Feminising the Masculine? Women in Non-traditional Employment*. Aldershot: Ashgate.

Yadav, P. (2007). *Gender Dimension of Conflict-Induced Internal Displacement in Nepal* (Masters), Asian Institute of Technology Thailand.

9 Conclusion

Rethinking social transformation

In this book, I have looked at social transformation in post-conflict Nepal from the bottom up by putting women's lived experiences at the centre of my analysis. I have argued that the existing discourse of social transformation would not look the same if women's lived experiences were put at the centre of the analysis. In this conclusion, I briefly reiterate the main points emerged from the chapters and will shed light on how the new space created by the armed conflict led to a significant social transformation in Nepal.

Despite the negative consequences and the hardship people faced during the decade-long civil war in Nepal, the People's War has created an enabling space for women's empowerment (Aguirre & Pietropaoli, 2008; Manchanda, 2001; Pettigrew & Shneiderman, 2004). The transformation of gender roles and relations in Nepal, which occurred within a short period of time, is an element of wider shifts in the sociocultural patterns of Nepali society. However, despite a great deal of discussion on women's empowerment as a necessary step for social transformation and as evidence of the significant gains that women have achieved during and since the war, studies on social transformation often seem to downplay or even ignore women's lived experiences, especially the gains that women have achieved since the war. This raises a key question: why are these gains not more prominent in scholarly literature, as indicators of social transformation? Four assumptions should be identified from the previous discussion:

1 *Social transformation as a desired political goal*: The assumption that social transformation is a desired political goal endorses a certain preconceived institutional framework and set of values, which leads to the validation of certain indicators over others.
2 *Structural focus*: The study of social transformation is heavily influenced by structuralist assumptions where the focus tends to be more on the transformation of objective structures and material conditions, rather than on subjective structures, or the lived experiences of people which are often complex, unpredictable, uneven and non-linear. The transformation of economic structures is still considered to be a permanent basis for sustainable transformation. It is only a short step to the assumption that the establishment of structural changes could consolidate the phenomenon of social transformation.

3 *Social transformation as an end goal and an intended outcome*: Social transformation is often understood as an end goal instead of a continuous process. Therefore, it is often taken as a mega-project, as in the current ways people are talking about social transformation in post-conflict Nepal. This assumption about an end goal limits the understanding of social transformation as if it is an intended outcome or a result of a planned intervention, leaving out the unintended consequences of unplanned actions, interventions and performances.

4 *Confusion between transformation and liberation*: Social transformation and liberation are two different concepts. However, there seems to be confusion between these two terms. Transformation is often mistaken for liberation and as a consequence, social transformation studies fail to recognize the local, bottom-up transformations that occur in parts. Society may not be liberated from all kinds of discriminations, but it may have gone through various levels of transformations.

Social transformation from the bottom up

Society is a relational space in which operative meanings are generated and circulated within certain discourses and are visible through the performance of social actors. Social structure is the arena for the discursive construction of collective beliefs. I have argued that social structure is a discursive habitus: each social structure is constructed through particular discourses. Not just subjective but also objective structures such as social rules, laws, rituals and even material conditions are constructed and perceived through a particular discourse. Due to the repeated practice of such discursively constructed rules, they become what Bourdieu calls the habitus of the people and of society. Habitus is the embodiment of those rules. Although habitus is generative and can be reproduced, due to its durable nature it lasts for a long time. Elements of habitus then become doxa, self-evident knowledge which is often taken for granted due to repeated practice in everyday life. These doxic norms often remain unquestioned, as they are considered normal, such as the white sari for widows in Nepal. People accept even discriminatory norms because they are attached to the everyday conditions of our existence (Butler, 1997, p. 2). We do not want to feel like an odd member of the society. However, these norms are not permanent, and neither is the social structure. I have argued that social structure is neither fixed nor material or virtual. Social structure is a discursive habitus, located within its material and embodied conditions, which becomes visible through the performance or acts of individuals.

Bourdieu, Foucault and Butler argue that whatever an agent does is reflective of social structure, but their actions are not only shaped by the structures: they also shape the structure through their actions. The shift in the habitus of a society may influence the performance of individuals and the changing performance of individuals may shape the social structures. It is a two-way process. When there is a shift in discursive habitus, social transformation occurs. I observed such a shift in the experiences of ex-combatants, tempo drivers, widows and women CA members in Nepal.

According to Bourdieu (1977, pp. 168–169), the possibility of social transformation arises when there is an "objective crisis," which breaks the harmony between the field and the habitus. This was seen in the example of a housewife becoming a CA member and suddenly needing to perform in a field which is different from what she was used to. Her habitus as a housewife did not fit with a different set of political rules. This posed a misfit between her new field and her old habitus.

Initially when a housewife becomes a CA member, it takes time for her to establish herself in a new field. However, as she learns about the new field, her habitus slowly starts changing. With her changing habitus, she is able to reflect on her previous roles and status and to start questioning the doxa, taken-for-granted norms. When people start questioning doxa, they are seeking new knowledge which may influence their performance. With her changing performance, her perception of herself and society's perception of her start changing. Bourdieu (1977, p. 169) argues that crisis is necessary for questioning doxa but it may not always lead to such shifts. He therefore emphasizes the importance of critical reflexivity in response to crises.

Open space for women led to social transformation

The change in political context due to the People's War proved to be fertile ground for women to participate in politics. For the first time in Nepali history, 33 per cent of women participated in such high-level political positions. This did not just provide an opportunity for women who were educated and had a long political background, but also for those who did not know how to read and write and had absolutely no formal political background.

Within the changing discourse of post-conflict Nepal, the inclusion of women became a key political agenda. There was a subtle competition between the political parties to prove themselves more inclusive. Therefore, like Devi, many women who could never have imagined becoming involved in politics had the opportunity to become CA members. In addition to the strategic decisions of the political parties to be more inclusive, which was the demand of that time, women were also given the opportunity to become CA members in recognition of the contribution of their husbands, who went missing or died during the People's War. Some of the widows who stood in the direct election won overwhelmingly.

Moreover, women's rights advocates, heads of leading NGOs were also nominated in the CA. As a result, the composition of the first CA was dynamic and diverse. Women from every sector – illiterate and literate; low to high education; rich and poor; and women leaders –participated in the CA to write the Constitution of Nepal. This rare opportunity, to have such diverse groups of women working together at the policy-making level, was possible only because of the changed political context.

Despite their diversity, all the women CA members I interviewed said they had experienced transformation in their lives since they joined the CA. Women who did not have a background in politics said they had become more confident and could now deal with any situation. They also said they received lots of support from their communities. Women who had been in politics for a long time felt it was easy to work in the post-conflict context. They did not have to do anything extra to prove themselves as leaders. People accepted them more easily as leaders now than in the past.

Almost all the CA members I interviewed said they experienced a great deal of transformation in their society, such as changing marriage practices, more girls going to school and more acceptance of women generally in the public sphere. A case study presented in Chapter 5 shows that the whole community has been transformed in many ways because of Devi's involvement in politics. The community, which once was neglected and enjoyed only scant recognition as part of society, now shares a better relationship with people from the upper caste community. There is more interaction between these two communities now than in the past.

Women of this lower caste community, whose names were hardly known to anyone, are now introducing themselves by their own name. They wear blouses without being worried about criticisms. When they wear a blouse, it makes them feel comfortable and gives them the confidence to participate in the public sphere. This is the same community where women were banned from going to a literacy class just a few years ago. This same community is now encouraging their daughters, sisters and daughters-in-law to participate in a range of development programs. Space for women has opened up. Their different performance is not only recognized but also respected and supported by family and society.

Certainly not all women could become like Devi, but they know that they are worth more. One participant in my focus group discussion (FGD) said, "*pahle hum sab kuwa ke beng chaliyeyi* [before we were like a frog in a well], but now we know a little bit but we want to know more." Pointing towards a man who was standing 20 metres away from us, she said, "we can't be dependent on them, we want to do things on our own." This was very different from what I had experienced in the past. I have been working as a researcher for over 15 years now. I used to go to the field for data collection a few times a year. Every time I went, the respondents used to ask me for monetary support, health support and so on, and I had expected the same from this community. However, I was surprised that instead of money, they asked for training.

If one uses a camera, change is not apparent. The infrastructure is still the same: the street is still muddy, people still live in small houses with thatched roofs. However, there is a significant shift in their habitus. The way they think about the world has changed. The way they think about women has changed. The way women view themselves has changed. One FGD participant said her daughter-in-law does not need to cover her face: "I asked her not to cover her face the day she came . . . paying respect to elders is fine but there is no need to cover the face" (Sabitri). That was an interesting sign of how perceptions are changing, because covering your face is like honouring your family values. However, this discourse has shifted. The honour now is no longer dependent on covering your face but on going out in public and doing something like Devi has done.

The second example that I have presented in this book, which suggests a radical shift in the image of womanhood, concerns women combatants. When the Maoists started their movement, no one had thought that it would introduce a new image of women in Nepal. Women's participation in the Maoist movement did not just transform the lives of women who were directly involved, but it also contributed to breaking down many gender stereotypes. Their participation in the Maoist movement changed the image of women from weak emotional beings to tough women in combat dress. Despite varied experiences among women, their participation in the People's War was not merely symbolic. They contributed directly to bringing change in various social structures. Once they proved themselves good combatants, they were recognized by the state as being capable for combat roles. As a result, the Royal Nepal Army (RNA) started recruiting women into the armed forces. Although the initial idea was to recruit women into the RNA to defend against Maoist women combatants, the assignment of women to combat roles rapidly became established as a practice in its own right.

The war between the Maoists and the state is over, but the recruitment of women into the Nepal Army is ongoing and has in fact accelerated. In all vacancy announcements, seats are reserved for women and women are encouraged to apply. The discourse about the recruitment of women into the Nepal Army has shifted from defence force to inclusive workforce. Moreover, when society saw the changing performance of women and their success in combat roles, people's perceptions also started changing. Women entering the Nepal Army is now seen as normal. It would have raised a lot of eyebrows if a woman from the Madhesi community would have joined the army in pre-conflict Nepal. But there are many women from Madhesh who have recently joined the army.

One of my close relatives (the wife of my cousin) got a job in the army 2 years ago. Although she is a medical doctor, she has to wear combat dress as in other armies and had to go through different training. Initially, during her training period, she had to stay in an army barrack. She had a 9-month-old daughter when she joined the army. When she went to training, her husband and mother-in-law looked after her daughter. There was no objection from the family, and everyone seemed happy about her job. There was certainly an economic aspect attached to it but if it was a pre-conflict context, the family would not have allowed her to work in an army barrack. Her ideal job would have been joining a hospital or operating a private clinic. However, there are no restrictions on her now. She went to South Sudan on a mission for 6 months. She posted her photos on Facebook with her colleagues in combat dress; her posts were liked by many and she received appreciative comments for her work. These may sound like little things, but it shows how the discourse has shifted and how open the society is now, especially accepting women in different roles.

The Maoist's main agenda was to fight against all kinds of discriminations and to establish a discrimination-free Nepal. Although personal experiences may vary, many women were given equal opportunities to participate in the movement. Women combatants said they did not feel any discrimination during the People's War based on their gender.

Because of the misfit between their previous and new roles, female combatants reflected on their own status as well as discriminatory sociocultural norms. The crisis situation forced them to do things they would not have done in normal circumstances, such as strategizing their every action to be safe and mobilizing their power to attack various government bodies, including army barracks. They did not just learn new skills through training provided by the Maoists but also learned new skills and strategies through their own lived experiences within crisis situations. An ex-combatant shared her experience of a narrow escape when a group of soldiers came to arrest her at her home. She said:

> My mum was making tea for me. I was very hungry so I asked my mum to prepare something for me to eat. She just had started cooking . . . a group of army came to our house. They asked my mum, "where is your daughter?" My mum said, "I don't know." When I saw them, I thought my life is gone today. But I still hadn't lost my hope. I jumped through the window from the back of my house and started running as fast as I could. I ended up in a jungle and slept in a cave all night with an empty stomach. My friends (Maoists) saw me and then they took me with them. My party had appreciated my courage.
> (Preeti)

One thing that stands out is her courage which she was able to gather only because that was her last resort to save her life. She also said that in her previous 'normal life' she would not have been able to do anything she did at that time.

Women in the Maoist movement learned various strategies, not only to attack but to escape as well. They had to walk from one place to another every day because staying in one place was tantamount to waiting to be found and killed by the army. Women with babies walked for hours. They visited unknown places with no money. They had to build a good rapport with the people so they could get support for their movement and also protection when needed. In addition, when they visited many rural remote villages, they also saw various kinds of discrimination against women. Their movement against polygamy, child marriage, alcoholism and dowry was very successful and had significant impacts in the community.

Received notions of family and marriage also started changing among the Maoists during the People's War. Usually, a proposal for marriage came through the party. The Maoist party used to organize a meeting where marriage proposals were presented. Women combatants had the opportunity to say no, but my research participants said that because it came from the party, people usually did not say no because the party was like their guardian at that time. They believed whatever the party decided was a good decision. There was no feeling of any caste or class distinctions among the people who were involved in the Maoist movement, and inter-caste marriage was seen as normal at that time. And at the broader level, when these couples went back to their homes, they became role models for others. These changes are not huge. For example, there is still reluctance to accept inter-caste marriage, especially when the marriage is between Dalit and non-Dalit (see Adhikari, 2014; *Gorkhapatra*, n.d.), but there is a somewhat greater level of acceptance for inter-caste marriage in Nepal now than in the past (see Basnyat, 2003). Efforts were also being made by the government to improve inter-caste relationships. The government of Nepal announced an award of NRs 100,000 (approximately US$1,031) in 2010 for people who marry someone from a lower caste, and some people have claimed this benefit (see *MyRepublica*, 2013; *Nepalnews*, 2014).

In the past, people would sometimes even kill their daughters, especially people from Madhesh, if they married a person from another caste, but such inter-caste marriage is slowly being accepted. There are several cases of women who married a member of another caste and this has been accepted (Basnyat, 2003), but it would be misleading to claim that this change occurred because of the Maoist movement. Other factors explain the changes. These include the influence of education, the people's movement, globalization and a media which prompts opportunities for citizens to reflect on their own lives and circumstances. However, the opening up of space in post-conflict Nepal and role models from the Maoists have created examples for many others to follow.

On a negative note, although the Comprehensive Peace Agreement (CPA) was a significant factor in bringing the country from the People's War through a post-conflict transition, some of the women are facing difficult consequences. After the Maoists left the jungle and entered into mainstream politics, they lost control over their cadres. There were political splits within the party. One faction supported the revolution and wanted a further revolution while another faction wanted to remain in mainstream politics. Their cadres became divided.

During the war, the Maoist cadres' needs were very limited, but after the CPA they needed to have jobs or some kind of income to survive. The Maoist leadership certainly could not provide jobs for everybody. As discussed in Chapter 6, combatants had to go through a verification process to be integrated into the Nepal Army. However, not all combatants qualified because of their age, physical compatibility or personal circumstances. It was even tougher for women because they had children. When the Maoist combatants became free and started a new life, they had to face many challenges. One of my research participants said her sister was left by her husband with two children because they had an inter-caste marriage and his family did not support this relationship; he later married someone from his own caste.

Women combatants had both positive and negative experiences depending on their personal circumstances. As Cynthia Cockburn (2001) argues, gendered power relations impact women in every stage of conflict: pre-war, during the war, during peacemaking and post-war. Women's status in the pre-conflict situation has an impact on their status during the conflict. In a post-conflict context, women's current status shows the influence of their previous status. For instance, girls from poor families joined the war when they were only 10–13 years old. Now these women do not have jobs or education and have poor financial status. They have children. They are facing difficulties but even though the situation is not very good for them, they are happy about what they have become – at least the women whom I interviewed. Jwala Singh said that if she had not been involved in the

Maoist movement, she would have been somewhere married to a man and would have been a housewife. She is now in what she considers a much better situation. Likewise, other women who were ex-combatants said if they had not been in the Maoist movement they would just have been housewives and would have had no knowledge about the outside world. Hence, despite the consequences they are facing, women are more confident and believe they have more agency.

Another example of the historic shift is the transformation of widowhood in Nepal. Widows faced extreme forms of violence and discrimination prior to the People's War simply because they had lost their husbands. During the armed conflict in Nepal, thousands of women became widows and most of them were young, under 40 years old. Many were much younger still. This sudden increase in the number of young widows took place in a society with no experience of dealing with such a situation. The traditional way was discriminatory and women used to be blamed for their widowhood. A firmly embedded assumption was that widowhood 'happened to them' because of their ill fate, their misfortune or their bad karma. Widows were not allowed to do things like normal women and faced restrictions on their food, mobility and dress. However, conflict-induced mass widowhood was something that Nepali society had never experienced before and did not have the skills to deal with. Imposition of the old rules was seen, in general, to be too harsh for these women.

The crisis also provided more space for widows to exercise their agency, meaning that when men died, widows were forced to do things outside their homes. A widow from the Western region said she never had to do anything outside her home when her husband was alive. She was only responsible for taking care of her family. After her husband died, she had to do everything by herself. She also said that although it was challenging for her in the beginning, as she did not know anything about the outside world, she now knows how to get official things done. Her husband was a police officer so she had to claim benefits from the government after he died. For that, she needed to negotiate bureaucratic procedures and attend various government offices, which she managed to do. During this process, she was not only able to accomplish the things she needed to do, but she also learned new skills and more about the world outside the domestic arena.

Another widow, who was also the wife of a police officer who was killed during the war, said she herself joined the police after her husband died; therefore she did not have to follow any of the traditional norms, as the nature of her job made it impossible. The Maoists opposed the discriminatory norms so women who were in the Maoists and lost their husbands during the war continued what they were doing. Despite their personal loss and emotional suffering, there was no pressure on them to follow any of the usual rituals.

At the wider societal level, on the one hand, the crisis situation impacted the normal functioning of sociocultural norms. On the other hand, the need for survival pushed women into the public sphere, which led to a misfit between their field and the habitus. This created the space for them to reflect. Moreover, with support from various organizations, widows started coming together. When they shared their suffering, they realized that it was not their problem or pain, but it was the discriminatory cultural norms which had placed them in such a situation.

When women came together, their collective power became strength for each other. They started supporting each other. With help from different organizations, they also obtained skills training. These women in groups started saving and giving loans to the members of the group which helped widows to start their own businesses. As Amartya Sen (1999) argues, the economic independence gave them flexibility and a better say within their families. Their contribution to the family was recognized.

Moreover, the red colour movement had a significant impact on widow's capabilities. When an increasing number of widows started avoiding the traditional white sari and started wearing other colours, it rapidly became accepted as normal. When I was in Surkhet in the Mid-western region of Nepal in 2007, there was a fair organized by the Business Association. A group for single women had a stall where they were selling *sell roti* (doughnuts made of rice flour) and curry. But people were hesitant to buy food at their stall, which suggests that their participation in the public sphere was still not fully accepted. However, the situation has changed so rapidly that today people are not concerned if a business is run by a widow or a married woman. There could be two reasons for this. First, they are not stigmatized as widows because the way they dress now does not say anything about their widowhood. Second, even if people knew, they accept them as normal women running a business. Societal attitudes surrounding widowhood have radically changed.

The high cultural visibility of prominent role models had a significant influence transforming widowhood in Nepal. Widows who started breaking discriminatory norms initially had to face many allegations about their character, but they paved the way for other women. Women's resistance to the white sari was not only about the colour of the sari but also about discriminatory practices. When other widows saw them performing differently, they followed suit. We also need to understand that we do not always act or react consciously; we act according to our habitus, as Bourdieu says. When people saw widows wearing other colours and performing differently, it slowly changed the habitus of people about widows. These widows look 'normal', like other women, and so they started being treated like other 'normal' women. People's attitudes towards widowhood also started shifting. In the case of young war widows, the honourable sacrifice their husbands and families made meant there was less inclination to blame them for their widowhood. So society was loyal and flexible towards widows. And when widows started performing differently, they were accepted as normal. In making these observations, I do not claim that there is no discrimination at all against widows. There are widows who still face various forms of discrimination, and their experiences vary depending on their individual circumstances and the context they live in. Despite the discrimination, this shift in widowhood was a major shift, which has both resulted from and contributed to social transformation.

The fourth category of women chosen for this research is women tempo drivers. There were no women tempo drivers before 1996 in Nepal. As discussed in Chapter 9, Sumitra, who was the first one to start, had to face open allegations of being a woman of 'bad character'. She was an educated woman and she wanted to bring more women into this occupation. Therefore, she started a driving training institute for women. The situation was favourable because during the conflict thousands of people had been displaced to Kathmandu and were looking for jobs. Because of the increased population in Kathmandu, finding work was a tough task. On the other hand, more people were using public transport. Sumitra had paved the way for many women to become tempo drivers. Some joined because their friends and relatives were already in the profession, while others joined because they got free training from various organizations. When women's participation increased in this occupation, it became acceptable in the society.

Inclusion was a significant political demand in the post-conflict context, including with the expanded presence of international non-governmental organizations (NGOs) and other organizations on the ground. Women drivers found opportunities with such large employers such as the United Nations Development Programme (UNDP) and the Swiss Embassy.

Women who had joined not only learned to drive but they also learned various life skills. They knew more about the public sphere. They had acquired broader social skills and knew how to deal with work-related situations. They wanted to do better for themselves and their families. My tempo driver research participants said they wanted to drive four wheelers now and that they are organizing to create a pool of women drivers, so if someone asks for a women driver, they can go through that community instead of advertising randomly. Such newly acquired political consciousness is not only limited to their own lives, but their families are also being transformed. These women tempo drivers are giving better education to their children, they have control over their income, share better relations at home and have improved status in the society.

From the examination of these cases, it is clear that social transformation is not something that can be captured solely by gauging the extent of institutional reconfiguration. It is also a bottom-up process. It can be initiated at the level of individuals and expanded as a collective effort. When Yogmaya, as discussed in Chapter 7, started protesting against discrimination against widowhood society was not ready to listen to her, but there now exists a more flexible attitude towards individuals such as Yogmaya.

When women participated in the public sphere, it did not match their own habitus. It created the possibility for critical reflexivity. When they reflected, they started questioning doxic practices. When they started questioning, they were seeking new knowledge. When they learned new things, they performed differently. When they performed differently and when people saw them performing differently, although there was some resistance in the beginning, the habitus of the people as well as of society started shifting.

Social transformation is embodied in the subjects of society and is demonstrated through the performance of people as well as structural and institutional change. A continuous process, it happens in everyday life. When we are faced with a new situation, although it may be challenging in the beginning, we learn through our experience. As Butler argues, we can never be the same once we are exposed to new knowledge. Foucault argues that knowledge is power. Once people have knowledge about their rights, they utilize this knowledge to enhance their capabilities.

The uneven nature of the transformation of gender relations illustrates Bourdieu's claim that "the habitus continues to work long after the objective conditions of its emergence have been dislodged" (McNay, 1999, p. 103). Since each field has its own habitus, and each habitus has its own history and logic, it is naïve to claim a radical shift in every structure of society at the same time. People's needs and desires are constantly evolving and so social transformation is a continuous process. It is possible for radical change to happen in some sections of society while others may remain the same or may only experience a little change.

This research suggests five important factors contributing to the significant changes that are taking place in post-conflict Nepal, which are the changed subject position of women, the emergence of new role models and the power of collective agency. These are facilitated by the opening up of space for empowerment and other internal and external factors such as globalization, people's movements, increased access to media and NGO interventions. Women are usually pictured as victims in post-war studies. This research reveals that women were not always victims, but they also benefitted from the war due to the rupture in restrictive gender norms. However, their achievements are often undocumented in peacetime, especially in the study of social transformation. To acquire a better picture of a post-conflict society, it is important to look at the gains that women achieved during the war. This not only helps in making plans for the reconstruction of the post-conflict society, but it also helps in bringing sustainable peace.

References

Adhikari, P. (2014, 1 January). Inter-caste Marriage Displaces Dalit Family. *eKantipur*. Retrieved 15 June 2014 from http://www.ekantipur.com/2014/01/01/national/inter-caste-marriage-displaces-dalit-family/383228.html

Aguirre, D., & Pietropaoli, I. (2008). Gender Equality, Development and Transitional Justice: The Case of Nepal. *International Journal of Transitional Justice, 2*(3), 356–377.

Basnyat, S. (2003, 26 December). Happily Ever After: Inter-caste, Inter-ethnic, Inter-racial. Nepalis Are Getting Married All Over the Place. *Nepali Times*. Retrieved from http://nepalitimes.com/news.php?id=11202#.U_lOP2OAoX8

Bourdieu, P. (1977). *Outline of a Theory of Practice* (Vol. 16). Cambridge: Cambridge University Press.

Butler, J. (1997). *The Psychic Life of Power: Theories in Subjection*. Stanford, CA: Stanford University Press.

Cockburn, C. (2001). The Gendered Dynamics of Armed Conflict and Political Violence. In C.O.N. Moser & F.C. Clark (Eds.), *Victims, Perpetrators or Actors?: Gender, Armed Conflict and Political Violence* (pp. 13–29). London: Zed Books.

Gorkhapatra. (n.d.). Society Still Reluctant to Accept Inter-caste Marriages, Couples Displaced. Retrieved 2 November 2015 from http://trn.gorkhapatraonline.com/index.php/69-life-style/4775-society-still-reluctant-to-accept-inter-caste-marriages,-couples-displaced.html

Manchanda, R. (2001). Ambivalent Gains in South Asian Conflicts. In M. Turshen, S. Meintjes, & A. Pillay (Eds.), *The Aftermath: Women in Post-conflict Transformation* (pp. 99–121). London: Zed Books.

McNay, L. (1999). Gender, Habitus and the Field: Pierre Bourdieu and the Limits of Reflexivity. *Theory, Culture & Society, 16*(1), 95–117. doi:10.1177/026327699016001007.

MyRepublica. (2013, 29 November). No Allowance for Inter-caste Couples. Retrieved 20 August 2014 from http://www.myrepublica.com/portal/index.php?action=news_details&news_id=65231

Nepalnews. (2014, 27 February). Couples Get Allowances for Inter-caste Marriage. Retrieved 15 May 2015 from http://www.nepalnews.com/index.php/news/31550-Couples-get-allowances-for-inter-caste-marriag

Pettigrew, J., & Shneiderman, S. (2004). Ideology and Agency in Nepal's Maoist Movement. *Himal Magazine*. Retrieved 30 October 2015 from http://www.himalmag.com/component/content/article/4272-women-in-the-maobaadi-ideology-and-agency-in-nepals-maoist-movement.html

Index